DATE DUE

FAREWELL TO THE FACTORY

FAREWELL TO THE FACTORY

Auto Workers in the Late Twentieth Century

RUTH MILKMAN

UNIVERSITY OF CALIFORNIA PRESS
BERKELEY   LOS ANGELES   LONDON

University of California Press
Berkeley and Los Angeles, California

University of California Press, Ltd.
London, England

© 1997 by
The Regents of the University of California

Library of Congress Cataloging-in-Publication Data

Milkman, Ruth, 1954–
    Farewell to the factory : auto workers in the late twentieth
century / Ruth Milkman.
        p. cm.
    Includes bibliographical references and index.
    ISBN 0-520-20677-0 (alk. paper). — ISBN 0-520-20678-9
(pbk. : alk. paper)
        1. Automobile industry workers—New Jersey—Linden.
    2. Automobile industry and trade—New Jersey—Linden.
    3. General Motors Corporation. I. Title.
    HD8039.A82U653 1997
    331.7'6292'0974936—dc20   96-22684
                                                    CIP

Printed in the United States of America
9 8 7 6 5 4 3 2 1

For Jonathan, and his generation

Contents

Contents

Figures and Tables

Figure

Tables

Acknowledgments

The work on which this book is based has been under way for nearly a decade, and I have incurred numerous debts along the way. First of all, I thank Cydney Pullman of the Labor Institute in New York City, without whom the project would never have been undertaken. She codirected the initial stages of the research with me and also shared in the difficult task of gaining access to the plant. After coauthoring a report on the initial research findings, as well as a journal article, we ended our collaboration in 1988 with an agreement that each of us could make independent use of the data. Pullman went on to write her Ph.D. dissertation based on statistical analysis of the in-plant survey data; I chose to conduct additional research (follow-up telephone surveys, interviews, library research, and archival work with National Labor Relations Board [NLRB] records), which—together with the jointly collected data—form the basis of the present work.

A project like this one, based almost entirely on original data collection, requires extraordinary resources. We were fortunate to have initial funding from the United Auto Workers (UAW) and General Motors (GM), supplemented by a series of small grants from the City University of New York (CUNY) Research Foundation, the University of California, Los Angeles (UCLA), Institute of Industrial Relations, and the UCLA Academic Senate. Every phase of the research was extremely labor intensive, and I drew heavily on assistance from graduate students at the CUNY Graduate Center and later at UCLA. For help in conducting the surveys, coding, data entry and cleaning, interview transcription, statistical analysis, and a variety of other tasks,

I offer heartfelt thanks to CUNY's Prisha D'Andrade, Zsuzsa Forgacs, Felipe Pimental, Matthew Schwarz, Steve Sconfienza, Vincent Seravallo, William Sites, and Betina Zolkower, and to UCLA's Alec Campbell, Christopher Campbell, Janette Lawrence, Benita Roth, Susan Stockdale, Eleanor Townsley, and Dolores Treviso. I also thank Ela Elfassy for her meticulous job as an interview transcriber, and Reza Behar and Mary Ellen Colten for their assistance in designing the initial survey questionnaires. Reza also provided indispensable advice as a computer consultant.

Special thanks are due to UAW Regional Director Tom Fricano; and to Lydia Fischer, Sheldon Friedman, Candace Howes, Mark Levinson, and Peter Unterweger, all then of the UAW's Research Department in Detroit. I am also grateful for the cooperation of UAW Local 595 officials Charlie Marshall, Guy Messina, and Joe Gentile. My deepest thanks go to the many workers, union activists, and managers at GM-Linden who shared their insights and experiences in the course of the research. I regret that they must remain anonymous here for reasons of confidentiality.

I am also much indebted to the insights of other researchers who advised me at various stages of the project, including Paul Adler, Barry Bluestone, Dorothy Sue Cobble, Steve Herzenberg, Jeffrey Keefe, Harry Katz, Nelson Lichtenstein, Dan Luria, Lowell Turner, and Maurice Zeitlin. Alan Wolfe solicited an article on the topic of this book for his edited collection *America at Century's End* (Berkeley: University of California Press, 1991), providing me with an early opportunity to formulate my ideas in print. I presented chapter 2 in preliminary form at a conference on "Work and Workers' Movements since World War II" at Duke University in 1994, and benefited greatly from the ensuing discussion. Early versions of chapter 4 were presented at the American Sociological Association's 1993 convention and to colloquia at the Cornell University School of Labor and Industrial Relations; the University of California, Berkeley; the Centre des Études de l'Emploi in Paris; and the University of California, Davis, all of which provided valuable feedback. Fred Block, David Brody, Michael Burawoy, Dana Frank, David Halle, Harry Katz, Gail Kligman, Nelson Lichtenstein, and Stephen Wood read the entire manuscript in draft form and offered extensive comments, which I found very useful. My editor at the University of California Press, Naomi Schneider, has been enthusiastic about this book from the outset and has been extraordinarily patient in awaiting its completion.

Over the past several years my attention repeatedly has been diverted from this project by other activities—among them a cross-country move, researching and writing another monograph (on Japanese-owned factories in California), the daily demands of university life, and most of all, the welcome duties of parenting my three-and-a-half-year-old son, Jonathan, to whom this book is dedicated. The manuscript could not have been written at all without the many hours of loving child care provided by Amber Linson, Alicia Maltzman, Andrea Sachtschale, and especially the Hill an' Dale Family Learning Center. Finally, I owe thanks to Jonathan's father, Nate Laks, who has lived with this project as long as I have, and whose companionship, criticism, love, and support sustained me during the long process of research and writing.

March 1996

Chapter One

Introduction

As advanced capitalist economies shift away from manufacturing, and as the manufacturing that remains is radically restructured, what is happening to industrial workers and their way of life? This book explores that broad question through a narrow lens, focusing on the recent experiences of workers from a single factory: the General Motors (GM) automobile assembly plant in Linden, New Jersey. First opened in 1937, GM-Linden was at the core of the mass production economy that flourished over the next several decades. Like the luxury Cadillacs it built during the postwar boom, this plant was a top-of-the-line operation, with high wages, excellent fringe benefits, and a strong union—the best America had to offer to unskilled, uneducated industrial workers. The system began to unravel in the 1980s, however, as GM struggled to meet the challenge of intensified international competition. Management introduced robots and other new technologies at Linden, and began reorganizing the work process as well. The plant also shifted to small car production, and all these changes combined to generate sharp employment cutbacks. In the mid-1980s, GM negotiated with the United Auto Workers' union (UAW) to establish a buyout program offering cash payments to production workers who agreed to give up their jobs—an option that proved very popular at Linden. The pages that follow assess these unsettling developments from the perspective of the workers involved—both those who accepted the buyout and left the plant, and those who are still employed there. Their stories reveal a great deal about the dilemmas industrial workers face in the postindustrial age.

Edward Salerno (not his real name)[1] went to work as an assembler at Linden when he finished high school. His father, a lifelong GM employee, got him the job—a common arrangement in the days before the auto industry started shedding old workers rather than hiring new ones. Salerno worked at the Linden plant for eight years until he accepted the buyout in 1987. Even before that, he was restless. "Let's face it, auto workers are not in the most intelligent occupation in the world," he said, "and you kind of get hung up in that type of lifestyle." The main thing that had kept him at GM was the high pay. "You come right out of high school, and all of a sudden you're making this big money!"

A couple of years before he left, when he learned that the plant was going to be modernized, Salerno had signed up for an electronics training course, hoping it would help him get a better job. He was laid off during the year-long plant changeover, and GM paid for his training under a union-negotiated tuition reimbursement program. "After I graduated, then they started calling us back, and my mind was pretty much made up: if I didn't get a job in the computer end, fixing the new robotics and all, I was going to leave." When it became clear that he could only return to GM as a production worker, and with his job security uncertain because of his relatively low seniority, Salerno decided to take the buyout, receiving about a year's pay, or $30,000. He got a job installing business telephone systems, but after a few months, he was laid off. So he went back to school again, this time to learn computer programming, and that led to a job in the payroll department of a large insurance company, where he works now.

The pay is less than at GM, but there is an excellent benefit package; and overall Salerno is much happier. "The working conditions and the atmosphere and the people—it's nice. It's such a great change for me, [better] than working on a line like that." He has no regrets about leaving GM:

I'm thrilled that I'm out of there—what can I say? The place was a hellhole. I really hated it. It was very belittling. It seemed like they were always trying to play games with you, always trying to degrade you. And there was always that struggle between management and union: we're enemies. You know, it was constantly that. Each side played [its] little games. They didn't like you; they were going to do what they could to get you. Where I am now, there's never any yelling or threatening or anything like [there] was at General Motors. The relationship is better. I get along fine with my managers, and there just isn't the need for that kind of nonsense like at GM. As far as my foremen or any of my bosses there, I can't say I hated them, but I've never been brought to such anger in all my life [as] I was at that place. The things that some of the guys would try to do! It's incredible!

Salerno knew when he left GM that the auto industry's glory days were over. Only a generation before, an auto worker could make a decent living. "You could buy a house and raise a family like my father did. Now, forget it. If you're working there, your wife *has* to work." GM, and with it the UAW, had gone downhill in the 1980s:

Let's face it, the auto workers just aren't what they used to be. They just don't have the power they used to, because there's not as many workers and there's always that threat, well, they can just pack up and leave—which is what they're doing. No one is listening to the union anymore. What are they going to do? They have no recourse. So, I saw all that coming, and I said, "I just don't want to be a part of this anymore."

I think if the unions want to stay, they are going to have to start infiltrating the white-collar jobs, because manufacturing in this country is just going down the drain. I think that if it ever did happen, they could probably become strong again, because in this type of deal, where I work now, you could strike and you don't have to worry about picketing—because who's going to go in there and do your job? You're the one that knows what is going on. Nobody is going to walk in and take over your work, because they don't know what you're doing. In that respect it would be very easy. But where I work, you even mention the union, and they call you a communist. You start talking about that, and they get rid of you quick. But I'll tell you, I think that's their only hope for right now. I don't think that factory jobs will be around much longer.

Even though he's a lot happier now than when he worked at GM, Salerno is still keeping his eyes open for something better. "Most of the promotions come within the first two or three years over here, and then you kind of level off. I'm not learning anything new now, either." He's going to school again at night, with his employer paying the bill, working for an associate's degree in computer science. "If something else came along, I would take it."

Dan Cooper took the buyout too. He worked at GM-Linden for

ten years, although he never liked it much, and like Salerno, he had
not really intended to stay as long as he did. He was twenty when he
was hired. "I was working at a warehouse making, I think, $5.00 or
$5.25 an hour," he recalled. "They were starting up a second shift at
General Motors and I heard guys talking about it and it was a lot more
money. I didn't think I wanted to be an automaker, but while I was
deciding what I wanted to do, I could make more money at it. I went
there, and when I first got there, I started thinking about maybe going
for a foreman or trying to work up the ladder, but then I got turned
off by that pretty quick."

Cooper has his own business now, as a chimney sweep, and he does
other odd jobs, like stump grinding and landscaping, on a freelance
basis. He started the chimney sweep business while he still worked at
GM, as a second job.

For a while my wife worked for AT&T, full-time. And so we had it made—
we had money flowing out of our ears. Then the children came and she quit.
All of a sudden our salary was cut in half, you know. And that's when I started
my business. Working days on production, I usually got out between three
and four in the afternoon, and so I could set up appointments after work or
on weekends. I'd read about chimney sweeping in *Popular Mechanics* years
before. I thought about it during the oil crisis, when people were going crazy
buying wood stoves, but back then I didn't have the need for another job.
So it had been in the back of my mind for a long time, and then I saw this
ad for the equipment. I think I paid $1,600 for the vacuum, brushes, lad-
ders, you know, basic things like that. I attacked my father-in-law's fireplace,
and then I did a few for the guys at work, just free cleanings. Then I went
around—I had a top hat and tails and I had flyers made up, and I'd go around
on a Sunday, handing them out, looking for people working on their front
lawns. And people start looking. I'd go in the liquor store and buy a six-pack
of beer with top hat and tails on. Everybody in the store wants a card, you
know.

For a few years Cooper built up the business while continuing to
work at GM. Meanwhile, it was becoming obvious that the auto industry was in trouble. "The last five years or so before I left there, it
just felt like I was giving back, I wasn't gaining anything. Once Reagan
got into office, unions, organized labor went right down the drain. But
before they offered the buyout, there was never any incentive to

leave." When GM did offer him the buyout, Cooper hesitated. "It was a hard thing to do. I had a house, a wife and kids, a mortgage. And benefits—picking up benefits is expensive. And security, you know, you get that weekly income. But I figured that I was young enough—I was thirty years old at the time—that I could fall on my face, you know, working for myself, and I knew I could still go out and get work."

Cooper expanded his business into a full-time operation with the help of the buyout money. "I didn't look at it as a lot of money, but it was something to help tip the scale. I looked at it more like a small business loan, rather than throwing it into our bank account, I bought a new van." He had never intended to stay at GM forever, but he realizes that if not for the buyout, he might have done so. "I was never really happy at GM, but I just never had the guts to say, 'The heck with it, I'm going to throw it in, take my ball, and go home.' " Now Cooper is much happier with his work:

To me, it's a utopia. I love when I'm doing the cleaning. . . . My main thing is getting people to love to use their fireplaces, educating them. That's how I get all the referrals, because Mrs. Jones loves to tell Mrs. Thomas any new information she finds out. And if [Mrs. Jones] can tell her this, that, and the other thing about a fireplace, Mrs. Thomas wants to know. I've got a business that—with advertising, I could probably put three trucks on the road, but I don't want the headaches.

I work probably the smallest area of any sweep in the state. I've got a circle on a map that extends out four miles, and if I go outside of there, people pay fifteen to twenty dollars extra to have me come. I try to discourage them. I don't need the whole county; I just want my little corner of the world, you know. And people love that. They like the idea that I sell myself, not my company. If you call and you have a problem, the only person you're going to talk to is me. There's not going to be a seventeen-year-old kid coming out to clean your fireplace. I like that, being a hometown boy. I grew up here, my father grew up here, and my in-laws live a half mile away.

When the economy plunged into recession, business became more uncertain, but so far Cooper has managed to hang on.

Usually, February, March, April, I keep myself semibusy; I've got maybe two jobs a day, three jobs a day, and take days off and stuff. But this year, for a while it was like I was getting two jobs a week. Everything went down, you know, all my income went down, and the bills were still there. Later the chimney cleaning picked up a little bit, and also I started the stump grinding. Now I'm working basically seven days a week. Usually, I don't get home till around eight-thirty; then I usually have about twelve calls on my answering machine. Sunday I was out from eleven until around six o'clock at night, doing stumps and running around. And before that, from like nine till eleven, I was out doing estimates. You know, I can see the end of it coming, but right now I'm working like a maniac.

Mostly he is glad he left GM, but Cooper has no illusions about the future. "I'm never sure if I did the right thing or not, because I don't know what's down the road. I could go for one slide, one fall, and never be able to climb again, you know, and that could be— whew, the whole business totally gone."

Almost a thousand GM-Linden production workers took the buy-out at the same time as Salerno and Cooper. Three thousand others declined it and instead returned to work in the newly modernized plant. Susan Roberts was one of them. She thought about taking the buyout but decided against it in the end. "I was considering buying a house, and I figured that it would be a good down payment," she recalled. "But I talked myself out of it because I didn't have another job to go into. I figured if I wanted to buy a house, I don't need to put that much money down. So then I says, 'What the hell am I going to do? Where am I going to find a job that has benefits like this? Okay, the job security is a little iffy, but I'm going to hang in there.' "

When Roberts returned to the plant, she went through a two-week training program, jointly sponsored by GM and the UAW, welcoming the workforce to the "new Linden" with great fanfare. Along with the new technology, the program introduced a range of organizational innovations, many of them modeled after the practices of the Japanese auto firms that are now GM's most formidable competitors. In a dramatic reversal of past practice, for example, workers were told to "build the car in the station," meaning that they should do each job in its assigned location rather than marking problems for correction later on, as they had in the past. If extra time is needed to correct a problem, workers were told, they should simply stop the line. In addition, the plant switched to a "just-in-time" inventory system, so that parts were delivered to workers on the line as they were needed, rather than in larger quantities—a hallmark of the Japanese auto industry that is often credited with improving efficiency. The "new Linden" also had Employee Involvement Groups (EIGs) that met to discuss production and quality problems, and there were other efforts to improve communications between labor and management. Workers were promised a larger role in decision making and problem solving on the shop floor as well.

Like most Linden workers, Roberts welcomed these changes. "I feel we're going in the right direction, finally," she said.

General Motors didn't wake up fast enough to what the Japanese were doing. They thought they were just so big that nobody could touch them. GM's a little slow; it took them a little while, but they're finally getting into it. They're finally realizing that it's not quantity—it's quality that is going to bring back the American people to buy these cars again, instead of going to Japan and Korea. And it's good that they have realized it, because they definitely got to make some changes.

The union's working with management more, which, I think, helps. We have to work together. I think there's more communication now; that's the key thing to me, communication. You got to talk. And management is really doing more for the people, you know, trying to get rid of the old dinosaurs and get them more into sync with us, 'cause we're the ones that do the job.

Roberts liked what she heard in the "new Linden" training program. She even volunteered to be an EIG spokesperson. "I like doing a good job; I like seeing a good job done. A lot of people called me Goody Two-shoes," she confessed. She was especially pleased with the just-in-time system. "The plant is cleaner; they cleared all the stock out, you know. [Before] they had racks of stock, and you couldn't even see outside. Everything was blocked up; everything was stuffy, it felt, you know, claustrophobic. Once they started doing that, it was like a whole new breath of fresh air, believe it or not. You could see sunlight, and that, that helped my day—it really did."

But her enthusiasm flagged as it became clear that the daily reality of life on the shop floor would not be quite what had been promised.

Yeah, build-in-station. If you had a problem—let's say, sometimes on the modules the clip would be shot where I would have to snap in my rod. So,

I would stop the line, go over, get a clip, stick it in there, stick the rod in, start the line up again. Which took maybe about fifteen, twenty seconds, you know, but they would go crazy, because, you know, you stop the line, and they're thinking right away they're losing money. Even though the concept was, this was how it's supposed to work. Oh man, they used to come running—unbelievable! You had the line down not even ten seconds, and, boom, they would come running, "Why's the line down?" "Uh, a clip is missing, and I was supposed to do my job in my area, so . . ." A lot of people were scared that they would get yelled at and so they went back to the old system where you take a job number down and eventually somebody else in another section would pick it up. They were so used to the old way that that's the way they wanted to keep it. You know, maybe to pamper us or satisfy us, they keep the buttons [to stop the line] in there, but it's kind of frustrating.

The EIG program—eventually abandoned altogether by the plant management—was another disappointment. "It didn't work well at all," Roberts reported. "And it's a shame, 'cause it was a good thing to have, but it just fell apart, and it was lack of communication, lack of interest. One of our complaints when we had EIG was to get the engineers to work with us on the line and see how these parts fit together that they say fit fine together on paper. But forget it. That never worked, we never got them in." She blamed the supervisors and middle managers for these failures. "A lot of foremans [*sic*], they never worked on the line, so they really don't know what it's like. And these people higher up, they just come in, they do the job, they get the money, and that's it. Sometimes I feel like they're trying to make me out like an idiot, that I don't know what I'm talking about—and that pisses me off. So I would like better communication, better understanding."

Fred Lawton also turned down the buyout and went back to work in the plant after the changeover. His assessment of the "new Linden" is remarkably similar to Roberts's, even though he is far from a Goody Two-shoes type. "It hasn't changed that much at all," he reported. "The supervisors—they always would refer to them as dinosaurs—the dinosaurs are still here. They may have been put to sleep for a while, but they're still here; they rise up every once in a while, and then they start hollering and screaming the same way they used to. You have to, I guess, put up with it. I let it go in one ear and out the other."

Like Roberts, Lawton pointed to the discrepancy between rhetoric and reality. "They [management] tell you, 'This is the way we want it; this is the way the Japanese do it.' Okay, if that's the way they do it, then let's do it that way too. But if you stopped the line, most of the time they would start the line and *then* ask what's wrong. It's going back to the dinosaurs: it's a numbers game; we need so many cars, 430 cars or whatever, and we'll do everything to get them out. They don't want that line to stop for any reason." He also questions the level of commitment on the part of both managers and workers to the EIG program: "I think it was just done to make it look good, as a show. I really don't think they were serious about it. Everybody would go to the meetings because they got a half-hour's overtime pay, so that's why people took part. We used to come up with some good ideas for them, but they didn't want any. You know, 'Okay, okay, okay.' They didn't want to hear us, you know. They would want numbers, not ideas."

In the 1970s, Lawton had been active in a dissident faction of the local union, and through his father, who worked in the plant for forty years, he was familiar with its entire history. He deeply regrets the union's recent loss of power:

My belief is that in the past five years [there have] been less grievances filed than were filed in, say, all of '77 or all of '78. Our local used to be considered the rebels, going way back. We were the ones! The metropolis, this city that this plant is in, has such a wide variety of people. They don't have the hicks from, you know, come off the farm; they got an intelligent workforce up here. But now, our local is just going along with everything. The union is playing more of a management role. Their whole attitude has changed. They seem to be too cooperative, and I think all labor unions are getting that way. I think they're all dying. They say you can't have the militance, but you need something there; otherwise, things are going to fall too easy, and that's when things go downhill. That's what happened to our union.

To him, this is part and parcel of the decline of the auto industry as a whole. Despite Lawton's negative evaluation of recent developments, he remains a loyalist in some respects:

It bothers me that we have engineers who pull up to work in Nissans. There's something wrong; there's got to be some loyalty somewhere. I mean, I have two cars; they're General Motors cars. I had a Plymouth before that—I felt uncomfortable buying it at first. I cannot see, especially these engineers and upper management, driving these other cars. People in union-appointed positions, too—[there are] guys driving Mercedes. "Hey, Mercedes is a great car; so is my other car, my wife's car, a Chevy." I said, "Well then, do me a favor; keep your Mercedes home; drive your Chevy to work. Park your Chevy in the lot; don't park your Mercedes here. If everybody bought Mercedes, where would you be working?" But nobody cares.

Although Lawton turned down the buyout, he has long aspired to leave the blue-collar world. He attended college at night and got a degree in accounting back in 1981, "with an understanding that I would be moved into a financial department position" at GM:

But then, when the time came, they said, "Go and be a foreman." Their major concern was "We don't move anybody from the hourly line into the front office."

I said, "Why not?"

They said, "We don't do that; you have to be a foreman first." I had three kids; I did not want to work six weeks days, six weeks nights, like the foremen do. I like to have some time for my home life. I mean, I coach two soccer teams; I coach baseball. I couldn't do that as a foreman, but as a straight salary worker, I wouldn't have a problem.

I was hurt and disappointed, and was ready to leave then. I even had gone to an employment agency, looking for other jobs. At the time, in '81, we were probably making $21,000 or $22,000 a year. I went looking for junior accountant jobs, and they were all starting at $13,000 and $12,000 and no benefits.

So that was tough, but they don't move from the line in. You have to go and be a supervisor first, and that bothered me.

Lawton continues to dream of leaving the plant to become an accountant. He thought hard about taking the buyout. But "I couldn't just do it; I would have to have something to go into. All my résumés went out, and I got nothing back. I have a whole folder in there, probably about two hundred responses back, and they were all: 'Very sorry, we'll keep your résumé on file. If something comes up, we'll let you know.'" So for Lawton, leaving the plant remains a fantasy, at least for now.

The Lack of Nostalgia

Social commentators in the past often lamented the destructive effects of capitalist industrialization on ordinary people; today, however, the focus of critical inquiry has shifted to the results of *de*industrialization. Despite the irony of this reversal, there is ample basis for concern—particularly from a labor perspective—about the structural transformations now under way. Radical economic restructuring inevitably renders less powerful groups newly vulnerable, and it threatens whatever forms of self-protection they have developed. Indeed, as manufacturing has moved to regions with cheaper, more tractable labor, and as GM and other American firms have seen their formerly unchallenged market position dramatically eroded by foreign competition, millions of people have been thrown out of work, and employers have launched bold attacks on labor organizations. Particularly in monoindustrial communities where alternative sources of work are few or nonexistent, many victims of plant closings or mass layoffs who once enjoyed middle-class incomes have been forced into long-term unemployment or into marginal, poorly paid jobs and have suffered a radical decline in their standard of living. Discarded, like obsolete machinery, by their former employers, they face a bleak future of economic deprivation and social humiliation. A considerable literature already exists documenting the devastating social effects these developments have produced in recent years.[2]

Even if this proves a transitional phenomenon limited to a single, lost generation of "displaced" workers, it represents a tragic and inexcusable failure of social policy. Without denying its importance, however, one can also recognize that this is only part of the story of industrial decline and restructuring. Some former high-wage factory workers like Edward Salerno and Dan Cooper have been able to make a relatively smooth transition into other types of employment; others, like Susan Roberts and Fred Lawton, are still employed in basic industry, although technological and organizational innovations have transformed their work. To be sure, neither those who left GM-Linden under the buyout program nor those still employed there are representative of the industrial labor force, past or present. The buyout takers are a self-selected, relatively youthful group who are in many ways atypical of the larger population of displaced workers; those who remain at GM-Linden are dependent on a firm that is undergoing extensive internal restructuring and whose survival, given the continuing shake-up in the global automobile industry, is far from assured.

But it is precisely their peculiar yet strategic social locations that make these two groups of workers particularly interesting. The buyout takers' post-GM employment trajectories suggest the problems and possibilities confronting young workers in the growing service-based "postindustrial" economy, whereas the situation of their co-workers who stayed at GM exposes the complexities of the process of work reorganization now under way in the shrinking, but still important, manufacturing sector. The recent experiences of workers like these may be more relevant for understanding the prospects for future generations of non-college-educated workers than the more dramatic stories of emiseration among former industrial workers in other settings that are so extensively documented in the literature on deindustrialization.

For both those who left and those who stayed at GM-Linden, the future is extremely uncertain, and they are painfully aware of this fact. Although so far, both groups have escaped the long-term unemployment, downward mobility, and accompanying social distress that has afflicted so many other workers, they know very well that they remain vulnerable to such a fate. As Dan Cooper put it, "I don't know what's down the road." And yet surprisingly few GM-Linden workers, past or present, express any desire to restore the old industrial system that is now collapsing around them. Their lack of nostalgia highlights a sad fact that is all too often forgotten in the age of deindustrialization: factory work in the golden age of mass production was deeply problematic in its own right. However much it fascinated some left-wing intellectuals, workers themselves never romanticized the assembly line—instead they mostly yearned to escape its relentless and dehumanizing rhythms.

In twentieth-century America, alienation at work has been a perennial theme of public debate, and the automobile industry has always been its prototypical symbol. In the prosperous 1950s, for example, Ely Chinoy's classic study *Automobile Workers and the American Dream* drew attention to the lack of opportunities for social mobility facing GM workers and to their daily frustrations on the line.[3] Two decades later, following the 1972 strike at the GM plant in Lordstown, Ohio, "blue-collar blues" were rediscovered and became the focus of the U.S. government's high-profile 1973 study *Work in America*.[4] But not long afterward, the frustrations and degradations of daily life in the factory were displaced from center stage as capital mobility and technological change suddenly brought up new questions. Whether mass production work would survive at all in the restructured, downsized economy, what to do about the abrupt erosion of real wages and fringe benefits, and the implications of the precipitous decline of organized labor—these were the issues that now captured the attention of social commentators. In the wake of the economic upheavals of the 1980s and 1990s, the classic questions of worker alienation and degradation have been virtually obliterated from public memory.

Yet for workers at places like GM-Linden, the daily humiliations of the assembly line continue to rankle. Even in the anxious 1980s, their long-standing desire to leave the factory was what motivated so many Linden workers to accept the buyout offer. And those who did so appear to have surprisingly few regrets, even though most are economically worse off now than when they worked at GM. Among the buyout takers I followed over a five-year period, almost all reported without hesitation that they would make the same decision if they had it to do over again—in large part because of their bitter memories of working at GM. Significantly, the few who did have regrets were disproportionately African Americans, who fared significantly worse in the outside labor market than their white counterparts.

Most of the Linden buyout takers landed on their feet; almost none of them joined the ranks of the unemployed, and a sizable subgroup became modestly successful small business owners like Dan Cooper. However, even among the majority, who were downwardly mobile and who now hold relatively poorly paid jobs, few have any nostalgia for GM. The Linden buyout takers had several key advantages over most displaced industrial workers: they were self-selected; they lived in a region with low unemployment; and crucially, they were relatively young (typically in their thirties) when they reentered the labor market. To be sure, in stating that they have no regrets, some may be making a virtue of necessity. Perhaps the buyout takers in serious distress are those whom I was unable to track in the later phases of the research. These caveats notwithstanding, the overwhelmingly positive outlook of those with whom I did maintain contact suggests that most former auto workers are not mourning the world they have lost.

Like the buyout takers, those who remain employed in the Linden plant have no kind words for the traditional system of mass production, GM style. Contrary to the popular assumption that blue-collar workers are committed to the work rules and other features of the status quo ante, few current GM-Linden employees complain about the new forms of work organization they now confront. However, many do express resentment about management's failure to implement fully the changes it promised to make when the plant was modernized in the mid-1980s. Those changes did *not* include the introduction of flexible teams of workers who rotate jobs Japanese style (the "team concept"), which have been the focus of so much debate among auto industry analysts.[5] But GM—with the local union's active cooperation—did introduce a range of other organizational innovations at Linden at the same time as it updated the plant technologically. In the postchangeover training period, workers were explicitly told to expect improved treatment at the hands of supervisors, better communication with management, and a larger role in decision making and problem solving on the shop floor. The build-in-station concept, just-in-time inventory systems, and EIGs were among the changes introduced. Most workers were enthusiastic about the cluster of organizational reforms that constituted the "new Linden," but like Susan Roberts and Fred Lawton, they were deeply disappointed when the much-touted promise of increased worker participation and responsibility proved empty.

A Lost Opportunity?

Many commentators presume that labor is deeply committed to defending the work rules and job classification systems that were embedded in the postwar mass production system, and is thus opposed to teams and related forms of work reorganization. For example, Mike Parker and Jane Slaughter, among the first and most insightful critics of teams, state: "In most instances where the team concept has been implemented, it was a management proposal which met opposition from the workforce."[6] However, there is surprisingly little research about what rank-and-file workers actually think about these matters.[7] Consider, for example, the highly influential 1990 book on the auto industry *The Machine That Changed the World,* based on research by scholars at MIT. The authors assert that the "lean production" system first perfected by the Japanese auto firms, key features of which are flexible teams and just-in-time inventory systems, offers workers a "humanly fulfilling" alternative to traditional mass production. Regrettably, however, the book presents no evidence whatsoever to support this claim. Apparently, none of the considerable resources supporting the research (the dust jacket boasts of a "5-Million-Dollar 5-Year Study") was used to investigate blue-collar workers' own evaluation of the lean production system.[8]

Other commentators have criticized the team concept and the lean production system on behalf of workers, pointing out the ways in which these innovations can increase the pace and pressures of work, but here too there has been little effort to document systematically the views of ordinary workers. If these critiques reproduce workers' perspectives at all, they tend to draw primarily on the statements of dissident unionists who have been vocal in their opposition to teams and other organizational reform efforts, notably the New Directions group within the UAW.[9] While this viewpoint certainly merits discussion, there is little evidence that it is widespread among workers. In fact, the typical rank-and-file viewpoint may be more accurately reflected in the dominant UAW policy, which generally has been one of cooperation with management's efforts to introduce work reforms—precisely the policy that motivates the dissidents' critique.

A major reference point for both advocates of lean production and for its critics is the GM-Toyota joint venture in Fremont, California, known as New United Motor Manufacturing, Inc., or NUMMI. This plant is run by Toyota, using flexible teams and various other so-called Japanese management techniques. (GM's responsibility primarily involves the marketing side of the operation—ironically, the only area where the plant has had serious problems.) The workforce is comprised almost entirely of former GM workers who were employed at the same plant before it was closed in 1982. In contrast to the wholly

Japanese-owned auto plants in the United States, called transplants, NUMMI's workers are all UAW members. Under GM, the plant had a reputation for low productivity and frequent strikes, but when it reopened as NUMMI in 1984, with the same workforce and even the same local union officers, it became an overnight success story, with productivity and quality ratings comparable to those of Toyota's plants in Japan. Efforts to emulate it inspired the organizational innovations at Linden and at other Big Three (GM, Ford, and Chrysler) automobile assembly plants around the United States.

Another showcase of workplace transformation is the Saturn plant in Spring Hill, Tennessee, a wholly GM-owned subsidiary of that corporation. Saturn opened in 1990, five years after the UAW and GM signed an agreement to launch it as an experiment in maximizing worker participation. Saturn too has self-directed work teams but carries the principle of labor-management cooperation even further, involving workers and the UAW directly in long-range corporate planning, as well as hiring and personnel policy.[10]

Many have praised the NUMMI and Saturn plants as models of workplace democratization; others, however, have severely criticized them.[11] Detractors argue that despite the rhetoric of worker control, the team concept and similar participatory schemes are basically strategies to enhance *managerial* control. In this view, far from offering a humane alternative to traditional assembly-line production, workers at team-concept plants participate mainly in the intensification of their own exploitation, mobilizing their detailed firsthand knowledge of the labor process to help management speed up production and eliminate wasteful work practices. As Mike Parker and Jane Slaughter argue in one of the first and most trenchant such critiques, "[T]he little influence workers do have over their jobs is that in effect they are organized to time-study themselves."[12] They argue that the team concept is a system of "management by stress," and see it as extremely treacherous, undermining union power in the name of a dubious form of participation in management decisions.

Despite its merits, this critique underplays a crucial point: namely, that workers themselves often find intrinsically appealing the idea of participating in what historically have been exclusively managerial decision-making processes, especially in comparison to traditional

American management methods.[13] This may be the case even where worker participation is confined to a very restricted arena, such as helping to streamline the production process or otherwise raise productivity. Parker and Slaughter themselves acknowledge that at NUMMI, "nobody says they want to return to the days when GM ran the plant."[14] Unless one wishes to believe that auto workers are simply dupes of managerial manipulation, the apparent preference of the workforce for the new system suggests that it has some positive features and cannot simply be dismissed as the latest form of labor control. It further suggests that whatever the obstacles U.S. companies must overcome to meet the challenge of Japanese competition, the problem is not resistance from workers to more participatory systems of factory organization.

At GM-Linden and in most other Big Three auto plants, things are far different than in NUMMI and Saturn. Management has made only tentative, surprisingly timid efforts (and in many cases even these have failed) to introduce truly participatory systems. What has stood in the way of change is not resistance from workers, who are ready to try anything in their desperation to escape the traditional system. Rather, management has proved itself unable (or perhaps unwilling) to implement even relatively modest changes like those announced with such fanfare at GM-Linden in the late 1980s. Since such reforms are typically introduced in the name of enhancing the plant's—and ultimately the firm's—competitiveness in a context where failure to compete can mean closing down entirely, any sustained resistance from workers would be surprising. But what is striking is not the mere acquiescence but rather the enthusiasm with which so many workers have responded to restructuring efforts of this sort. They dislike the traditional system of management so intensely that they desperately want to believe in the promise of a new one. Yet GM has failed to capitalize on this opportunity, and at most of its plants, the traditional system—with a few cosmetic modifications—has been preserved intact.

At GM-Linden, some local union leaders are skeptical about the team concept, but to date, local management has not proposed this particular form of organizational change, even though it has had several opportunities to do so. The changes management has initiated at

Linden, however, that do move in a participatory direction have been
accepted by the local union with little difficulty. Indeed, at the time
of the changeover, the "new Linden" program was jointly developed
by the local union and management. As for the rank and file, those
who are not particularly active in the union, my research suggests that
the vast majority welcomed the reforms introduced at Linden with
great enthusiasm. Like their co-workers who left to take the buyout,
the workers who returned to the plant after the changeover detested
the old system and were delighted by the prospect of replacing it with
something new—especially since they were led to believe that the
degrading and humiliating treatment they had so often endured from
supervisors would be eliminated. Ultimately, workers' criticism of the
postchangeover situation focused, not on the reforms themselves, but
rather on management's failure to live up to its professed commitment to carry them out. In all this, GM-Linden is far more typical of
American auto plants than such highly visible showcases as NUMMI
and Saturn.

Uncertain Futures

The responses of both former and present GM-Linden workers to the
dilemmas and challenges they now face are powerfully influenced by
the past. But their view of that past is complex and ambivalent. On
the one hand, with their high pay and strong union, auto workers see
themselves as they often have been seen by others: as an aristocracy
of labor, the supposed millionaires of the working class. But on the
other hand, as far as their actual shop-floor experience is concerned,
they see themselves as victims. It is not so much that their jobs are un-
imaginably boring and routinized—the classic prototype, after all, of
alienated labor—because most workers accept that as an inevitable
feature of mass production industry. What they hate far more intensely, and what virtually none sees as inevitable, is the abusive and
degrading treatment that so many workers routinely endure at the
hands of first-line supervisors. This has created a deep reservoir of
resentment and frustration (and also an important foundation for the
adversarial industrial relations system for which the United States is
now famous worldwide). Their bitter memories of all this are precisely

what lead so many past and present GM-Linden workers to welcome the possibility of change, even without knowing whether they will be winners or losers in whatever socioeconomic order emerges from the present disarray.

From an outsider's perspective, the auto workers' future prospects hardly look promising: they have few economic resources; little education (the average level for both the buyout takers and those remaining in the plant is eleventh grade); and the political influence they formerly could exercise through the UAW, always modest, has declined precipitously. Yet having thus far successfully eluded the unambiguous marginalization so painfully inflicted on the obvious losers in the restructuring process—the long-term unemployed and the growing underclass—the workers whose voices are reproduced in these pages are remarkably hopeful. Those still in the plant, who retain most of the economic advantages historically associated with employment in the auto industry (despite some erosion in pay and benefits after a wave of concession bargaining in the 1980s), have difficulty imagining that a reorganized work process or a changed industrial relations regime could be any worse than what it would replace, and many dare to hope that it will be better. As for those who took the buyout, they are well aware of what they gave up economically, but they still hope that the noneconomic advantages of their pact with the devil will be worth the price of lost wages and fringe benefits.

The hopes of both groups may well be disappointed. But it is crucial to understand their contempt for the dinosaurs of the old industrial regime and their eagerness for something better. To take their perspective seriously is to abandon any effort to restore the world of mass production industry as it existed in the past—which is probably impossible in any case. If we look forward rather than backward, the real challenge is how to enhance the resources with which workers might confront the newly transformed world of work now taking shape. Unionism, their major resource in past years, is now hopelessly besieged in the shrinking manufacturing sector and largely nonexistent (outside the public sector) in the vast new postindustrial service-based economy. How can an organization like the UAW, once widely admired as a paragon of democratic industrial unionism, adapt to the radically new situation facing its current and former members?

The record so far is not inspiring. At the national level, the union has yet to forge an alternative to its long-standing habit, institutionalized in the aftermath of World War II, of ceding basic decisions about how to organize production to management. The UAW faces vast new challenges in the shape of huge job losses in the domestic auto industry, as well as the rapid erosion of unionism in the industry (thanks to the growth of the nonunion Japanese-owned transplants and of a growing domestically and foreign-owned nonunion auto parts sector). In this crisis the auto union has concentrated on trying to preserve the security of both employment and income for its dwindling membership. That has led to some positive achievements, among them the buyout program that was so popular at Linden. But the UAW has yet to come to terms with the changes in work organization that are now under way in the plants, changes that often render traditional modes of resistance to managerial domination obsolete.

Even more tragically, in view of the vast overcapacity that still exists in the domestic auto industry, and especially at GM (a reality that makes future plant closings inevitable), the national UAW has failed to prevent management from pitting workers in one factory against those in another run by the same company—what auto industry insiders call whipsawing—leading to dramatic erosion in the power of local unions. In this context, challenging management too forcefully at the local level simply invites the ultimate sanction of a permanent plant closing. This is one reason that Linden's local union, UAW Local 595, which enjoyed a reputation for militancy until the mid-1980s, has been largely quiescent in the face of the dramatic events of recent years. Linden's former and present workers may be hopeful about the future, but few express any faith in the ability of the profoundly weakened UAW—or any other union, for that matter—to assist them with their current dilemmas. The union's diminished strength is far more troubling to many of them than the erosion and transformation of factory employment itself.

The GM-Linden story, then, is largely one of the failure of both management and union to respond effectively to rapidly changing circumstances. On the management side, GM's internal organizational structure and traditional corporate culture have remained largely intact, despite much ballyhooed efforts to institute changes. GM has been unable to reap the full advantages of new technologies or to make a successful transition to a more participatory system of workplace management, even though the firm has invested considerable resources in both areas. Sadly, management's own inertia has been reinforced by the weakening of the UAW in this critical period. Long habituated to a reactive stance toward management initiatives, in recent years the union has left the challenge of reorganizing the workplace largely to management while warily embracing "cooperation" in hopes of slowing the hemorrhaging of jobs in the auto industry. The net result has been an increasingly uncompetitive status for GM, which in turn has further weakened the union, creating a vicious circle of decline.

Because so much of the recent behavior of both GM management and of the UAW and its members is rooted in the past, the first step toward understanding the current situation is to look back at the history of the system of mass production in the automobile industry and the accompanying pattern of labor-management relations. Chapter 2, accordingly, explores the experience of workers under the traditional system as it existed at GM-Linden in the postwar years. The role of the UAW in that system and the ways in which the dramatic transformations of the 1980s affected the union are the subject of chapter 3. Chapter 4 examines the effects of the job security programs the UAW negotiated with GM and takes a closer look at those who chose to leave the factory entirely—buyout takers like Edward Salerno and Dan Cooper. Finally, chapter 5 returns us to the factory itself, exploring the ways in which the new technology and the new industrial relations introduced in the 1980s affected Linden's workforce.

Chapter Two

Prisoners of Prosperity

Auto Workers in the Postwar Period

Most commentators agree that the American industrial relations system stabilized in the immediate aftermath of World War II, following a period of protracted labor turbulence. The postwar settlement was centered in the automobile industry and especially in the transformation of the relationship between GM and the UAW, then, respectively, the world's largest corporation and the world's largest labor union. In 1945, just after the war's end, the UAW launched its ill-fated "open-the-books" strike against GM, demanding that the giant auto firm open its books to public scrutiny if it insisted on linking higher wages to higher car prices. In this struggle, led by Walter Reuther, the UAW sought to extend union power into the sphere of corporate decision making and thus into the wider society. This effort proved unsuccessful, yet shortly afterward Reuther triumphed over his adversaries within the UAW, becoming the union's president in 1946 and consolidating his power thereafter. Rather than using his new position of strength to expand the broad, progressive agenda he had championed for the previous decade, Reuther gradually retreated, accepting a more limited role for organized labor. Against the background of a national resurgence of conservatism in the late 1940s, the UAW increasingly restricted its efforts to improving wages and working conditions for union members, while ceding to management all the prerogatives involved in organizing the production process and in economic planning. In 1950, Reuther signed an unprecedented five-year contract between the UAW and GM, the "Treaty of Detroit," signaling a new era of labor peace. This was the preeminent symbol of Reutherism and of the broader postwar capital-labor accord that would endure until the late 1970s.[1]

The industrial order that emerged from these events is often characterized as Fordist, although it was actually a historically particular variant of the global mass production system that that term denotes. What is beyond dispute is that the postwar labor settlement in the U.S. auto industry was predicated on, and at the same time reinforced, a system of work organization established decades earlier—well before the UAW even appeared on the scene. Indeed, to understand the dynamics of the postwar settlement as it shaped life on the factory floor requires a brief review of this earlier history. After sketching the evolution of the system and its stabilization after World War II, I examine the ways in which workers at the GM-Linden plant actually experienced it in the period prior to the sweeping economic transformations of the 1980s. This adds an important dimension to the image of the capital-labor "accord," for although the overall contours of the industrial system were no longer in question, the factory nonetheless remained a site of intense conflict and deeply rooted discontent. "Settlement" at the national level obscured ongoing turmoil at the local level, where workers' experience was forged.

Fordism and the Social Relations
of the Shop Floor

Whereas the earliest car manufacturers had depended heavily on skilled craftsmen to make small production runs of luxury vehicles for the rich, during the 1910s the industry was transformed into a model of mass production efficiency by systematically removing skill from the labor process through scientific management, or Taylorism (named for its premier theorist, Frederick Winslow Taylor). The Ford Motor Company, then the leading automotive firm, perfected not only de-skilling but also product standardization, the use of interchangeable parts, mechanization, a moving assembly line, and high wages. These were the key elements of what has since come to be known as Fordism, defining not only the organization of the automobile industry but also that of modern mass production generally.

As rationalization and de-skilling proceeded through the auto industry in the 1910s and 1920s, the proportion of highly skilled jobs fell dramatically. The introduction in 1914 of Ford's famous Five Dollar Day (then twice the going rate for factory workers) both secured labor's consent to the horrendous working conditions these innovations produced, and helped promote the mass consumption that mass production required for its success. Managerial paternalism, symbolized by Ford's Sociological Department, supplemented high wages in this regime of labor control—although this was one feature of the original system that would prove short lived. Early Ford management also developed job classification systems, ranking jobs by skill levels and so establishing an internal labor market within which workers could hope to advance.[2]

De-skilling was never complete, however, and some skill differentials persisted among production workers. Even in the 1970s and 1980s, auto body painters and welders had more skill than workers who simply assembled parts, for example. But these were insignificant gradations compared to the gap between production workers and the privileged stratum of craft workers known in the auto industry as the skilled trades—tool and die makers, machinists, electricians, and various other maintenance workers. Nevertheless, the mass of the industry's semiskilled operatives united with the skilled-trades elite in the great industrial union drives of the 1930s. In the UAW, both groups were integrated into the same local unions and remain so today, although this alliance has suffered periodic strains.

The triumph of unionism left the industry's internal division of jobs and skills intact, but the UAW did succeed in narrowing wage differentials and in institutionalizing seniority (a principle originally introduced by management but enforced erratically in the pre-union era) as the basic criterion for layoffs and job transfers. For the first decade after unionization, much labor-management conflict focused on the definition of seniority groups. Workers wanted plantwide or departmentwide seniority to maximize employment security, while management sought the narrowest possible seniority classifications to minimize the disruptions associated with workers' movement from job to job. But once the UAW won plantwide seniority for layoffs, it welcomed management's efforts to increase the number of job classifications for transfers, since this maximized opportunities for high-seniority workers to choose the jobs they preferred. By the 1950s, this system of narrowly defined jobs, supported by union and management alike, was firmly entrenched.[3]

While the union did little to ameliorate the actual experience of work in the postwar period, with the job classification system solidified, those committed to a long-term career in the industry could build up enough seniority to bid on the better jobs within their plants. While the early, management-imposed job classification systems had been based on skill and corresponded closely to wage differentials, the union eliminated most of the variation in wage rates. Indeed, the payment system the UAW won, which persists to this day, is extremely egalitarian. Regardless of seniority or individual merit, assembly workers are paid a fixed hourly rate negotiated for their job classification, and the rate spread across classifications is very narrow. Formal education, which is in any case relatively low (at GM-Linden, both skilled-trades and production workers averaged twelve years of schooling in the late 1980s), is virtually irrelevant to earnings. At GM-Linden, production workers' rates in 1988 ranged from a low of $13.51 per hour for sweepers and janitors to a high of $14.69 for metal repair work in the body shop. Skilled-trades workers' hourly rates were only slightly higher, ranging from $15.90 to $16.80 (with a $.20 an hour "merit spread"), although their annual earnings are usually much higher than those of production workers due to extensive overtime.[4]

The grueling nature of production work in the auto industry changed relatively little over the postwar decades. Any hopes for improvement in the deadly tedium of the work or for a moderation in its intensity were relegated to the realm of fantasy. Extending the original logic of the Five Dollar Day, the UAW continued to extract improvements in the economic terms under which its members agreed to submit to these conditions, and for many workers this was the only incentive to return to the factory gate day after day. Rising wages and excellent health, pension, and supplemental unemployment benefits, gradually accumulating into the equivalent of a private welfare state, made auto workers into the blue-collar aristocrats of the age. Throughout the postwar period, they enjoyed continual increases in pay, both in absolute terms and relative to workers in other sectors, and their real wages rose as well until the crisis of the 1980s. The ratio of auto assemblers' to all U.S. nonsupervisory workers' hourly earnings increased from 1.18 in 1950 to 1.55 in 1980. And total hourly compensation costs (including fringe benefits) for an auto assembler rose nearly 400 percent in real terms between 1948 and 1981.[5] This was the quid pro quo for the rapid productivity growth of the period under the terms of the postwar settlement.

The settlement also established new mechanisms to regulate and contain shop-floor conflict. The UAW's rise already had set limits on the arbitrary exercise of power by supervisors; indeed the original goal of institutionalizing seniority rights was precisely to undercut the long-standing traditions of favoritism and other managerial abuses. But the shop-steward system that had enforced workers' new rights in the 1930s and 1940s, always relatively tenuous at GM, was weakened in the postwar period. Industrial conflict was now channeled into more predictable patterns, most importantly through the increasingly complex grievance process. This was the basis of the highly bureaucratic and adversarial industrial relations system that would later be criticized as a drag on U.S. productivity, along with the proliferation of job classifications and seniority-based work rules.

This system functioned reasonably well until the emergence of new international competition for the U.S. automakers in the late 1970s, yet workers' resentments smoldered just beneath the surface calm of Fordism and Reutherism. Peace prevailed at the national level between the union and the corporations, but in local unions and among the rank and file, the managed retained a fierce animosity toward management. Fed by a steady diet of degrading treatment at the hands of supervisors, this hostility found expression in an expanding volume of grievances and exploded occasionally into wildcat strikes.

Most auto production workers became resigned to the physical rigors of factory work, the Taylorist division of labor, and the resulting tedium as inevitable features of modern capitalist manufacturing. Although virtually none found this system appealing, few could imagine any possible alternative. The deal brokered by the UAW, trading high pay and good benefits for managerial control over production, was also accepted by most of the giant union's members as a necessary evil—at least until management broke its side of the bargain in the 1980s. Workers' deep antagonism toward management was rooted

elsewhere: in the social relations of the shop floor, especially the military-style regimentation to which workers were subjected and the insensitivity of many first-line supervisors to the basic human needs of
those in their charge. The rise of the union and the system of industrial jurisprudence it helped institutionalize had set some limits on
managerial power, yet foremen still faced unrelenting pressure from
above to get production out, and this often led them to behave in ways
that workers found simply intolerable. Unlike Taylorism itself, this
behavior was something few workers could simply accept as a business
necessity.

The combination of mindless, monotonous work, unrelenting regimentation, and inhumane supervision made the workers feel like prisoners, and they routinely employ the metaphor of the plant as prison
in discussing their jobs. They entered the factory gates willingly
enough, since for most, lacking any specialized training or educational
credentials beyond high school, it was their only opportunity to share
in the unrivaled prosperity of the postwar boom years. But once they
grew accustomed to the high pay and benefits, most began counting
the years until their "sentences" (typically thirty years, when they became eligible for retirement) would be up. Like auto workers elsewhere in the nation, those at GM-Linden served out their time with
deep feelings of bitterness, as prisoners of prosperity.[6]

GM-Linden: The Division of Labor

The Linden, New Jersey, GM plant sits on an 85-acre lot about 15
miles south of New York City. It first opened in May 1937, shortly
after the UAW first won recognition from GM, following the massive
sit-down strike in Flint, Michigan, the previous winter. After building
Buick, Oldsmobile, and Pontiac cars for a few years, the Linden plant
was retooled for U.S. Navy fighter plane production during World
War II and then reconverted to automobile assembly in 1946. In the
1960s, it became the first plant outside Detroit to make Cadillacs
(Sevilles), along with Buicks (Rivieras) and Oldsmobiles (Eldorados).
These large luxury cars were built at Linden until 1985, when the
plant shifted over to smaller car models.[7]

For most of the postwar era, GM employed 4,000 to 5,000 blue-

collar workers on two shifts at Linden, although as with the auto industry as a whole, employment fluctuated sharply over the business
cycle, and at times the plant operated with only one shift. Most of the
plant's hourly employees were unskilled or semiskilled production
workers, complemented by an elite corps of skilled-trades workers
in the maintenance division. In 1985, Linden had 4,343 production
workers and 376 skilled-trades workers on its payroll. The overwhelming majority of these workers were male, for women were largely
excluded from auto assembly jobs after World War II. Virtually no
women worked in the plant during the 1950s and 1960s. GM did hire
women during the 1970s, but by 1985, they were less than 15 percent
of the Linden production workforce, and less than 1 percent of the
skilled trades. Men of color were a more substantial part of the automotive workforce, both at Linden and nationally. In 1985, 61 percent
of Linden's production workers were white; 27 percent were African
American; and 12 percent were Latino; however, 91 percent of the
skilled-trades workers were white.[8]

Linden conforms to the typical auto assembly plant organization,
with the vast bulk of the production workforce divided among four
main departments: the body shop, where the metal frame of the car

TABLE 1.   GM-Linden Production Workers by Department and
Selected Characteristics, 1985

Department	Number of Workers	Percentage of Workers	Mean Seniority (years)	Percent Female	Percent White
Trim	1,330	30.6	10.8	21	61
Chassis	1,114	25.7	9.8	16	60
Paint	608	14.0	12.9	16	57
Body	595	13.7	9.5	4	65
Material	306	7.0	17.6	3	68
Inspection	235	5.4	18.0	10	65
Maintenance	155	3.6	21.9	0	66
All Production Workers	4,343	100.0	11.8	15	61

SOURCE: Computed from data obtained from GM-Linden management.

is assembled; the paint shop, where the bodies are painted; the chassis department, where the motor, engine, and wheels are assembled and united with the car bodies; and the trim shop, where the seats, electrical wiring, glass, and instrument panels are installed. As table 1 shows, 84 percent of the plant's production workers were in these four departments in 1985, with well over half in chassis and trim alone. Smaller units include the inspection area and the material department, where parts are stored and distributed. There is also a small crew of unskilled janitors, sweepers, and other unskilled workers responsible for plant upkeep, who are assigned to the maintenance department (along with the skilled-trades workers) and deployed as needed throughout the plant.

Although wage differentials are rather small, they are by no means insignificant to workers. Still, the key to the informal de facto hierarchy among production jobs is not pay rates, but instead what workers themselves perceive as desirable job characteristics. While individual preferences always vary somewhat, the consensus is reflected in the seniority required to secure any given position. In general, any job "off the line," where workers can pace themselves rather than be governed by the assembly line, is much sought after. As table 1 shows, mean seniority levels are much higher in the inspection, material, and maintenance departments—where almost all jobs are off the line— than in the four assembly departments. While comparing departments in this way suggests the broad contours of the plant's hierarchy of job desirability, a more detailed picture can be derived from analysis of the job classifications that are enshrined in the local union contract.

Table 2 lists the 30 production worker classifications (from among the plant's 89 populated production classifications) in which the median seniority level was 20 years or more in 1985.[9] These extremely desirable jobs employed only 11 percent of the Linden production workforce in 1985, most of them high-seniority workers. The list includes inspection and repair positions throughout the plant, as well as many classifications in the material and maintenance departments, where all jobs are off the line. Also highly prized are subassembly jobs where workers can build up stock or "bank" their work. Examples include the "Assemble seats A" and "Assemble all glass" classifications

TABLE 2. Selected Characteristics of Production Classifications at GM-Linden with Median Seniority of 20 years or more in 1985

Classification	Department(s)	Number of Workers	Median Seniority (years)	Percent Male	Percent White
Inspect trim and hardware	Inspection	71	20	94	69
Sweeper	Maintenance	81	21	100	65
Operator-power equipment	Material, Maintenance	75	21	100	59
Clean equipment	Paint, Maintenance	45	21	100	56
Trim repair-new car conditioning	Trim	34	21	100	80
Light repair	Chassis	15	21	100	80
Inspect metal finish	Body	5	21	80	60
Inspect wire & accessories	Inspection	5	21	80	40
Oiler	Maintenance	5	21	100	20
Power sweeper	Maintenance	4	21	100	100
Baler & shredder	Maintenance	3	21	100	66
Assemble seats A	Trim	8	22	100	88
Metal repair & ding	Body	8	22	100	88
Material handler	Material	2	22	100	100
Repair after duco	Paint	30	23	97	50
Yard laborer	Maintenance	7	23	100	71
Assemble all glass	Trim	5	23	100	100
Miscellaneous parts inspection	Inspection	6	23.5	100	83

TABLE 2 (continued)

Classification	Department(s)	Number of Workers	Median Seniority (years)	Percent Male	Percent White
Car washer	Chassis	2	24.5	100	100
Inspect welding	Body	3	25	100	100
General	Material	21	26	100	81
Major salvage repair & inspection	Chassis, Inspection	2	27	100	100
Elpo attendant	Paint	6	28	100	83
Paint	Material	2	29	100	50
Inspect final new car conditioning	Inspection	25	30	96	72
Bonderite equipment operator	Paint	4	32	100	0
Stockman-car conditioning	Material	3	32	100	33
Radio and electrical repair & inspection	Trim	1	32	100	100
Receiving inspection	Material	3	33	100	100
Driver-outside	Chassis	2	33	100	100

SOURCE: Computed from data obtained from GM-Linden management.

shown in table 2, both in the trim department. "The good jobs, to me, are the 'subs,' what we call subassemblies," said Raymond Perry, who worked at Linden for over 15 years. "This job is off the line. You work at your own pace. You stop when you get ready. You take your own breaks. It don't compare to working on the assembly line. You can't go anywhere—you're tied, you're pinned there." Most subassembly jobs are in the trim and chassis departments, although body and paint have some off-line jobs of other types.[10]

Wage rates for production workers at Linden, which varied very little in any case, were *negatively* correlated with seniority in 1985.[11] Perhaps the ultimate testament to the intensely alienating nature of work on the assembly line is that among the jobs auto workers prefer most are those of sweeper and janitor, even though these jobs have the *lowest* hourly wage rates. At Linden in 1985, the median seniority of sweepers was 21 years and that of janitors was 19 years—compared with the 9-year median seniority level of production workers in the plant as a whole.[12] Some sweepers were workers who had been injured and could no longer do a normal job, but most were old-timers who got the jobs through the seniority system.[13] "It was a combination," Carl Block, a former Linden worker who was a union committeeman for several years, explained: "Sometimes they were hurt people who had what was called light duty, a temporary job as a sweeper. And the rest of the people were very high seniority, because it was freedom from the line. You could make your own time; you could hang out. Also as a sweeper, you usually worked through [model] changeovers, so you got some extra money. . . . It wasn't the kind of thing where people said, 'He's a wimp,' or anything like that. It was just: 'This is an old guy.' It was a little bit of justice, almost, you know, that this person, after being there for so many years, could get this job."

Among the four large production departments, as table 1 shows, average seniority levels varied relatively little in 1985. But the distribution of desirable jobs across these departments, as well as such factors as the quality of supervision, nevertheless gave each shop a distinctive reputation. Most workers agreed that the paint shop was the best place to work in this period, the body shop the worst, and trim and chassis somewhere in between—as the average seniority levels also suggest. "The paint department was considered like the rest home of the plant," said Jonathan Fox. "There are no tools, no guns, no welding." Similarly, Sean O'Brien recalled moving to the paint shop from the body shop: "I came from the body shop; I went up to paint. My first day there, they sent me over to the bumper line to wipe off bumpers and I'm sitting here doing this job and I'm saying, 'You actually get paid here for doing this, huh? I've been in the body shop for how many years killing myself?' And then the biggest kick I got out of the whole thing was the relief man came over and gave me a relief. I said, 'I actually get a relief on this job too?' The guy looked at me. I said, 'Where was this part of the plant before?' "

By contrast, jobs in particularly hot or dirty parts of the plant, or those in areas where supervision was especially brutal, were shunned by workers whose seniority gave them any choice. Until the mid-1980s, when robots replaced workers on many of the jobs involved, the worst area was "the jungle," the part of the body shop where car bodies were welded together. "It was filthy over there," Matthew Larson, who worked there in the late 1970s, recalled. "You'd walk through there three times, and you'd have an extra two inches on your shoes, from the grease on the ground, the oil and all. When I worked in there, you'd have to scrape it off the bottom of your shoes." As Mike Evans, who worked there in the early 1980s, explained: "They called it the jungle because of all the spot-welding guns. They had these little cables and they looked like big tree branches, and they had them hanging from the ceiling and all that, and you couldn't see down the line. I still have burn scars on me from the welding. Even though they'd give us coveralls, we'd only get one pair a week. Working in the body shop, especially when you get this really hot, humid weather, by the end of the first day the coveralls are drenched in perspiration, and they're covered with grease and dirt. By the end of the week, forget about it, you can stand them up in a corner because they're so caked out." Carl Block, who represented workers in "the jungle" for several years, had a similar view:

It was unspeakably bad. People had scars on their faces. Women sometimes would pull down their shirt a little bit and show me across their chest where they were all scarred up. You could cut yourself very easily. And I would say 35 to 55 percent of the people there had carpal tunnel syndrome, which you got from repeated use of heavy vibrating machinery. The noise was deafening. And the foremen drove you to the ground. There was not even a semblance that you had a kind of semiskill. It was strictly pulling the gun down, bang, bang, bang, doing your forty-seven welds, and then pulling another gun down; there was not even a pretence of a skill. So you were treated, accordingly, worse in that area. Foremen would just treat you like absolute scum.

In 1985, over a third of the workers in the body shop were spot welders, and no other job classification anywhere in the four main production departments had a lower median seniority level (6 years).[14] To be sure, this department also contained some more desirable, relatively skilled production jobs, like the metal finish operation, which involved fixing dents on the unpainted car bodies. "It looked like it was easy work, but you had to be pretty well skilled; you had to know what you was doing," recalled Tom Peterman, who did this job from when he was hired in 1979 until he took the buyout. "You don't want to hit it [the dent] real hard, because then you're going to push it way too far out; you just want to tap it till you get it just about out or just a little bit more than you want, then just file it down smooth." He knew how lucky he was to have had this job instead of one on the line. "There were some jobs there, I just couldn't see how people could do them. Twist this way, grab this, grab that. Some of them guys didn't have time to blink their eyes! Where in our department, man, we sat down, looked at a little spot, maybe filed it down a little bit. We wasn't on the line. Matter of fact, we could sit there and take the car off the line if we wanted to." Unlike many of the plant's more desirable jobs, this one included numerous low-seniority workers (the median seniority was only 8 years in 1985), many of whom, like Peterman, had outside experience in auto-body repair work. In this case, a nominally unskilled operation actually required considerable skill.

Seniority has a major bearing on the distribution of jobs, since under the terms of the union contract, high-seniority workers can transfer into more desirable jobs as vacancies occur. In cases like the metal finish job, where special qualifications were required, seniority was less important, since unqualified senior workers could be bypassed. And even for ordinary production jobs, seniority was by no means the sole determinant in matching jobs with individual workers. As Sean O'Brien put it, "One-third works on seniority, one-third on luck, and the other third on who's kissing whose ass." The initial job assignments given to new hires—controlled entirely by management—played a key role. Sometimes a worker's first job assignment was just a question of luck. Dan Cooper, for example, was hired in 1976, when the plant added an entire second shift. "My first job there was putting taillights in," he recalled, "and I found out I was one job away from being the person that put undercoating on the cars, where I probably would've walked out the first day. You know, I would've gone in there; they would have put me in a pit with a respirator, spraying black stuff; and I would've said, 'Good-bye.' "

Workers with connections could sometimes get assigned to highly desirable jobs from the outset. Actually a large percentage of the workers, especially the white males, had already made use of family ties for purposes of getting hired. All through the postwar period, until the company stopped hiring new workers altogether in the 1980s, it was routine for men who worked in the plant themselves to help get their sons, nephews, or other relatives jobs there. "My father kind of got me in, I guess," recalled Eddie Soares, the son of an official in the local union. "That's how the whole place is." Indeed, just about every white male I interviewed had a similar story to tell:

My uncle worked there. I had been putting applications in, and nothing was happening. He found out, and he said, "Well, give me your application." I gave it to him, and the next week I was working there. Plus I had my dad, and another uncle also, retired from GM.

(Mike Evans)

My wife's dad, one of his best friends worked at GM for thirty-five years, and he's the one that got me in.

(Tom Peterman)

My father worked over there and told me they were hiring. He said, "They're starting a second shift back again." He didn't want me to go there; he says, "No, don't work in there. Sick place in there," you know. So I said, "Well, I'll give it a try." He said, "You won't last," and my brother said the same thing—he'd worked there for a little while, and he couldn't take that. So, I took them up on their bet, and I stayed there. If you had an in—like most of the guys that were hired in '76, either a father worked there or an uncle or somebody. A lot of my friends around here signed up, filled out applications, but they didn't get hired because they didn't know anybody.

(Matthew Larson)

My mother-in-law got me the job. She worked in management, in accounting. She gave me the application and—you can put in an application for
General Motors, you don't know anybody, you're never going to get hired,
unless they get down to the bottom. And I gave my mother-in-law the application, and like the next day, they called me in for a physical.

(Ben Kowalski)

This was less often the case for women or minorities, many of whom
were hired in 1976, when the plant added a second shift and when
affirmative action was on the agenda.[15]

High-seniority workers who were particularly well connected
sometimes could do more than simply get their kin hired: they could
also influence the crucial initial job assignment. For example, one
worker who regularly drove the shop chairman (the most powerful
officer in the local union) to work got his son a highly prized job in
the paint shop. Pulling strings in this way was rare, indeed sometimes
impossible, for women and minorities. Moreover, race and, to a far
greater extent, gender seem to have played a role in initial job assignments.

In the plant's production departments, as table 1 shows, racial segregation was not much in evidence at the aggregate level (actually
whites were slightly underrepresented in the highly ranked paint
department). However, some workers suggested that race played a
role in matching people with jobs, at least in some departments. Carl
Block's impression was that in the late 1970s and early 1980s, "there
were more blacks in the jungle than in other parts of the body shop."
And Ben Kowalski remarked that of the women who worked near him
in the body shop, "most of 'em were black ladies." Indeed, of the 25
women employed in the body shop (an overwhelmingly male department) in 1985, 20 were African American—a much greater proportion than in the other three large production departments.

African-American and Latino workers were distributed through
most of the production job classifications (see appendix 1 for details),
but they were underrepresented in some of the most desirable jobs,
as table 2 shows. Nine of these 30 top classifications were exclusively
occupied by whites, although these jobs only accounted for a handful
of the plant's workers. White workers were overrepresented in some
of the other desirable jobs as well, although the disparities were far

smaller than in the skilled-trades workforce, which was 91 percent white. One reason for the underrepresentation of nonwhites in the best production jobs was the fact that white production workers had somewhat higher seniority—an average of 12.2 years in 1985, compared with 11.5 years for African Americans and 10.8 years for Latinos.

While there may have been some race typing associated with job assignments, the overall record is ambiguous. The same cannot be said about job segregation by gender, which was pervasive throughout GM-Linden. In 1985, as table 1 shows, women were distributed unevenly among the plant's production departments. They were almost entirely absent from the skilled trades (there were 2 females among the plant's 375 skilled-trades workers in 1985). Among production workers, women were almost as scarce in the smaller and especially desirable off-line departments (material, inspection, and maintenance). And among the highly desirable jobs listed in table 2, all were at least 80 percent male in 1985, and 25 of the 30 job classifications were 100 percent male. Of course, this was partly because women's average seniority (9.5 years in 1987) was considerably less than men's (15.5 years).

Despite this seniority differential, women were *overrepresented* in the plant's trim department, where the bulk of the light work in the assembly process was located, and underrepresented in the very unpopular body shop. Moreover, women were highly concentrated in relatively few production classifications. In 1985, 31 percent of Linden's women workers (compared to 13 percent of the men) were in a single job classification, hang and/or adjust doors and lids, in the trim department. And fully two-thirds of the plant's women workers were concentrated in only 5 production classifications. (These 5 classifications accounted for only 30 percent of the male production workers.)[16]

Since access to more desirable jobs was viewed as something that had to be earned by serving time in the plant—that is, as tied to seniority—the effect of this blatant pattern of job segregation by gender was to delegitimate women's right to work in the plant at all. "I had a lot of guys say, 'Oh, you're a woman; you shouldn't be here; you're taking away a man's job,'" Susan Roberts recalled. Most male workers made it clear that they viewed women as interlopers, even in speaking to a female interviewer. Indeed, there was a widespread perception among both male and female workers that management tended to give women easier, less physically demanding jobs—creating considerable resentment among men. "Women were put on jobs, and if they weren't able to handle it, they would try them on something else," Joyce Cowley recalled. "If they could do it, fine. If not, they would find them something else. In some cases, they would work their way down to an easy job, because they wanted the money and the benefits but not the work. And see, I didn't mind the work." Susan Roberts saw it a bit differently: "I hate to say this, but they have 'women's jobs' and they have 'men's jobs.' They try to put the women on the easier jobs or whatever. But there were some guys there that wanted easy jobs too; they don't want to work that hard." And Ben Kowalski complained:

The women, see, they get, I guess you'd call it preferred treatment. You know, there are some jobs in there that are hard. Like putting on gear boxes: you have to hold the gear box with one hand, and it's like about thirty-five pounds, and you have to lock it in and hold it in such a way so that you can drill into it. But the women, they're not going to give them the gear box job, unless they ask for it. They're not going to give them the tougher jobs. They're going to cater to them, which to me isn't fair. If they want to work there—anyone who makes the same amount of money that I do—they should be willing to do and capable of doing the same job I do. Because with a guy, they put you on a job, and if you can't do it, you know, they'll try a couple of jobs—they're not any easier—and if you can't do it, they'll just tell you, you know, "There's the highway."

Fred Lawton agreed: "Women are definitely given the less strenuous jobs. In paint, they were always given the nice, easy jobs, just wipe the car off. And in trim, it's the same thing: they don't get the job climbing in and putting the seat in the job, in the car; they'll get the job of putting the hood ornament on it, you know, something like that." Like Kowalski and most male workers, Lawton was strongly opposed to this policy: "Equal pay should be equal work, that's my feeling—if they want to work there."

Since gender and perhaps race, as well as luck and connections, often influence initial job assignments, not every production worker starts at the same point in the internal labor market at GM. Still, under the terms of the union contract, as a worker accumulates more seniority, he or she can request a transfer to a more desirable job. This is in fact a fundamental aspect of the principle of industrial justice embedded in the seniority system, second in importance only to the role of seniority in dictating the order of layoffs. But the system has some loopholes, so that in practice, management can influence job transfers in ways that conflict with seniority rights. "I knew that the longer you were there, the better job you can get," Ben Kowalski recalled. "But they can give you the runaround. You know, they might want to sneak one of their friends in there or something like that." As Carl Block explained:

Sometimes when you bid for those jobs, in terms of seniority, you didn't get it. Politics came in, and a foreman who owed a favor to somebody who had done something for the foreman, that person would get it. People really, really, really resent that! The contract says, where merit and ability are equal, seniority will rule. So they can play games with merit and ability. . . . [17] [For instance,] when you drove the car, the actual finished product off the line, and [went to] park it, that was a car driver. They got loads of overtime, and they were driving cars—I mean, you would jump into this $20,000 car and put on all the beautiful stereo and sit there, and maybe, in the hot weather, you could get three minutes of air-conditioning on you. So that was a really nice job, and there were lots of politics played in getting that job. It wasn't strictly done by the transfer system, under the contract. There was a young woman that I represented in the body shop who hired in in '76, and inside of four or five months, not only was she out of the body shop, she was driving cars on Saturdays and Sundays. And it turned out she and the general foreman were making it—it was that kind of stuff.[18]

Mike Evans angrily recalled another case of favoritism:

I was on the night shift, and I had a job off the line. It wasn't a bad job because we would build up our stock, and then we could sit down for ten to fifteen minutes. But I was tired of being on the night shift, and I wanted to go on days. They kept trying to block it, even though I had the objective right to go on days. . . . They kept trying to stop me. They told me, "Okay, for days you have to go to a different job classification. You can't keep the same job." I was willing to do that just to get on days. But then I found out that a guy I was working with, who had less time than me, they sent him days before me, and they put him on the same job on days. And I found out that his dad carpooled with the general foreman.

Job transfers within the ranks of production workers were often attainable, despite these problems. But there was another trajectory that was almost completely blocked, namely movement from a production job into the skilled trades. Elusive though it was, this was an aspiration a significant minority of workers longed to fulfill. Most skilled tradespersons were recruited from outside the plant; and there were many complaints that the few apprenticeships for which production workers could apply were distributed on a highly political basis. White male workers especially disparaged the affirmative action aspect of the in-plant apprenticeship program, although the truth was that since only a handful of apprenticeships were available to *any* production workers, even without affirmative action one's chances of entry to the elite preserve of the skilled trades were minuscule.

Still, with persistence, one could eventually move to a better job within the production departments. There were also some ways to speed up the process. For example, day-shift workers could sometimes move out of a particularly undesirable job by switching to the night shift. Another relatively rapid route upward, for those who were sufficiently versatile and who disliked the monotony of most assembly jobs, was to transfer into a relief, repair, or utility classification. These were known as premium jobs because the workers in them also received some extra pay—$.10 an hour or slightly more. All three included workers whose seniority levels were relatively low.

Relief positions involved briefly replacing other workers during their breaks and thus involved performing a range of different jobs. (This classification was eliminated in 1986, when the plant changed from a system of staggered breaks to "mass relief.") While most relief workers were relatively experienced—their average seniority level was 18 years in 1985—quite a few were not. In 1985, 100 of the 351 relief workers in Linden's production workforce had 9 or fewer years' seniority. Repair workers, who did troubleshooting and case-by-case repair work on cars or components that had been assembled improperly on the line, also had varied and relatively skilled work, and most worked off the line.[19] Their seniority status was similar to that of relief workers, with an average tenure of 14.5 years but with many low-seniority individuals as well—half of the 250 repair workers the plant employed in 1985 had 9 or fewer years' seniority. A utility worker, the supervisor's "right-hand man" (the vast majority were indeed male), filled in for other workers who were absent or pulled off the line for purposes other than breaks that relief workers covered, as well as assisting with a variety of supervisory responsibilities. Utility positions were even more accessible than relief and repair jobs to low-seniority workers: in 1985, the average seniority level of utility workers was 11 years (about a year less than for production workers generally), and more than two-thirds of the plant's 461 utility workers had 9 or fewer years' seniority.

However, these were the exceptions. On the whole, the most junior workers were stuck in the least desirable jobs. Counterbalancing this, however, was the absence of any financial reward for accrued seniority. Not only was the overall wage spread very narrow, as I have shown, but also a worker who had worked in the plant for thirty years was often paid at the same rate as one who had been there only a few months. For many families, this meant a newly hired eighteen-year-old son could earn virtually the same income as his father. Indeed, the fact that seniority and pay were negatively correlated, as noted earlier, meant that new workers often earned slightly more than their older counterparts. Workers who had accumulated some seniority had several reasons to remain at GM—the realistic hope of moving to a less onerous job and, eventually, of collecting a pension. For new recruits, however, the high pay was the main reason to return day after day to a job with few other redeeming features.

Indeed, many young workers lured to GM by the high wages hired in with the intention of leaving after a short time. "I said, 'I'll just stay here until I get my bills paid off,' because I'd just bought a new truck," Mike Evans recalled. "It was real good pay—and somehow I went on staying there for seven years." Raymond Perry told a similar tale: "I stopped school, intending to go back after I got some money. And meanwhile I was looking around, and someone told me about General Motors in Linden, that they were hiring a lot of people, so I said, 'Well, maybe this is a good opportunity for me to go and get this money,' 'cause they said the money was real good and you made it quick. And I said, 'That sounds all right.' So I went up to GM, and they hired me. And the money was coming good, and I waited—I made a mistake by waiting too long. I was young and, you know, get-

ting that much money at that short a period of time." This was the
typical process of incorporation into the plant's internal labor market.
It was difficult to give up the high pay after even a short stint at GM.
And workers who were married and had children became especially
dependent on the fringe benefits, making it even harder to leave.
"One of the biggest things with GM was the benefits, you couldn't
beat 'em," Carl Block recalled. "A lot of people had kids, and it was
just—you *had* to have those benefits; they were incredible. They were
a chain that kept you in the plant." Indeed, many workers saw the
benefits as the main compensation for the many indignities associated
with the job. "I can live with all the garbage that goes on in there,"
explained Matthew Larson, who worked at Linden for over fifteen
years, " 'cause, you know, you have the *best* benefits."

While temporary (if sometimes lengthy) layoffs were a frequent
occurrence, their financial impact was cushioned by the supplemental
unemployment benefits the UAW had won for its members in the
1950s. And since the seniority system provided recall rights for those
laid off, long-term job security seemed assured until the late 1970s,
when it became clear to everyone that GM was in trouble. "You
figured, General Motors, you got a set job," Mike Polansky said, looking back to when he was first hired at the Linden plant. "This was
1976. People buying cars, and you couldn't see too many Datsuns and
stuff like that. You seen 'em, but not like today." And George Brown,
who was hired in 1971, recalled, "I felt at that point that corporations
like GM and Ford, the Big Three, these places are living dynasties—
they'd never go down." Those who worked in the plant for more than
a few years thus became resigned to staying for the full thirty, until
they could leave with a pension.

Workers typically spoke about their time in the plant as if they were
waiting out a prison term. "Now my case, I'm forty years old, and I got
like fourteen and a half years in there now," explained Ben Kowalski.
"If I go start another job at forty—you know, I *got* to work here till I
retire." Ivan Kovac was closer to the end of the ordeal: "I've got seven
more years, I'll be sixty-two." Matthew Larson made the comparison
to incarceration explicit: "It's not a great place to work. I always took
it as a prison. It was like going to jail, like a work-release program.

You work all day, and you take a lot of guff and work hard—but at least you're getting good pay for it. And you get to go home at night." Other workers referred to the plant as "the joint," "a compound," or even compared it to slavery or to a concentration camp. In principle, of course, they were all free to leave anytime, but most felt bound to the job by their family responsibilities. "You always think of quitting," said Sean O'Brien, "but when you got a wife, kids, and mortgage, you're talking about going back to $18,000 after you're used to making $35,000. It just doesn't cut the mustard. You can't pay the bills."

Bitterness on the Line

The metaphor of imprisonment was central to the self-conception of most GM workers not simply because of the "thirty and out" pension system, but also because they hated their jobs so intensely. There was no shortage of things to dislike. Auto assembly work is the prototype of alienated labor: the combination of the Taylorist division of labor and the moving assembly line makes for extremely boring, monotonous work. "It's the same thing over and over and over and over and over. You could do it in your sleep," George Brown complained. This was not true for every single job in the plant but certainly characterized the vast majority. In addition, although most jobs involved relatively simple tasks, the process of physical adjustment was often difficult. Carl Block described the bodily discipline demanded by his first job in the body shop, on the door line:

As the cars come down, you pick the door up and set it with its hinges onto the car, and then you have these guns that you screw the doors onto the car with. It was just the noise and the heaviness of it and the fact that you always have to watch that your foot's not run over by the truck that the car is set on as it goes down the line and, you know, falling and getting yourself cut up. And your arm's totally coursing with pain from holding the air gun. It vibrates so much that—it's like somebody with Parkinson's, you know—your hand shakes when you pick up a cup when you're first doing it. And sometimes you wake up at night, you can't find a position for your body, because your body's not used to it. Just learning how to do the job and keep up with the job was really, really hard. I think, within about ten days, I more or less could do it, but it took months before I knew the tricks and could relax.

Even getting used to jobs that were less physically strenuous was pain-ful because of the fast pace and repetitive character of the work. "I was so sore, my wife used to help me out of the bathtub," Dennis Tucker recalled. "And I was in the best shape of my life. You could take a professional athlete that's receiving millions of dollars a year, being that he's in such good shape. You put him on that assembly line; you teach him an operation; his muscles are going to be sore—he's going to wish he was back on that football field."

Workers generally dislike the physical aspect of their jobs and the monotonous nature of the working day, but they find it virtually im-possible to imagine any alternative to the long-established Taylorist system of job design or to the relentless pressure to get production out as rapidly as possible. They accept these conditions as necessary and inevitable features of efficient manufacturing. "GM is a product-oriented company, obviously. They are very hard lined as far as how much output you have to get out every day," noted Tim Murphy. "See, I look at a company where they're renting your time, but you're not there to just sit and collect your paycheck. You have to do a job for the people. It's not like I'm going to sit on the sand in the Bahamas and collect fourteen dollars an hour."

By contrast, many GM-Linden workers are extremely critical of the way in which they are treated by management, both of the com-pany's overall policies and practices and of their immediate relations with first-line supervisors. To workers, the brutality of social relations within the factory hierarchy is neither necessary nor justifiable for business efficiency or profitability. On the contrary, many believe that production would proceed more efficiently and that quality would improve with a different, more humane style of management. John Pierce told a story to illustrate this point, one of many such parables workers routinely invoked: "I had a supervisor once; we had a beef about something. And he told me, 'I'm your boss, and you do what I tell you to do.' I said, 'Sir, that's the wrong answer.' I said, 'I can make you or break you, because I'm the worker. So therefore if I want to give you good work, I can give you good work, but don't harass me. It's not going to get you good work. Only thing that's going to do is make me angry and [not] want to work for you.' 'Cause to me, people is the resources you have in business." Ironically, in response to the profitability crisis GM faced in the late 1970s and 1980s, top management eventually came to hold a rather similar view—although so far (as I will show in chapter 5) it has been spectacularly unsuccessful in transforming the character of plant-level management.

Workers complain far more bitterly about their treatment by GM management personnel than about their subordination to the plant machinery or to the assembly line itself. As Sean O'Brien put it, "It isn't so much that you hate the job—you hate General Motors, hate being there." Some of the specific grievances may appear trivial to an outsider, but in the worldview of workers, each small insult resonates as part of a coherent whole, a pattern of continual degradation in a variety of arenas. "You know, the simple things," John Pierce explained. "You could ask your supervisor for a pair of gloves. He'd say, 'I'll be right back.' And you know, you might not get those gloves all day." The military-style regimentation also provoked resentment. "Everything had to be done by whistle, you know, a whistle to stop, a whistle to go," Patrick Nolan complained. "In GM, if you're late a minute, you're six minutes late; if you work overtime, you work six minutes," Eddie Soares added. "It's just like the army, you know. It's just a compound."

Another issue that came up in virtually every interview was access to bathroom facilities. "When you're on the line, a simple function like going to the bathroom, you have to raise your hand like a little kid," Dennis Tucker lamented. "It's a major project; everybody's got to know your business." The fact that relief and utility workers do not always respond promptly to such requests contributes further to workers' feelings of humiliation over this issue. Many workers also resent the policy prohibiting production workers from receiving phone calls (or even messages) on the job, except in a serious emergency.[20] Dan Cooper recounted one of many stories turning on this:

One time I had gone to the bank after work and cashed my paycheck, and when I got home, it was a hundred dollars short. I hadn't looked at it; I went through the drive-in window. So I talked to my wife about it. "Call the bank first thing in the morning; tell them what happened," I said. "When they do their count, they should come up a hundred dollars off, which is our money." So, I gave her a call around eight-thirty. She said, "I didn't call yet; they don't open till nine." I had already had my first relief of the day and I wanted to get on this quick because it was Friday and I didn't want it going through the weekend. She was pregnant at the time. The baby wasn't due until September, and this was July. So I said, "I already had my relief. Just call back up and tell them to give me the message that everything's okay, or that I should contact the bank." So, she tried to call, but they wouldn't put a message through. She hung up, and called again and said, "I'm having a baby; get my husband." So the foreman comes walking over; he says, "Congratulations!" "Congratulations on what?" He said, "Your wife's having the baby." I said, "What? She better not be," you know. "She's not due till September." I had no idea she was going to do this! So he brought the utility man and said, "You better go call her." So I call her, and she goes, "Oh, I tried to call, and they wouldn't let me leave a message. So I told them I'm pregnant." And I said, "Okay, screw them—I'm coming home." So I get off the phone, and I go, "Geez, I don't know what's going on." Now the foreman feels like stabbing himself—he feels like shit, you know, that he came over and had to give me this news, you know. He thought it was all happy, and now he thinks it's something wrong. So I come home, and there's a box on the table; it's anniversary paper. "Whose anniversary is it?" She says, "Ours!" Oh, God, this was some day! Well, we got our hundred dollars back, and I went out and got her an anniversary present and went back to work and said, "It was a false alarm." So, everything worked out fine. But it burns you up that, you know, I had to leave in order to get a message. It was things like that that just drive you out of your mind. That you're like trapped there.

Workers also spoke bitterly about the mandatory overtime that management could impose on them without advance notice. "Sometimes you had to work nine hours a day, six days a week. You had no family life. You had no life," Patrick Nolan complained. "At GM, I never went to work there any day knowing I'd be off a certain time," recalled George Brown. "That line ran until management felt it was time to shut it down. You couldn't make any plans. If they tell you, line time is two o'clock, you stay on that line until two o'clock, simple as that. So you had, I don't know, a slave tactic there. The people, they were like robots, that had been there for like a long time, and their foreman and supervisors were more or less [slave drivers]."

The sharp demarcation between workers and managers was also a source of irritation. "They even had separate cafeterias," Mike Evans observed. "A friend of mine, whose husband worked there in management, said that her husband was told that people on the line were like animals, and you have to treat them like animals. And that's how they acted. I remember being on the line in the summertime, dying in the heat and the humidity. And the foreman would be sitting in this little air-conditioned office that he had." Carl Block recalled yet another affront to workers' basic sense of dignity: "People would get hurt, and they would be forced to go on the line and work hurt. That happened all the time."

Almost every worker recounted at least one incident of managerial insensitivity, often something that had occurred many years before, but which was so offensive to the teller that it was seared indelibly into his or her memory. When Frank Leone's baby niece was hospitalized after an accident, for example, he left the plant during his lunch break to visit her in the hospital, which was three miles from the plant. Before he left, he told the supervisor where he was going and requested that his job be covered in case he got back late. "The guy tried to convince me not to go," he recalled. "He said, 'There's no need for you to go; it won't make her better. You're not her father.' I went anyway, and I stayed the rest of the night. That was the first time I'd ever missed a day of work, after six years and three months in the place. After that, though, I figured, screw them. An inch of snow, a cold, I'd call in sick."

Like Leone, most GM-Linden workers were convinced that management had little concern for the humanity of the managed. Moreover, they believed that this was not due to the shortcomings of individual foremen but was rather a systematic company policy. "If you were the kind of supervisor who would lead your people instead of driving them, you didn't last long at GM," George Brown asserted. "You had to be a slave driver." Leone commented with cynical understatement, "GM is not an 'employee-oriented place.' You're a machine, an object, a piece of equipment. If it breaks, they'll replace it. They don't care about the individual." John Pierce agreed:

I've seen people working there in tears, because of the way you were treated. You were treated fairly bad, you know. Because at General Motors, the attitude was: You're here, you weren't asked to come here, you came here on your own, so you got to do what you have to do in order to make the money. You know, you can't make this money on the outside, because you're unskilled labor. So, we'll treat you how we want to treat you.

Most of the supervisors there were from the old school, okay; they were from the school that they carried engines on their backs, let's say. . . . And you know, it was just mind control because, see, when everyone first comes in, everyone is excited because they're making more money probably than they ever made, so they're hyped up about it. And okay, after that, once they get in and they see how you are treated to earn that money, they say, "Whoa!" I've seen people come in and work for two hours and walk out.

Those who do not walk out instead grudgingly accept the terms of the Faustian capital-labor accord. The quid pro quo for the inhumane management practices they endure, however, is workers' minimal level of loyalty to their employer. One salient badge of this for many workers is the car they choose to drive. While most are fiercely nationalistic in this respect—almost none would dream of buying a foreign car—many shun GM products, although they can purchase them at a considerable discount. Tom Peterman made a point of the fact that he had three cars: a Thunderbird, a Cougar, and a Dodge, none of which is made by GM. Similarly, "GM was never my cup of tea," Eddie Soares told me. "I always was a Ford man, you know. I just like the way they do everything. GM would think of something and put it in their cars whether it worked or not." He drives a Thunderbird.

On the job, workers develop creative ways of lessening their burdens. Any excuse to get off the line, even for a short time, is eagerly seized. "Whenever that blood bank came around, I gave blood just so I could get off the line," Edward Salerno confessed. "I'd go down there for like an hour. *Anything* to get off the line!"[21] Those who are lucky enough to be able to manage it "double up" with co-workers, with one worker doing two jobs while the other takes an extended break:[22]

I'd do his job and my job, and he'd take off for an hour. So I was reading like three newspapers a day and a magazine, doing crossword puzzles.

(Dan Cooper)

I was a wet sander. We had six people just on my line. And the cars came out; the hoods and the fenders came out and the deck lids. And we had to sand them on the sander with water. But see, our foreman, our department ran so good and we were all way in the back and he didn't see us. We would double up. And I mean, so I would take off for two hours.

(Patrick Nolan)

We used to help each other out, you know. You get a few guys that really knew what they were doing; they could sit there and do each other's jobs, and somebody else [could] take a break.

(Tom Peterman)

Workers also turn to a wide variety of distractions from the day-to-day drudgery. At least until the late 1980s, drugs were readily available in the parking lot, and many workers routinely drank on their lunch breaks. "The work conditions are horrible, awful," Patrick Nolan stated. "You know, that's why half of the young people were on drugs." The general perception was that management was well aware of this and basically looked the other way. Raymond Perry was among those who sought solace in religion. "As long as you got something outside of work, you can make it," he asserted. "You have to have an outlet."

One such outlet was taking a second job while working in the plant. Often this involved some type of entrepreneurial activity, ranging from selling things in the plant (licit or illicit) to various home-based sidelines. "A lot of people had side jobs," Carl Block recalled.

Some people knew mechanics or did wallpapering or home remodeling. Some people had those little trailers that hook onto the back of your car and that, you know, you can sell hot dogs out of. Or they'd work in a friend's body shop. People did have their different hustles. But you got to remember that with the boom and bust, when we were working—they can make you work nine hours a day and then two Saturdays in a row. That's an awful lot of time. And you were wasted and exhausted. And some guys still had something on the side. It represented—it wasn't just the extra income; it was a potential of getting released from that, you know, punching in, punching out, and once you're in there, getting hounded to death. And *nobody* would put it down. They just didn't.

All these activities allowed workers to find meaning outside of the daily grind in the plant.

Union activity, with all its symbolic (and often genuine) devotion to fighting back against the company, was another outlet that some workers found appealing. The postwar capital-labor accord set limits on the challenges it could mount, yet at many points the Linden local union did offer an avenue for resistance to the inhumane treatment that was the source of so much discontent among its membership.

Strikes, grievances, and other union-sponsored challenges to corporate authority were continually fueled by this discontent. Even if they were ineffective in transforming the social relations between management and labor in any fundamental or lasting way, these union efforts were a crucial vehicle for expressing workers' frustrations and yearnings for dignity—at least until the postwar accord was suddenly and unilaterally abandoned by GM in the early 1980s, as the U.S. auto industry confronted an unprecedented crisis. The UAW's activities at Linden and the rapid decline in its power in the 1980s are the subject of the next chapter.

Chapter Three

Adversarialism and Beyond

The UAW in Uncertain Times

Relations between management and labor in the U.S. auto industry generally, and at GM-Linden in particular, have always been highly adversarial. Indeed, the Linden plant is a classic example of the conflictual industrial relations system that has long distinguished the United States from most of its international competitors. Trust between management and managed is minimal, and their relationship is governed by an elaborate, highly bureaucratic structure of industrial jurisprudence. A complex body of contractual rules constrain shop-floor behavior, enforced by a system of progressive discipline for workers who violate them, on the one hand, and by a multistep grievance procedure offering redress against managerial abuses, on the other.[1]

In the interstices of this adversarial system, GM-Linden workers have constructed an elaborate local union culture, with its own language and rituals, and rich in political intrigue. Under the union shop clause in the labor contract, all nonsupervisory employees in the plant are required to become members of UAW Local 595, after a brief probationary period. And although most workers participate only marginally in the UAW's official activities, virtually all are aware of its dynamics, and most feel some allegiance to one faction or another among those vying for local power in what has long been one of the nation's most democratic unions. In all this, GM-Linden is fairly typical of the U.S. auto industry, although local conditions have also shaped the contours of labor relations in the plant.

The rise of a militant caucus (the Linden Auto Workers, or LAW) within Local 595 in the 1970s, and local management's intransigence toward it, heightened the long-standing tensions at Linden and made the union more appealing to many workers. In the early 1980s, however, national developments intervened, undermining the UAW local and radically tilting the balance of power in favor of management. The growing economic troubles of the nation, and of the domestic auto industry in particular, set the stage for this change. Starting in the early 1970s, the energy crisis and the surge in demand for imported cars threatened the viability of the domestic auto firms and the stability of the world their workers inhabited. Along with deindustrialization, these years brought rapid deunionization, especially after the 1980 election of Ronald Reagan unleashed unprecedented political attacks against organized labor.

Two critical events made the local transformation at Linden in the 1980s especially dramatic. First was the wave of concession bargaining that swept the nation after the August 1981 air controllers' strike was crushed by the U.S. government. In the spring of 1982, as corporations throughout the nation capitalized on labor's newfound weakness amid the worst recession since the 1930s, GM and the UAW signed a new agreement containing $2.5 billion in union givebacks. Although Linden's workers voted overwhelmingly against this contract, it was narrowly ratified by GM workers nationally. Immediately after this defeat, members of Local 595 elected a new, maverick leadership drawn from the Linden Auto Workers caucus that had emerged in the 1970s. But in early 1983, less than a year after it won control of the local union's top offices, LAW suffered a major setback. The U.S. National Labor Relations Board (NLRB), which was just then coming under the control of Reagan appointees widely seen as biased against unions, dropped a major contempt case against GM stemming from charges LAW leaders had filed starting in the mid-1970s—charges that had until then provided the caucus with an unbroken string of legal victories.

While GM-Linden workers disagreed among themselves about how their union should respond to these developments, it quickly became obvious to all concerned that Local 595 (like the UAW as a whole) had lost much of its economic and political muscle. As the 1980s wore on, this reality was underscored when GM's deepening crisis of overcapacity, in the face of growing international competition, led it to play off one local union against another by threatening to close "uncooperative" plants—a tactic auto industry analysts dubbed whipsawing. Faced with this, the national leadership of the UAW chose the path of least resistance. Reasoning that UAW members would have no jobs at all if the domestic auto firms failed to become competitive in the global marketplace, the national union gingerly embraced the notion of cooperation with management and began to concentrate its energies on enhancing its members' job security.

Some local UAW leaders, including many at Linden, were openly skeptical about this nonconfrontational approach, most prominently associated in the 1980s with the union's General Motors Department director, Donald F. Ephlin (until his 1989 retirement).[2] But once the national UAW lent its official imprimatur to the strategy of labor-management cooperation, local affiliates were left with little room to maneuver. Local unions that balked at management's demands could find themselves threatened with the ultimate sanction of a plant closing. The contrast between the years before and after 1982 for Linden's UAW Local 595 vividly illustrates the consequences of "Ephlinism" at the local level. Indeed, the dramatic power shift that took place in the mid-1980s can only be understood against the background of the union's earlier history.

Shop-Floor Conflict
and the Local Union, 1940–1982

In May 1937, at a dedication ceremony for what was then the corporation's newest and most modern plant, GM president William S. Knudsen welcomed Linden's two thousand workers to the GM "family," promising them that "we are going to treat you squarely." He must have had the UAW in mind as he spoke, since the union had triumphed over the company only a few months earlier after its dramatic sit-down strike in Flint, Michigan. "I can't think of anything I'd like better than to have those fellows in our other plants tell me, 'You, here in Linden, make better cars than we do,'" Knudsen told the assembled workers.[3] But if he expected labor relations to become more harmonious as the company decentralized production, Knudsen must have been disappointed. In the spring of 1940, GM-Linden's production and maintenance workers voted overwhelmingly in favor of UAW-CIO representation, along with their counterparts in many other GM plants around the nation.[4] And on November 6, 1941, a strike closed down the Linden plant for two weeks as the fledgling UAW Local 595 demanded improvements in working conditions and adherence to seniority rules.[5] As this early walkout demonstrates, conflict between management and labor would prove as intractable at Linden as elsewhere in the GM empire.

The Linden plant had its share of strikes in the postwar years, most of them relatively brief, unauthorized wildcats. The fragmentary record suggests that the strike issues were similar to those provoking walkouts at other auto plants in this period, ranging from production-line speedups to mandatory overtime to disciplinary action against local unionists to delays in processing grievances. In July 1953, for example, when a Linden repair worker was indefinitely suspended for refusing to work overtime one evening, the entire plant struck in support. Over the previous few months, workers in the repair area had been required to work twelve hours a day, seven days a week, and others had faced disciplinary actions for refusing to comply.[6] The following February there was a brief work stoppage in the plant's trim department, apparently provoked by management's effort to discipline a union committeeman.[7] Stanley Aronowitz, who had a relative employed at Linden, recalls in his memoir of the "unsilent fifties" that speedups provoked several more walkouts there in the summer of 1955; that same year another unauthorized strike took place in the plant shortly before the expiration of the 1950–1955 national GM-UAW contract, involving a local dispute over shift rotation.[8] In September 1958, Linden workers walked out again, this time as part of a national dispute over grievance handling.[9] And a four-hour work stoppage at Linden in April 1961 over working conditions and speed-up was followed by an eighteen-day strike over the same issues that May.[10] Although specific data for Linden are not available, at GM as a whole the rate of unauthorized strikes fell in the 1960s and 1970s, relative to the 1950s, a decline only partly offset by an increase in authorized strikes.[11]

Of course, strikes are but one expression of shop-floor discontent.

Another less dramatic, but still revealing, formal avenue open to unionized workers is to file a grievance in protest of managerial action. Grievances are limited to issues covered by the union contract, are processed in a highly bureaucratic fashion, and may languish unresolved for long periods of time. Yet, as one GM-Linden manager put it, "grievances are a way of letting off steam."[12] Grievance rates can be affected by many factors, including the degree to which the parties involved are willing or able to resolve problems informally, as well as the personalities of foremen and union committeemen—elected union stewards who handle grievances for union members (called committeemen even in the rare cases where they are female!). Still, the overall grievance rate is a crude barometer of shop-floor tension.

At GM nationally, the number of grievances rose steadily over the postwar years, multiplying tenfold between 1947 and 1980, well above the 30 percent growth in GM's UAW membership over the same period.[13] Most observers, whether union or management affiliated, recalled that the volume of grievances at Linden peaked in the late 1970s, although unfortunately systematic plant-level data for the postwar period as a whole are not available. The majority of grievances in the years before 1982 concerned a few key issues: the intensity of work, discipline, health and safety problems, violations of the seniority rules governing job transfers, various types of managerial harassment, and supervisors performing work contractually reserved for union members.[14] Although grievances often dragged on without resolution, and sometimes were dropped outright in the course of local bargaining with management, they did express workers' day-to-day concerns—at least those within the purview of the union contract.

Among the most common grievances were those concerning production standards, popularly known as 78s, or overwork grievances, covered by Paragraph 78 of the GM-UAW national contract.[15] "There [were] a lot of times when they would overload a job and you couldn't do it, or you had a lot of trouble and they were just like: 'You do that job or else,'" Edward Salerno recalled. "So, you know, it would be this whole little procedure you'd have to go through." A representative overwork grievance reads, "I charge management with violation of Paragraph 78 of the National Agreement whereas my job is overworked. I demand that this extra work be removed from my job so

that I may work in a safe and normal manner."[16] Management's standard answer was that "employee has ample time to do the operation,"
although often these grievances did achieve the desired result of reducing the workload. "One of the strongest pieces of the contract
when I hired in there was overwork," declared former body-shop
committeeman Carl Block. "If the elements of your job changed, you
could file a 78, and that was the only time, according to the contract,
you could let the work fly down the line without doing it and without
getting disciplined for it. It was one place where labor could get [its]
foot in the door."

Other grievances dealt with seemingly mundane matters that nevertheless were major sources of aggravation on the shop floor. "There
were things as minimal as when you have to go to the bathroom, you
pull a whistle, and someone's supposed to come over and give you
relief, and often times that wouldn't happen," Block recalled. Other
examples include these grievances filed in the body shop between
1980 and 1982:

I charge mgmt. with bargaining in bad faith inasmuch as you agreed to pay
me the sum of $5.00 for damaged clothing as well as to return to me the
article of damaged clothing. I demand that mgmt. live up to its agreement
and immediately pay me for my loses [sic] and return my damaged clothing.

I charge mgmt. with violating my health and safety rights inasmuch as un-
sanitary conditions exist in the restroom (women's). I demand that these conditions be cleaned up and maintained regularly.

I charge management with violation of Local contract provisions and Mgmt's
own work element operator assignment sheet inasmuch as I have been denied coveralls (3 pair & coverall locker) and proper safety glasses with side
frames. I demand I be immediately supplied with coverall locker, 3 pairs of
coveralls and dark green safety glasses w/side frames.

I charge Mgmt. w/viol. of H&Safety as well as viol of Par 5a of N.A. [National
Agreement] inasmuch as fan at Column U-28 which disappeared from elec-
tric shop in February of 1982 has still not been replaced as had been committed. Demand immediate replacement of stated FAN.

I charge management with violation of my minimum health and safety requirements as well as provisions of local contract inasmuch as I was kept

waiting almost 1 hour for a hospital pass. I demand [names of two supervisors] be instructed as to their obligations under the local contract and that this behavior be stopped.

I charge management with violation of LD [Local Demand] #4 in as much as I was kept waiting 4 hours to be released fr. work for an emergency. I demand an explanation of this delay as well as a commitment by mngt that the newly negotiated provisions re: emergency calls will be lived up to as well as the provisions previously negotiated.

I charge management with violation of minimum health and safety requirements inasmuch as lights in solder grind booth are obstructed by dust on the glass covers. I demand that a regularly scheduled cleaning program be set up so that the operator will be able to see his work.

Workers also used the grievance mechanism to secure job transfers in line with their seniority, when management violated the contract provisions on transfers (in most cases Paragraph 63 of the National Agreement). A typical grievance of this type reads: "I charge management with violation of Par. 63 of the N.A. I demand I be moved immediately in line with my seniority and that I be made whole for all losses." Most such cases seem to have been settled to the plaintiff's satisfaction, with the transfer occurring within a week or two after the complaint was filed. In these instances the facts were seldom in dispute, and it was simply a question of enforcing the contract.

Other types of grievances were far less straightforward. For example, it was not uncommon for workers to file grievances alleging harassment by foremen. In such cases, since it was inherently difficult for workers to provide proof, the union was less likely to be successful, as the following examples (both from early 1978) suggest:[17]

Charge Foreman A with useing [sic] abusive language + threatening me. Demand this practice be stopped at once + foreman A be instructed in the proper manner to address employes [sic].

Management's answer: Nothing in Management's investigation of the instant case, nor in the Union's presentation to date, substantiates the charges as contained in the grievance. The Union's charge is completely unfounded with no basis of fact, and is accordingly denied by Management. Investigation of this matter disclosed that on the day in question the grievant was properly instructed and cautioned by his supervisor concerning the unnecessary use of the "foreman call whistle." Accordingly, Management sees no cause for grievance. The charges and demands contained in the grievance are emphatically denied.

I charge Foreman B with undue harassment. Request that Foreman B stop harassing me every time I am absent by saying he will get me sooner or later.

Management's answer: Nothing in the investigation of the instant case, nor in the Union's presentation to date, substantiates the charges of harassment. This charge is completely unfounded, with no basis of fact, and is accordingly emphatically denied. Management states that this charge is nothing more than an unsuccessful attempt by the Union to becloud the real issue, which is the grievant's own misconduct. In view of the facts, the charges and requests contained in the grievance are denied.

Sometimes grievances were simply used as ammunition in the ongoing war between supervisors and workers. In one otherwise typical overwork grievance, for example, two body-shop workers demanded "that a sufficient amount of work be removed from our operation so that we may work in a safe and normal manner," and management answered: "Charge and request denied. Employees have more than enough time to do their operation as instructed—this is only retaliation by employees because we took away their reading material." Under some circumstances, grievances could even be manufactured to give the union extra leverage. "If somebody got in a little trouble for something, a few of us would write up a grievance," Tom Peterman remembered. "Well, the union would throw away these grievances if they'd let this guy come back."

Some grievances were satisfactorily and speedily resolved, but others dragged on and on, with management intransigence growing as a case worked its way to the upper levels. Cases that could not be resolved by the individual committeeman could be brought before the shop committee, an elected body of committeemen and other union representatives that met weekly with plant management.[18] These meetings resolved few grievances, however: Of 91 cases discussed at 31 shop committee–management meetings held between early 1978 and late 1981, only 1 was settled! In the other 90 cases, management's position was "charge and request denied"—sometimes "emphatically denied."[19] Such unresolved grievances could be settled or withdrawn later on as part of informal local bargaining, or they could be appealed to the national level. Typically, either course meant a long wait, and workers often grew frustrated with the delays. "I'll be honest with you," John Pierce recalled. "Out of all the years I was there, any problems I had were never totally satisfied. It was always, 'Well, it has to go to the next step.' I remember writing up a supervisor for harassing me, and I wrote up several jobs for being overworked. Nothing ever really got resolved. Once, when I had written up something, I found out that my committeeman sat on it for over two months. It never even left his hands!" Joyce Cowley complained that some committeemen played favorites: "If their friends had a grievance, they would do their darnedest, and with anybody else, they would tell them, 'Yeah, we'll take care of it, and it was just shelved somewhere and it was never done.'"

In addition, some committeemen were less conscientious than others. Workers who won union office tended to have relatively aggressive personalities. "A lot of your union guys are ex-bullies, tough guys, streetwise—not your mild-mannered nice guy," Jonathan Fox pointed out. "You have to be, and that's what people wanted: loud, foul-mouthed, strong, pushy guys—literally fighters." Still, once elected, some unionists became enamored of the perquisites tied to their positions. Indeed, while being a union officer involves a great deal of responsibility and can be extremely time consuming, it is one of the few avenues of upward mobility open to production workers, who typically have little formal education and whose work offers few intrinsic rewards. Ely Chinoy's observations on this point, made decades ago, are still apt:

Paradoxically, the collective pursuit of common goals has provided many individuals with opportunities for personal advancement. . . . [T]he personal risks to which organizers and active [union] members were once exposed are virtually gone. Indeed, workers who assume a full-time union office usually do not even lose their seniority standing in the plants from which they come; they are given leave for the duration of their union assignment and can return to their previous jobs at any time. . . . Even as shop stewards at the bottom of the union hierarchy, workers cannot help becoming aware of the concrete rewards to be gained in union office. They immediately derive some advantage from their own position: they are given top seniority status in their districts.[20]

This dynamic could lead to complacency or worse. "The trade-off is you get off the line, and to stay off the line and to stay in good graces, you're not too aggressive in representation; you just kind of let things slide," Carl Block recalled. "So some grievances get flushed down the toilet, or you never hear anything more about it. There were even some horrible committeemen who would actually punch their card in and would be out at the local bar drinking, on company time, and they certainly weren't available."

Nonetheless, even highly dedicated committeemen could not always win grievance cases. And union officials became entangled in many conflicts that spilled beyond the boundaries of the highly legalistic grievance machinery. Sometimes the mutual antagonisms between labor and management exploded into physical violence. In May 1978, a few days before the plant's annual union elections, the *Local 595 Shop News Bulletin* complained of an unprovoked physical assault by a plant guard against the local union president. Immediately after the attack, according to the bulletin, the plant manager ordered the president to leave the premises and actually had the local police escort him out on the basis of a trespassing charge. (Union officers' access to the plant is governed by specific rules, and in this instance GM contended the president's presence was unauthorized.) The same bulletin lists several other assaults on workers by supervisors that allegedly occurred in the plant shortly before this incident, including one case where a superintendent "pushed and shoved" a worker in the maintenance department "for not working fast enough to suit him during a line breakdown."[21]

There were also occasional allegations of physical assaults by workers against their supervisors—an infraction that could lead to the worker's discharge. While the facts in the two examples that follow (extracted from minutes of shop committee–management meetings) are contested, they effectively evoke the flavor of the plant's social relations:

Union's position: This employee was unjustly discharged, inasmuch as he did not assault the foreman as charged, but merely grabbed the supervisor's arm in an attempt to reason with him. The Union further asserted that mere contact does not constitute assault. Therefore, the discharge penalty is too severe. . . .

Mgt's. Answer: Management states the instant case arose on Thursday, January 12, 1978 when the grievant was properly discharged for assaulting a member of supervision. Contrary to the statement contained in the Union's position that the grievant merely grabbed the foreman's arm, Management stated the grievant physically grabbed Supervisor X, and struck him in the face with his fist.

Union's position: This employe [*sic*] was unjustly discharged, inasmuch as he was provoked into whatever altercation that might have taken place. Specifically, the Union claimed when this employe [*sic*] was called into Supervisor Y's office for smoking in a no-smoking area, Supervisor Y said, while pointing his finger in the grievant's face, "I got you now nigger, I'm throwing your black ass out." Thereafter, when the grievant pushed his supervisor's hand out of his face, Supervisor Y grabbed the grievant and ripped his shirt pocket. Accordingly, the Union claimed the grievant was provoked into this altercation and therefore the discharge was unjust. . . .

Mgt's. Answer: The instant case arose on Thursday, May 21, 1981 when, shortly after the 6:30 A.M. starting whistle had sounded, Supervisor Y observed the grievant smoking in a no-smoking area. Accordingly, Supervisor Y put the grievant on notice for this misconduct and then instructed him to report to his (supervisor's) office. Subsequently, when Supervisor Y returned to his office, the grievant assaulted him. After the grievant struck his supervisor three times, he was restrained by another hourly employee who enabled Y to exit the office. After the grievant was released he picked up a stick and started after his supervisor. The grievant was then restrained by several employes [*sic*] while his supervisor ran from the area. A short time later the grievant appeared at the entrance way to the foreman's cubicle . . . where he threatened Foreman Y, in the presence of Foreman Z, by yelling, "I'm going to get you, your [*sic*] no f——k—— good. I'm going to get you outside, sooner or later you'll have to come outside." Subsequently the grievant was escorted to the Plant Protection Office and interviewed in the presence of his Union Representative.

"Adversarialism" here was no mere academic conceit but a grim day-to-day reality for many workers and managers.

Grievances like these, and others involving workers disciplined or discharged "for cause," enjoyed top priority on the local UAW's bargaining agenda. Indeed, the two workers involved in the cases just cited were ultimately reinstated.[22] UAW members knew that when their job was at stake, the union could be relied upon to defend them vigorously; yet this practice also bred cynicism among the rank and

file. The problem was that for every discipline case in which management abused its powers by targeting union militants or other so-called
troublemakers, there were several others involving workers whose
performance was less than exemplary, and the latter seemed to receive a disproportionate share of the union's attention. "The union
will use all their power to get somebody back on the job [who] should
have been fired three years ago," Ben Kowalski complained. "And
then they'll say, 'Well, look, we got this guy back in here.' The guy
don't deserve to be back in here. I don't care if he's a union brother,
union sister, or whatever. The guy's no good! They work so hard for
this person that really isn't worth it." Mike Evans agreed: "It seemed
like the guys who were good workers, conscientious, reliable people,
were always getting the shaft. We would have to give up our grievances, so that these other guys—we used to call them deadwood—
could get their jobs back."

This widespread perception fostered a broader view of the union
as devoted mainly to protecting the incompetent—not only in discharge cases but more generally—and many workers concurred with
this perception. "The union only helps people that can't do a job,"
declared skilled tradesman Henry Adamic. "You got an idiot that don't
know nothing and don't do nothing—he needs a union. The unions
are to keep jobs for deadweights. That's the only purpose they serve
in life." Production worker Dennis Tucker put it slightly differently:
"The union basically is a lawyer, and if you don't have that many problems and you do your job, you're not really going to need a lawyer."
Even former committeeman Eddie Soares agreed. "The good guys
are never in trouble," he said, "so they don't need the union to go to
bat for them."

Despite all this, most workers saw the union as a positive force and,
at least until the early 1980s, as a significant power base. "I admit I
never really needed it, but it was nice to know it was there," Tom
Peterman said. "The union is a necessary evil," declared skilled electrician Max Funk. "Without it, we'd probably be working twelve hours
a day, making two dollars an hour." The fact that so many of those
employed at GM-Linden in the 1970s and 1980s were second-gen-
eration auto workers injected a historical perspective into the rank-
and-file culture that reinforced the prevailing sense of loyalty to the

UAW. "Guys before us made it easy for us. We didn't have to fight for a lot of things, because they had gone and done it for us," Peterman stated. "I believe in unions," said Matthew Larson. "I've been a union member for a long time—my father was too—and I think you need 'em, because otherwise you would end up in sweatshops. I mean, they'd just take advantage of you." Ben Prindle, a skilled-trades committeeman whose father had been a union officer decades earlier, expressed similar sentiments: "With GM, you must have a union—there must be some kind of protection for the workers—or else you'd have to come in here with knee pads and kiss the foreman's ass, so you don't get fired. That's the way it would be if there was no union."

The Rise of the Linden Auto Workers

In the 1970s, the nation rediscovered blue-collar discontent, which had been obscured from public consciousness in earlier years by the glow of postwar prosperity. Now a new generation of industrial workers shaped by the social turmoil of the 1960s began to rebel, most conspicuously in the dramatic 1972 strike over working conditions at GM's Lordstown, Ohio, assembly plant. What *Business Week* dubbed "the spreading Lordstown syndrome" was much in evidence at GM's Linden plant, where the level of shop-floor conflict intensified in the 1970s as a caucus of young, militant union activists took shape and began to challenge management in ways that galvanized rank-and-file support.[23] GM-Linden managers took drastic measures against the caucus leaders, including many actions that would later be condemned by the NLRB and the federal courts as violations of national labor law. Ironically, however, managerial intransigence served, not as a deterrent, but as a spur to the steady growth in rank-and-file support for the caucus, culminating in 1982 when it won control of top offices in the local union.

The first battle in what would be a decade-long war began one night in September 1973, when GM-Linden management suspended union committeeman Douglas Stevens. Stevens had worked in the plant since 1965 and already had been suspended twice since announcing he would run for union office. The 1973 suspension came a few months after he was elected committeeman. Rumors flew around the plant that evening about the situation, and 105 workers walked out during the night shift's lunch break to protest the suspension, forcing the plant to close down early. The next night, there was another walkout by 63 workers, including 49 who had participated in the first wildcat. GM immediately fired this latter group, who became known as the 49ers. All of them were from the plant's chassis department, where Stevens also worked. After this mass firing, Stevens's original suspension was rescinded, but management warned that it would investigate his role in the walkouts, which violated the no-strike clause in the UAW-GM contract.

According to GM officials' own later testimony, at the time the 49ers were fired, all of them stated that no one had asked them to walk out, and that the strike was a "spontaneous combustion–type affair." An investigation by the NLRB concluded that Stevens had not led the strikes, and that on the contrary, he had urged the workers involved to return to their jobs when they assembled at the union hall (next door to the plant) during the lunch breaks on both nights and also at a union meeting held the afternoon after the first walkout. Nonetheless, three months after they were fired, 36 of the 49ers signed statements to the effect that Stevens and his alternate committeeman, Thomas Towell, *had* led the walkouts. On that basis, GM reinstated most of these workers and in turn fired Stevens and Towell on the grounds that they had "demonstrated positive leadership causing a group of employees to engage in a concerted action resulting in unauthorized work stoppages."[24] It was these firings that led Stevens and his supporters to file a formal complaint against GM with the NLRB, alleging that management was interfering with Stevens's union activity, in violation of a fundamental provision of U.S. labor law.

The leaders of UAW Local 595 played an important role in these events. Although Stevens and Towell were elected union representatives, apparently they were abandoned by the top local UAW leaders as part of a deal to get the 49ers their jobs back. The NLRB found that "[u]nion officers did advise employees [the 49ers], in effect, that they would be reinstated if they gave or made these statements" implicating Stevens. Evidently, not only management but also some local union officials saw Stevens as a problem. The local's most powerful officer, the shop chairman, in conversations with one of the 49ers, allegedly called Stevens "a communist and pinky and everything." Several of the 49ers testified before the NLRB that both GM and the UAW were "out to get" Stevens and Towell, and that they had been told that they could only get their jobs back by signing the statements.[25]

In June 1975, the NLRB ordered GM to reinstate Stevens and Towell with back pay and to stop "interrogating . . . restraining, or coercing employees." However, GM did not comply until the NLRB's decision was enforced by a federal court order in April 1976, leading to Stevens's and Towell's reinstatement more than two years after they had been fired.[26] Long delays of this kind (not unusual in NLRB cases) usually redound to the advantage of management, since even if the workers prevail legally, the company's ability to keep them out of the plant and without wages for so long a period leaves the impression that management can fire troublemakers with impunity. This case was different, however, because the period of delay coincided with a long-term layoff affecting the Linden plant's entire second shift. In January 1974, about a month after Stevens and Towell were fired, the second shift was placed on indefinite layoff in the wake of the energy crisis. Stevens and Towell were reinstated in early May 1976, just as the plant's second shift was being called back to work.[27] The layoff affected the 49ers and virtually everyone else involved in the 1973 wildcats, which had included night shift workers only. When they came back to work in 1976, they found Stevens and Towell in the plant, able to boast of their legal victory.

During the layoff period, Stevens, as well as some of the 49ers and their supporters, formed a new local union caucus, the Linden Auto Workers, or LAW. As one activist in the group later testified, LAW "began putting out leaflets on a monthly basis from January 1974 . . . and took collections from union members to support the newsletter. Generally we handed out 1,500 to 2,000 leaflets. . . . I would personally hand out approximately 500." Some of the LAW leaflets publicized the NLRB hearing on Stevens's and Towell's firing (held in June and July of 1974). When the second shift came back to work two years later, LAW immediately enjoyed great prestige, thanks to the court order reinstating Stevens and Towell.[28] The caucus continued to build support, particularly on the night shift, and some of its leaders (including Stevens) were elected as union committeemen and alternate committeemen.

Shortly after Stevens's and Towell's reinstatement, LAW members began filing new charges with the NLRB, alleging continuing management discrimination against the caucus supporters in defiance of the court-enforced NLRB order. The order had stipulated that management "cease and desist from . . . discriminating against employees for being and acting as union committeemen" and from "interfering with, restraining, or coercing employees in the exercise of their rights."[29] Several workers signed sworn affidavits complaining that they had been subjected to unusual disciplinary measures in retaliation for their participation in LAW or for their association with caucus members. The following examples are representative:[30]

My lateness record is better than the majority of the workers in my department. . . . In addition to being treated differently from other workers who have been late and who have not been disciplined, it was also highly unusual, indeed extraordinary, that the company disciplined me for failing to provide a note the first day after being late. . . . I believe that the reason that the company suspended me was because . . . I have been an alternate committeeman of the UAW since April of 1977 and . . . I have been an active supporter of Linden Auto Workers and ran on the Linden Auto Workers slate. I have continually and do to this time associate myself in work with [name deleted] and the other members of Linden Auto Workers and am viewed in the plant as being a leader of Linden Auto Workers.

On Friday, November 11, 1977, I felt badly, feverish and had pains in my chest. . . . I called in sick and told the absentee clerk what was wrong. I tried going to work on Saturday, November 12, 1977 and when I got to the G.M. plant at 4:30 P.M. I spoke to General Foreman [name deleted] who I informed that I still wasn't feeling very well. . . . At about 5:40 P.M. I was feeling badly and approached Foreman [name deleted] for a Hospital pass. He said, "Well, never mind that, I just got told I've got to throw you out." In my 11½ years at G.M., I do not recall any time . . . where the order for the discipline came from higher management. I was brought to the bullpen and [name deleted], Supervisor of Labor Relations interviewed me and I told him . . . it was absolutely unfair and discriminatory to discipline me before giving me an opportunity to substantiate my reason for absence. As a committeeman, I told him, I've settled many many cases where employees are given time to substantiate their reason for absence.

I was approached by [name deleted] who I have known all my life as we grew up together. [He] is a labor relations man. [He] said, "You got a call," and I asked him from where, and he said, "From your wife, she was ill but she is o.k. now." I said I was going to have to go home. He said, "Don't cause alot [*sic*] of trouble because you're already in trouble now." I said explain what you mean. He said, "Well I don't have time to tell you now but you have been seen associating with, talking with and communicating with commie groups and the wrong kind of people. [Name deleted] is one of those people and he's in one of those commie groups" or words to that effect. He went on to tell me that I should not tell [name deleted] anything about this conversation and he walked away. . . . I arrived home about 11:00 P.M. and received a call within an hour or so from [name deleted]. He again told me that I was associating with the wrong kind of people. He said, "The groups you're associating with are commie groups. You're causing alot [*sic*] of trouble down there. You have a bad attendance record and you've been late constantly and you're not doing your job properly. If you listen to me you'll get a clean start."

Other new charges were filed with the NLRB, alleging that when the plant's second shift was restored in 1976, GM had refused to re-hire several workers associated with LAW's activities, including some of the 49ers. This did not violate the union contract, which had a "time for time" provision stipulating that an individual's recall rights expired if a layoff's duration exceeded the time he or she had worked for the company. However, at this time GM did rehire many other laid-off workers whose contractual recall rights also had expired, and hired large numbers of people with no previous experience as well. After some of the 49ers, as well as others who had testified on behalf of Stevens before the NLRB or who were active in LAW, applied for jobs at the plant and were rejected, they testified in sworn affidavits that GM's refusal to rehire them was illegal discrimination based on their union activity. For example:[31]

I never missed handing out a [LAW] leaflet. . . . I personally handed leaflets to my former foreman [name deleted] on two occasions. I clearly remember on one of those occasions him saying, "Out here again, [name deleted]?" . . . In mid-March of 1976, I went to Linden-G.M. and filled out an application as a new hire. I subsequently heard that they were rehiring people who had worked at Linden-G.M. but had less seniority than I did [so I went back]. Then [name deleted] called me into his office. . . . he said, "[Y]ou're here about not being recalled?" I responded, "Yes." He stated that General Motors had no contractual responsibility to rehire me and I said that I knew that but I also knew of people with less seniority than me and with discipline on their records being recalled. He stated, "We have a recommendation that you're not suitable for hire." When I asked him where he got the recommendation, he said probably your foreman. I responded that I thought my foreman retired in February of 1974. . . . I said the only reason you're not hiring me is because of my union activity.

In September, 1973, I was one of a group of 49 employees who walked out for 2 nights. . . . In March, 1976, some of my friends who had worked at GM got notices to come back to work. I thought I'd get one too, and when I didn't, I went down to the plant at Linden. I went to the personnel department and filled out an application. I said I had worked at GM previously. I asked whether I'd be rehired, and I was sent to a tall dark-haired man who I believe is personnel director. He said [my foreman] had not recommended me for rehire. I asked him: Is it because I'm a 49er? He said the reason's not here, it just says your foreman did not recommend you for rehire. . . . I know of several people hired after me who are now back at GM.

When I put in the application I told the labor relations rep (I don't know his name but he is tall with dark hair) that I wanted to speak to someone but he said I couldn't and they would treat my application like any other application. I believe he knew when I applied that I was a "49er" because I saw him at various trials we had when I and the others were discharged. . . . At the time I put in this application my time for time had expired. I put in two applications since the first one. The same thing happened. . . . People who I know who live near me put in applications around the same time I did and were hired.

I was one of the "49ers," and I was subsequently subpoenaed by General Counsel and G.M. to testify at the unfair labor practice hearing at the National Labor Relations Board. . . . In the Spring of 1976, my brother told me that General Motors was hiring a second shift. I believe I also heard about the hirings on television. In late April 1976, I went to the General Motors plant with a friend of mine. When I arrived at the Guard shack I asked one of the guards if I could see labor relations. The guard asked me why. I responded that I wanted to try to get my job back. The guard asked me if I was one of the "49ers"; I told him I was. Then an older fellow with a suit and tie on, who I now believe to be [name deleted] head of Labor Relations, said to me, "you're not getting your job back if your [sic] one of the '49ers.' " I said, "Hasn't G.M. hired some of the 49ers?" He responded, "Didn't you testify against General Motors at the trial?" I said I had. [He] then said,

"Well, your [*sic*] not getting your job back." I said, "Well, I want to try any-way." He responded, "Well, go ahead and try but it won't do you any good." When I went upstairs I spoke with Supervisor of Labor Relations [name deleted] who I told I was interested in getting my job back. He said, "You're not recommended for rehire." I asked him why and he said because you have two lates and two absences. I said, "Well that can't be the reasons, there are thousands of people who are late and absent here." He said well you're also one of the "49ers."

I was one of the employees who walked out on the job 2 consecutive nights in September, 1973, i.e. one of the "49ers." . . . Sometime in December, 1973, I met a friend who told me that he had heard through the grapevine that if we gave GM a statement about certain people, we'd get our jobs back. . . . On or about January 4, 1974, when GM reopened after the Christmas–New Year holiday, I went to see [name deleted] in the Labor Relations Depart-ment and gave him the statement they wanted. He wrote it all down, then gave me a layoff slip. He told me my record would reflect the fact that I had a 90 day suspension. . . . In February 1976, I heard through the newspapers that GM would be calling back some employees, so I went to the personnel office to notify them, that my address had changed. [Name deleted], the head of personnel, saw me, but didn't say anything. He and the other people in the personnel office gave me looks, that made me realize they knew who I was, and were not particularly glad to see me. . . . In April, 1976, I went back to the company to apply for a job. . . . A man who worked in personnel [. . .] took my file out and handed it to [name deleted], the head of person-nel. [He] told me I was not being recalled, that I was on a list of people not recommended for recall. I asked him why. He said that's obvious, isn't it. I said yes. It was understood that we were talking about the walkout, but nei-ther of us said that word. I said, but that's the only thing on my record. He said isn't that enough? What would you do if you were me and I had done this to you? I said, I would weigh the circumstances[.] I said I spent 2 years here on the street, I think I paid my dues. He didn't say anything to that, but said there's nothing I can do for you. I asked him if I could fill out another application and he said yes. I asked him what my chances were of being accepted and he said not good at all. So I left. . . . I know of at least one employee [name deleted] who had less seniority than me who is now back at work. I'm not sure whether he was involved in the [walkout], but I think he was not.

As the volume of NLRB charges grew, in 1977, someone in man-agement leaked a copy of what came to be known as the Stevens Log, a log book recording Douglas Stevens's activities in the plant in great detail on a nightly basis. The accumulating evidence of GM's defiance of the 1976 court order eventually led the NLRB to threaten contempt proceedings against GM. The agency's regional director summarized the situation in a 1978 memorandum:

On May 3, 1976, Stevens was reinstated. General Motors immediately began to surveil his activities and those of other employees who supported him. They also began to keep a written "log" regarding these incidents of surveillance. . . . In late October 1976, General Motors began a policy of discriminatorily enforcing discipline in that portion of the Linden plant in which Stevens was the committeeman. The purpose of this plan was to discourage Stevens from filing grievances or in other ways representing the employees in his district. . . . [During the next seven months] there were 63 unlawful disciplines involving 44 employees. . . . General Motors implemented a policy of refusing to bargain in good faith with Stevens concerning the adjustment of grievances. In March 1977, General Motors transferred an employee into Stevens' district to facilitate that employee's campaign against Stevens for union office. It also allowed this individual and other individuals opposed to Stevens to solicit and distribute literature during working time and in working areas but refused to allow Stevens to do the same. Also in March 1977, a supervisory level employee at General Motors threatened employees with discipline if they supported Stevens or associated with him.[32]

"It went beyond Doug Stevens' wildest accusations," the attorney who represented him before the NLRB told a journalist several years later. "Stevens didn't know GM had set spies on him in the plant, transferred people to his district to undermine him, disciplined workers for dealing with him."[33]

In April 1978, after a long series of procedural delays, GM agreed to a court-approved settlement stipulating that it reinstate, with back pay, nine of the workers who had been excluded from recall; stop surveillance of Stevens's union activities; and expunge a variety of disciplinary measures from the personnel records of Stevens and a long list of other workers.[34] As is customary in NLRB cases, GM was required to post an official Notice to Employees in the plant for sixty days "in conspicuous places," detailing the company's commitment to comply with the terms of the settlement. The notice reads in part:

WE WILL NOT surveil the union . . . activities of Douglas Stevens and other of our employees. . . .

WE WILL NOT allow candidates for office in U.A.W. Local 595 opposed to the candidacy of Douglas Stevens to solicit and distribute literature during working time in working areas while at the same time refusing to allow Douglas Stevens to do the same.

WE WILL NOT transfer employees into that portion of our Linden plant for which Douglas Stevens is the U.A.W. Local 595 Committeeman in order to further those employees' campaign for office against Douglas Stevens. . . .

WE WILL NOT maintain a "log" or any other written record of the activities of Douglas Stevens of a kind that is not kept for all other employees similarly situated, i.e. U.A.W. Local 595 committeemen. . . .

WE WILL NOT discipline employees in that portion of our Linden plant for which Douglas Stevens is the U.A.W. Local 595 committeeman for the purpose of discouraging Douglas Stevens from filing grievances. . . .

WE WILL destroy the written log and any and all other written documents relating to the activities of Douglas Stevens. . . .

WE WILL offer to the following employees immediate and full reinstatement to their former jobs [a list of nine names follows].[35]

The effect of this second legal victory was to enhance further the status of LAW generally, and Stevens in particular, in the plant. Indeed, many years later, workers vividly remembered the case and Stevens's role in it. In a 1991 interview, for example, Ben Kowalski recalled: "Doug's a good man, you know. I mean, Doug gets things done. Back when, I think it was like '75, when they had the gas shortage and everything, they laid off people, and when they called the people back, there was a group of people they didn't call back in the right order. They weren't going to call them back at all, because they didn't want these people. And Doug is the one that went to court with all those people, and he won their case for them, and they got back pay and everything."

Before 1978, LAW had grown relatively slowly. A few of its members were elected as committeemen or alternate committeemen, mostly on the night shift, but the higher local union offices remained under the control of the old guard. After the second NLRB case was settled in LAW's favor, things began to change. In the May 1978 elections, held just a few weeks after the settlement, LAW supported a slate of candidates for several of the union's most powerful positions, and two of these candidates were elected: Doug Stevens won "shop-at-large," the highest night-shift position (which he had sought the previous year and lost by a close vote), and another LAW stalwart won a spot on the shop committee, also for the night shift.[36]

But management remained intransigent, as events just after the settlement suggested. The first sign of trouble was the timing GM chose for posting the Notice to Employees cited above. The notice appeared on the plant bulletin boards during the August 1978 model changeover period, when the bulk of the workforce was laid off for a few weeks. This meant that a considerable part of the mandatory sixty-day posting period elapsed while only a small proportion of the work-force was in the plant. Only after Stevens complained to the NLRB, which in turn notified GM that this arrangement was unacceptable, was the posting extended for an additional month.[37]

That GM-Linden's plant management had no intention of abiding by the other terms of the settlement soon became apparent. The same pattern of harassment of LAW activists that had led to the earlier NLRB and court cases continued unabated. More complaints piled up at the NLRB (forty separate charges were filed between the 1978 settlement and 1982), and in 1980, the agency's regional office rec-ommended a civil contempt suit against GM for its violations of the 1976 and 1978 court orders. By late 1981, NLRB headquarters had approved going ahead with such a contempt case, the first such action in GM's history.[38] As the NLRB argued in a court petition in December 1981:

The Company and its agents . . . continue to disobey, fail and refuse to comply with, the Court's judgements herein by discriminating, and threat-ening to discriminate, against Union committeemen and former committee-men because of their grievance-handling activities and their membership in, and activities on behalf of, the Linden Auto Workers ("LAW"), a caucus within the Union at the Company's Linden, New Jersey facility. Further, the Company has discriminated against and threatened to discriminate against employees because they were represented by LAW committeemen; refused to deal with said committeemen over grievances; physically assaulted and threatened committeemen in the course of their grievance-handling or other protected activities; denied employee requests for assistance from their com-mitteemen; engaged in surveillance of, and discriminated against, employees because of their LAW candidacies for Union office; discriminated against employees because of their participation in [NLRB] unfair labor practice investigations . . . all in violation of said decrees of this Court.

The petition went on to detail seventeen specific allegations of discriminatory acts by various GM-Linden managerial officials, starting in November 1978, including these incidents:

On or about April 12, 1980, Union committeeman and LAW member [Carl Block] met with General Foreman A to attempt to resolve a grievance, involving employees within his jurisdiction, concerning that [*sic*] they had not been provided break time during their shift. Despite [Block's] contractual right to represent the employees in this matter, A refused to deal with [Block] over the grievance. . . . When [Block] persisted in his attempt to deal with A over the grievance, A physically assaulted him and expelled him from the office. . . .

On or about August 20, 1980, the Company assigned former Union committeeperson [Judy Chisholm] to a job involving the movement of heavy equipment which was never before filled by a woman and which it had reason to believe [Chisholm] was physically unable to perform. Said assignment was made in retaliation for her former activities as Union committeeperson and as chairperson of the LAW caucus. On or about September 12, 1980, Company Foreman B in further retribution for [Chisholm's] protected activities, removed an employee who had been assisting [Chisholm] in the performance of the job, resulting in [Chisholm's] injury. . . .

In or about September 1980, employee [Tony da Silva] was a candidate for Union office on a LAW-sponsored slate. From on or about September 15 to September 22, 1980, Company Foreman C surveilled and more closely supervised [da Silva] by, among other actions, timing [da Silva's] breaks and following him into the bathroom, because of his candidacy on behalf of LAW.

In or about October 1980, Union committeeman and LAW member [David White] met with Company General Foreman D to discuss the transfer of employee X. Foreman D threatened that as long as [White] was a committeeman, D would not deal with him and that anything [White] requested would be denied; D further indicated that, in effect, he could prevent [White] from being reelected as committeeman inasmuch as D would see to it that [White] did not get anything accomplished. . . .

On or about January 20, 1981, Union committeeman and LAW member [Carl Block] and employee Y met with General Foreman E over a grievance concerning the Company's transfer of another employee with less seniority ahead of Y. . . . Foreman E refused to discuss the grievance with [Block], threatened to suspend him when he protested E's refusal, and assaulted [Block].[39]

Although the contempt case this petition introduced was never brought to trial, the charges involved suggest that by the early 1980s, the conflict between GM and LAW had greatly expanded in scope, going far beyond the original vendetta against Douglas Stevens and the 49ers. By now, numerous GM officials were involved; in fact, twenty-seven different individual plant managers were mentioned by name in the contempt petition. However, as in earlier phases of the struggle between GM and LAW, management's efforts to thwart the caucus's progress backfired, contributing to, rather than undermining, the growing support LAW enjoyed among GM-Linden employees. As an NLRB attorney involved in the cases recalled many years later, the Linden managers were no match for the intelligence, creativity, and strategic ability of Stevens and the other LAW leaders. "They [LAW] could run circles around those [management] guys," he exclaimed.

LAW captured the imagination of a generation of auto workers who, despite their lack of higher education, came of age in a period of widespread questioning of the status quo. This was especially true on the night shift, where the younger workers were concentrated. Fred Lawton, a LAW supporter, explained: "The LAW was, actually, the majority were people who were hired in '76, who have a limited education, who ask questions. When they're told to do something, they ask why. They want a reason. And I think that's why we're looked at as adversaries. If you tell me to do something, I want to know why I'm doing it and what the importance of it is." Charlie Ferraro, a LAW leader, agreed. "They were usually younger workers; they didn't take as much bullshit," he recalled.

The incumbent union leaders, whose control of Local 595 began to be seriously challenged by LAW in this period, knew that their relationship to the plant's younger workers was tenuous. "The Young Man in the Union," an article published in the October 1978 issue of the local union newspaper, poses the problem this way: "Why doesn't he feel like his dad felt in '36? A barrier exists between the young man in the union and the older man. . . . The young man in the union . . .

doesn't like paying dues every month, because he feels that if the union would take as much interest in him as the dues he pays, he would be a lot better off. . . . He feels he's being held down on his job . . . , that the majority of union representatives don't want to hear his complaints, they give him the brush-off. . . . The biggest thing about the young man is his impatience: he doesn't seem to care about 20 years from now, he is only concerned with today."[40] The old guard union leadership, although aware of the disaffection of younger workers, never succeeded in bridging the generation gap. Instead, the incumbent leaders tended to resist the changes LAW advocated, further alienating the young workers. "There [were] certain guys in the union that didn't want a lot of things to happen," Tom Peterman recalled. "They wanted it their own way, a lot of the older ones. They didn't want to see the changes. . . . It seemed like all the younger ones was in [LAW]."

LAW activists rejected the careerism that had dampened the effectiveness of so many earlier waves of union activists. As Charlie Ferraro explained years later:

Let's say you want to get involved with the union. And they [the old guard] say, you know, "We'd like you to come with us. We can give you access to the union hall, time off from work; we'll pay you to do the job; we got some trips going to Detroit; we'd like you to go out there." Then you come up to me and Stevens, you say, "What are you going to do for me?" We say, "Well, we can get you fired, we can get you thrown out every day, we can get people to call you a commie, we can get people to throw shit at you outside the plant. You want that? No problem." Most of them are doing it for themselves, unfortunately. Any place you have money involved and power involved, whether it be the Elks Club or the Congress, unfortunately the people who are out for themselves will work the hardest. It's hard to get somebody to work hard for a principle. Most of them, they're career men, they want careers in the union. . . . I was a popular guy. I had the personality; people loved me. I could make people feel that they were part of the union. They would perceive a committeeman as "the union." I would never accept that. I said, "What are you guys fucking talking about. I used to work with ya. What am I? You elected me; I'm something different that you?" Always kept that. Me, I feel comfortable; the day I stopped being committeeman, I felt just as comfortable. It don't make no difference to me. I've had people confide in me—I used to go home and cry. Stuff they wouldn't tell their own mothers and fathers. They trusted me that much; they needed somebody to talk to. That job is more than just reading the contract. I got people to stand up for themselves that you wouldn't believe. Guys that were there twenty-five years and never called for a committeeman—screaming at a foreman. But they knew I was right next to them to back them up. If you don't think that screws a foreman's day up, young lady, you've got to be kidding!

At times, LAW's opponents resorted to explicit red-baiting, making reference to commies in the plant in electoral flyers and in one case equating LAW with "Russian Governance."[41] Such rhetoric may have cost LAW some support, but it was not enough to counteract the appeal of the caucus to many workers. In fact, almost all of LAW's leaders were ordinary auto workers, entirely disconnected from the resurgence of youthful radical activism that was so much in evidence on college campuses around this time. The one clear exception was Carl Block, a college-educated Jewish radical who got himself hired at Linden in 1976 with explicit political purposes in mind. Although Block ultimately became one of LAW's most effective leaders, the infrastructure of the caucus and its militant reputation were already well established when he arrived. Indeed, Block often took his cues from the plant's homegrown militants, rather than the other way round. LAW stalwart and then committeeman Charlie Ferraro recalled his initial contact with Block, who had just been elected as a night-shift committeeman from the body shop, this way:

[Block] was with the Communist Party at the time, a regular member of the Communist Workers Part [CWP] or whatever. So he's gung ho, you know, he's going to save this plant and all this shit. . . . I was the kind of committeeman with a big district, geographically. Every night I'd walk the district, stop and talk to people. The body shop used to be my first stop. Well, one day, [Block] sees me coming up, and he comes running behind me; he says, "Excuse me, can I talk to you?" I says, "Yeah, what's up?" And he says, "I'd like to talk privately with you." And he's coming on strong. This little short dwarf. He says, "Well, I realize that you're a shop committeeman and I've heard a lot of good things about you, but I'm just letting you know that I'm going to do this job the best that I can. I'm a member of the CWP, and I know you're going to hold that against me, but I still think I should tell you that I'd like to work with you." I says, "Let me tell you something, all right, pal? Might as well get it straight. I'm a member of the shop committee. My job is to help committeemen. I don't give a shit if you're with the CWP, the

EWP, or the TWP. I don't give a fuck what your political views are. It means nothing to me at all. I don't care if you're a Democrat, Republican, Communist don't even faze me. These people elected us to do a responsible job. If you want my help, I will give it to you. If you choose not to, that's your choice. But I'm going to tell you something, pal. From what I can see of your group there, they're so busy trying to save the tea in China, or whatever the fuck those meetings are about . . . wait till you try and get some guy on the line a pair of gloves. Then you're going to accomplish something." There was something I felt about the guy, you know. Now he's coming to me every day; I'm showing him the ropes. Well, about a month later, he's got to get a guy a pair of gloves, and he can't get the frigging gloves for the guy. As time evolved, a few months later, he dropped out of the CWP; he saw it for what it was. He got a lesson about what the real working world was about; that a pair of gloves is important to some individual. And we got tight after that; we had a lot of respect for each other. He came to realize that that was all bullshit; this is the real stuff here, you know.

LAW developed a reputation for aggressively pursuing grievances, demanded that management address a variety of health and safety concerns, and on this basis gradually built up more respect and support among the workforce. As Matthew Larson recalled:

It's like there was two unions at that time. I always used them [LAW], you know, because they work a little better. They weren't siding with the management. They were, like, radicals. . . . Stevens, he's the right person for you. He's the one who'll stick up for you. He doesn't give in to the management— you know: "We'll give your friend this job, or we'll do this, if you keep your mouth shut." He doesn't work that way. He never did. What's right is right, you know. Like he'd stop the lines for floods. The other union would get you boots, and you'd work in a half a foot of water. He'd stop the line, saying, "The water shouldn't be there, and your job description does not say you should work in boots."

Stevens remained the group's most visible leader and was reelected several times to the night-shift shop-at-large position after first winning this office in 1978. Block also was widely admired by workers. As Tom Peterman recalled much later, "He was always behind the worker. He wanted to get things straightened out and done. He wouldn't let nobody run over him or anything."

With two of its leaders installed in highly visible local union offices, and with two major NLRB victories to its credit, the group continued

to increase its political effectiveness. The caucus sold clothing marked
with the LAW logo for supporters to wear in the plant. "People loved
the jackets and the shirts," Block told me later, adding, "It was a presence kind of thing. The people who bought the stuff were on a continuum from dyed-in-the wool activists to people who couldn't care
less and probably voted against us in elections. There were a lot
of people who wore LAW jackets that couldn't care less about LAW
but hated their foreman. People loved that paraphernalia, and it
made some kind of statement. It said LINDEN on it and it said AUTO
WORKER on it and it wasn't given out by the company. I'm sure now
there are wonderful company T-shirts, but we were faster on the take
with that."

While there were other caucuses in the local union as well, and
individuals occasionally shifted alliances, starting in the late 1970s,
the main competition was between the older group of incumbents
and LAW, which most workers saw as more militant. "It was like two
political parties," Edward Salerno, a LAW supporter, recalled. "The
night shift, the radicals dominated that." Eddie Soares, partly out of
loyalty to his father, opposed LAW but saw the situation in very similar terms: "The Linden Auto Workers, they were like the rebels. My
father was with the union, the United Auto Workers. The LAW, they
had their own jackets, they had their own people, but they were still
all-union. Just like the Democrats have their people in the House,
and the Republicans have their people—that's exactly how it was, a
Democratic-Republican kind of thing."

Workers who were not directly involved in the factional struggles
inside the local union had a wide range of opinions about the situation.
Some, like Ben Kowalski, expressed a critical view: "When they had
the two caucuses like that, they had the black coats and the other
people had orange coats, and they didn't work together the way they
should have." Mike Evans agreed: "I'm sure the company lapped it
up because these guys would be bad-mouthing each other over this
or that. We were supposed to be a union! It seemed sort of self-de-
feating." On the other hand, Joyce Cowley felt the effect of the internal divisions was positive. "You can't have everybody in a place [hav-
ing] the same opinion," she reasoned. "If you have two groups, the
people with one type of opinion can go here and the other there, and

they can work it out. If there was only one group, then the ones that weren't in with that group, where would they go? They couldn't speak their opinion. So I figure having the two different things was good."

But the overt factionalism of the 1970s became more subdued by 1980, as LAW forged an alliance with a key member of the old guard, Tony Fernandez, who for several years had held one of the local union's top two offices, that of shop chairman.[42] His name appeared on the official LAW slate in the 1980 local elections, and in 1981, LAW supported his bid for the local union presidency. Fernandez won and rewarded LAW by appointing Stevens editor of the local union newspaper (in addition to his shop-at-large position). Previously, LAW had occasionally issued an oppositional newspaper of its own, also edited by Stevens. Now, the official local union paper became part of a broader effort on LAW's part to question the direction the national UAW leaders were taking in responding to the deepening problems of the U.S. auto industry. With Fernandez's support, LAW organized an extensive educational program for the membership. As it turned out, the unprecedented crisis of both GM and the UAW provided LAW with new opportunities for leadership. By 1982, Stevens would be elected shop chairman, and LAW candidates would win a majority of the positions on the local union's executive board. However, gaining control of the local union at this historical moment proved a hollow victory, as the UAW's power was being undercut by national developments beyond local unionists' control.

The Industry's Crisis and the 1982 Concessions

LAW's rise in the early 1970s coincided with the beginning of the U.S. auto industry's long decline, signaled by the energy crisis and the surge in demand for imported cars. These developments, along with the recession of the mid-1970s, hit GM-Linden especially hard. Demand for the expensive luxury cars built there had always been sensitive to the business cycle, and the shift to smaller, more fuel-efficient vehicles added to the problem. It was these developments that led to the massive 1974 layoffs, when GM eliminated the Linden plant's entire second shift. When these jobs were restored two years later, many hoped for a return to normalcy. Indeed, employment in the U.S. auto industry as a whole expanded in the late 1970s, reaching an all-time high in 1978.[43]

By the decade's end, however, it was obvious that the industry's troubles were far from over. Chrysler, the nation's third largest automaker, hovered on the brink of bankruptcy, and imported cars had captured an unprecedented share of the U.S. market. In late 1979 and early 1980, as a quid pro quo for the government bailout of Chrysler, the national UAW agreed to grant the firm unprecedented wage and benefit concessions, valued at over $650 million. As part of the deal, the UAW secured a seat for its president (then Douglas Fraser) on Chrysler's board of directors, an achievement the union touted as a link with its past traditions of innovative bargaining and its vision of industrial democracy.[44]

The Chrysler concessions turned out to be the tip of the iceberg. In 1982, in the depths of a new recession, a massive wave of concession bargaining swept the nation. Whereas Chrysler had extracted concessions on the basis of a desperate profitability crisis, now even healthy firms began to demand that workers give back wages, benefits, and work rules won in more prosperous years.[45] With unemployment at a postwar high, and with the memory still fresh of the Reagan administration's dramatic destruction of the air controllers' union after its August 1981 strike, many unions caved in to the escalating corporate pressure.

The UAW was at center stage in this national drama. Ever since it had agreed to a new round of concessions at Chrysler in early 1981 (linked to additional government loan guarantees granted at that time), the auto workers' union had been resisting demands from Ford and GM to reopen the three-year contracts then in effect. At first, the union rejected the idea outright, but the companies grew bolder after the air controllers' strike. In October 1981, Ford announced a 50 percent wage cut at its Sheffield, Alabama, plant and threatened to close the plant if workers refused to go along. The UAW rejected this ultimatum but did allow its Ford local affiliates to negotiate changes in work rules not covered by the national contract. A wave of local work-rule concessions ensued, in the face of management threats to move work away from "uncooperative" plants. Against this background, in

December 1981, the UAW's national executive board reversed itself and voted to reopen the Ford and GM national contracts.[46]

In the spring of 1982, UAW members were asked to vote on new contracts with Ford and GM containing $1 billion and $2.5 billion in concessions, respectively. Both were ultimately ratified, although in GM's case only after a protracted struggle inside the union and by an extremely narrow margin. Whereas the fact that Chrysler and Ford had been losing money helped persuade workers to go along with concessions, GM had turned a $333 million profit in 1981, and at the time, its share of the domestic car market was stable. Many GM workers around the nation opposed concessions for this reason, with fully 48 percent voting against ratification of the new contract. Indeed, it might not have been ratified at all if GM had not stepped up the pressure in February, after the first round of talks with the UAW broke down, announcing plans to close seven plants. The clear message was that GM would find a way to reduce its labor costs whether or not workers agreed to concessions.

By any standards, the givebacks were extensive. The annual wage increases that had been a standard feature of UAW contracts for over three decades were eliminated for the two-and-a-half-year term of the new agreement, and three quarterly cost-of-living increases were also deferred for eighteen months. In addition, all nine of the "paid personal holidays" to which each worker previously had been entitled were eliminated. The 1982 contract also empowered GM to unilaterally reopen local work-rule and wage agreements, whether or not the local unions involved were interested in such discussions, and stipulated that unresolved local disputes would be automatically referred to the national level after sixty days.

In return for all this, GM called off four of the seven plant closings it had announced in February, and agreed to a two-year ban on further plant closings due to outsourcing, or obtaining parts formerly manufactured within GM from independent suppliers (foreign or domestic). The company also agreed to establish a new program, the Guaranteed Income Stream, which guaranteed high-seniority workers lifetime incomes (at half their GM pay level) under certain circumstances. Protecting workers against job and income loss was already a vital concern for the UAW, for by 1982, the number of production workers employed in the auto industry nationally had fallen to two-thirds of the peak 1978 level.[47] Real wages in the industry, which had risen steadily in the previous twenty years, also began to fall after 1978. Despite some fluctuations in the 1980s, auto workers' real wages have essentially leveled off at about the 1980 level, as appendix 2 shows. (On the other hand, since workers in other sectors have suffered declining real wages since 1973, the *relative* wage advantage of auto workers has actually increased slightly in the 1970s and 1980s.)

The UAW's national leadership tried to put the best possible face on the concessions, arguing that the silver lining in the dark cloud was the prospect of expanding the terrain of collective bargaining to include issues other than wages, benefits, and working conditions. In return for reduced living standards, the argument went, the union might gain new influence in spheres that had been sealed off as sacred managerial prerogatives under the postwar labor-capital accord.[48] As it had characterized the appointment of Fraser to Chrysler's board two years earlier, the union presented the 1982 contract reopening as part of a renewal of its historical quest for a role in management decision making. Thus in January 1982, the UAW and GM jointly announced an agreement to link any wage concessions to lower car prices, dollar for dollar. This idea (which was later dropped) explicitly invoked the memory of the UAW's celebrated 1945 open-the-books strike, when the union had boldly suggested that if GM could not afford to meet its demand for a 30 percent wage increase without increasing car prices, it should prove it by giving the public "a look at the books."[49]

But the invocation in the 1980s of the rhetoric of the 1940s obscured the crucial differences between the two periods. In 1945, union strength and militancy were at their peak. Organized labor then embraced over a third of the nation's nonagricultural workers and 67 percent of those in manufacturing.[50] Unions were a central force in the Democratic Party and a vital influence in public debate, with an agenda that went far beyond the narrow, sectional interests of their members. Indeed, the UAW's 1945 open-the-books strike had put forth a broad social program as a supplement to basic economic demands. By contrast, in the 1980s, what appeared as a renewed attempt to challenge managerial prerogatives, while couched in the language used four decades earlier, was in fact a tradeoff for economic concessions from a position of union weakness and timidity.

The grim reality was that management had unilaterally abandoned the postwar accord, capitalizing on the dramatic decline in labor's power. By 1983, unions represented only 19 percent of nonagricultural private-sector workers, and only 31 percent of those in manufacturing—roughly half the 1945 levels.[51] Moreover, in the 1980s, organized labor was so isolated from the larger society that the right-wing characterization of it as a special interest prevailed unchallenged, and public approval ratings of unions were lower than at any time since World War II.[52] Under these conditions, the UAW's invocation of symbols from its glory days belied the underlying and fundamental power shift from labor to management—a shift in exactly the opposite direction from that which the union's discourse sought to project.

In fact, the UAW national leadership's thinking at the time was based precisely on the calculation that GM workers could not be expected to sustain a serious strike against the giant auto firm in the recession year of 1982. Car sales were severely depressed, nearly 150,000 auto workers were on indefinite layoff at GM alone, and the threat of more plant closings loomed large. Taking these factors into account, along with an obviously hostile administration in Washington, the union's leaders believed that it was in GM workers' interests to reopen the contract in early 1982, rather than risk being forced into a difficult and costly strike when the 1979 agreement expired in September. During a strike, the reasoning went, GM would sell off its inventories, save on wages and benefits, and perhaps close more plants, while auto workers stood by helplessly. Fearing that even greater concessions would ultimately be made in the event of a strike, the UAW sought to trade givebacks in wages, benefits, and work rules for guarantees of job security over the short term, in a holding action designed to tide the union over until conditions improved.[53]

The union leadership expected that the rank and file would see the situation in these terms as well. There had been substantial support among UAW members for the concessions granted to Chrysler in 1980, which were endorsed by 80 percent of those voting on the question. The 1981 round of Chrysler concessions was approved by a closer, 60 percent to 40 percent vote, but there was still no organized opposition to givebacks within the union. By the spring of 1982, however, when UAW members were presented with the Ford and GM concessions proposals, dissident secondary UAW leaders had formed a national organization, Locals Opposed to Concessions (LOC). Among its members were Linden's Douglas Stevens and other LAW leaders. LOC published its own detailed analyses of the Ford and GM contracts, and urged workers to reject them.

At the Linden plant, LAW led a massive educational campaign, with official sponsorship from the local union. Stevens was now chair of Local 595's education committee, and he enlisted the assistance of a group of labor educators in nearby New York City to develop classes for the membership, laying out an in-depth case against the concessions.[54] "We did an enormous amount of educational work," Stevens recalled later. "We began to bring people down to the union hall, at the rate of about forty per week. We'd arrange to excuse the people from work . . . [to] attend a special class about the situation of the industry and the company."[55] In March 1982, the education committee also held an anti-concessions conference in Linden with participants from twenty-three different UAW locals, most of them active in LOC.[56] The local union newspaper (still edited by Stevens) published a special issue entitled "GM's Road to Survival: Con-crete or Con-Game?" which presented detailed arguments against concessions. It argued that GM would use the funds obtained from concessions to finance investment in new technologies and in outsourcing, thus *accelerating* UAW job losses rather than saving jobs, as proponents of concessions claimed.

Basically, LAW tried to persuade workers that GM's economic problems were not serious enough to justify concessions, and that the company was simply trying to capitalize on the political weakness of organized labor. As Stevens explained in a 1982 interview:

It's true that Chrysler is in real trouble, and clearly something had to happen there in the way of concessions. But General Motors is not doing so badly as they like to claim in the press. They can jockey the figures around to show that they are losing money here, or making it there. But even their own stockholders' report shows that last year (1981) they earned a $750 million profit here in the United States, while losing $400 million overseas. Miraculously, their losses abroad become the responsibility of American workers! You notice that they didn't ask for concessions in Europe, because it was obvious that they'd get nowhere. They did try it in Canada, and were told to go pound salt. . . . What they wanted, and what they ultimately got was a worker subsidy to their plants. This was something they never would have thought they could get away with before. But last year, they realized that the climate was perfectly ripe for it. . . . [The labor movement's] failure to mobilize a strong support for the PATCO [Professional Air Traffic Controllers' Organization] strike was a green light to the corporations. They saw that Reagan could at one blow smash a union. . . . So they realized then that it was a perfect time to go after workers in other industries.[57]

LAW also argued that the pay gap between Japanese and American auto workers was smaller than it appeared, and pointed out that "the biggest gap of all is between US and Japanese auto executives! . . . $219.64 per hour."[58]

Many GM-Linden rank-and-file workers opposed concessions on a more basic level. "I just can't see giving anything back," Mike Polansky said. "If I'm doing the same work, why should I give something back?" Ben Kowalski agreed: "We fought hard to get these things. Why give 'em up? Management didn't have to give up [nearly] as much as we did. Now we don't make any money, but [then-GM chairman] Roger Smith gets a two million dollar a year bonus!" However, not everyone in the workforce was against concessions. "I was grateful I was making the money I was at the time," Tim Murphy recalled. "I'd rather have a $15 an hour job and give back $3 an hour and still make $12, than go out and work for $8 an hour. So, I really had no opposition to the givebacks, because if we get $15 an hour and they have to shut the place down, I will make zero dollars an hour. So, where am I going to be after that? You have to look at it realistically." Indeed, the fear of a plant closing was palpable. "We were told, more or less, either take concessions or there was the possibility that the plant would be closed," John Pierce recalled. "The idea was, this is an aging plant, and your quality of work is down. It was either concessions or walk, or no jobs." As Jack Giordano saw it, "We had to get real with the times."

At Ford, such fears neutralized the opposition to givebacks: in February 1982, the concessions were approved by almost 75 percent of those workers voting. At GM, however, where no one could argue that concessions were economically necessary for the firm to survive, LOC's arguments almost carried the day: the contract was ratified by a bare 52 percent majority in April 1982. The GM pro-concessions vote was concentrated in the parts plants, where the company's job losses had been concentrated in the 1970s, making the threat of new plant closings that much more salient. Workers at Linden and other GM assembly plants, in contrast, felt relatively secure, and overwhelmingly rejected the concessions. The vote was especially lopsided at Linden, where over 84 percent of workers who voted on the 1982 contract rejected it.[59] Even in plants where local union officers supported concessions, most GM assembly workers voted "no." At GM's Lordstown, Ohio, assembly plant, for example, the contract was rejected by a three-to-one margin, and a month later, workers voted to oust the local union president, who had favored concessions.

At Linden, the LAW activists who led the campaign against the contract consolidated their control of the local union in the May 1982 election (held just a month after the contract ratification vote). LAW won a majority on the Local 595 executive board for the first time, and Douglas Stevens was elected shop chairman. But LAW's electoral triumph occurred precisely at the moment when the UAW as a whole was facing its greatest crisis since the end of World War II. Already weakened by political defeats and steep membership losses, it now had to confront the implications of economic restructuring and globalization.

While the concessions may indeed have spared the UAW a potentially disastrous strike (as the union's national leaders believed), they did not succeed in stemming job losses. In fact, one of LAW's most cogent arguments was that concessions would simply accelerate GM's restructuring, leading to further employment cuts. "Actually, more jobs have been lost since the concessions went through, and as a direct result of them," Douglas Stevens pointed out in an interview that took place a few months after the 1982 contract vote. Stevens detailed these job losses: "The paid personal holidays which were lost cost 430 jobs right away in our plant alone, and across the country this alone cost over 10,000 jobs. . . . That $2.5 billion GM got from its workers is going to be poured directly into robotization and the reorganization

of their operations on a worldwide basis. . . . As they begin to auto-
mate away our jobs in this country, and move other jobs out of the
country, the future employment prospects for auto workers here are
very grim indeed."[60] This dark prognosis turned out to be quite accurate: if anything, it was insufficiently pessimistic, for GM's share of
the U.S. automobile market, which for many years had held firm in
the range of 45 percent, declined precipitously starting in 1985, leading to new layoffs and employment cutbacks in the second half of the
decade.[61]

Industrial restructuring and the growing internationalization of the
auto industry rapidly eroded UAW strength. Union coverage in the
auto-parts industry had been falling since the mid-1970s, and in the
1980s, the establishment of new Japanese-owned auto transplants created a nonunion beachhead in the otherwise solidly organized assembly sector.[62] As the domestic industry's growing excess capacity led to
wave after wave of plant closings and layoffs in the 1980s, GM, Ford,
and Chrysler launched a new campaign to discipline labor by playing
one plant off against another. Everyone knew that these firms would
close some of their plants, so management could credibly threaten
to target those with the least cooperative workforces. As Douglas
Stevens explained in 1982, "Locals have to compete with each other
to get or keep work in their plant. If your plant and my plant are
building similar products, then it simply becomes a question of who's
going to give up more—you or me? Whoever gives up the most gets
the work. We've been told, point blank, by management in our local
negotiations here at Linden, that we're competing. It's not really a
typical case, as we build top-of-the-line luxury cars here, and we are
the only GM plant in the world that does this work. But when I asked,
'Who are we competing with?' the personnel director's reply was that
we are competing with every other plant in the GM system."[63]

The UAW's long history of accommodation to management decisions in regard to such matters as investment and the organization of
the production process left its leaders ill equipped to come to terms
with the dramatic restructuring of the 1980s. The union's national
leadership had long focused its attention on bargaining over company-
wide wages and benefits, leaving local shop-floor concerns to the local
unions to resolve on their own. With the emergence of whipsawing in

the 1980s, this UAW tradition of local autonomy became a major liability. The national union increasingly concentrated its efforts on minimizing the pain of industry downsizing for its members, negotiating a variety of new job and income security programs, while uncritically accepting the notion that new technology, increased worker participation, and other strategies adopted by management were the best way to meet the challenge of foreign competition.

Many local union activists, including the LAW group now in control of the local union at Linden, disagreed with this strategy, but they were powerless to influence the larger forces that were transforming the UAW as a whole. Then, less than a year after the concessions vote, LAW suffered another major blow when the contempt case that the NLRB had been preparing against GM, based on LAW's charges, was abruptly dropped, only a week before the trial was scheduled to begin. Although the official records regarding the decision to drop the case have been destroyed, the timing itself is circumstantial evidence of a political motive. In the early 1980s, the newly elected Reagan administration had begun making a series of appointments to the NLRB that briefly transformed it into an extremely anti-union agency, and in early 1983, when the case was dropped, Reagan's appointees were in the process of gaining majority control of the agency.[64]

At Linden, the double whammy of contract concessions and the NLRB's abandonment of the contempt case made the aftermath of LAW's 1982 electoral victory bittersweet. "So we had a local. What could we really change?" Carl Block recalled in an interview. He added:

They were creaming us with harassment, the line speed being changed, with our credibility thereby being undermined, because here was this bad-ass group that had taken over the local union, and while we might write more grievances than anybody ever would, what was the real change? So there was a sense of disillusion, even though we now had positions of power. The more people you have in, the more management is really in a power position to dilute your power, combined with the fact that some people who won LAW jobs started taking care of themselves. . . . Your life could be made pretty easy, both through the International [UAW] and through the company if you just backed off a little bit—or backed off a lot. As time passed, we were back with the sense of, well, now we're stuck with concessions; there's some people even within our own caucus who are kind of [lying] down; and even the people that are working real hard, what can they do? So it got very hard.

Over the next few years, LAW's influence gradually waned. Deeply disillusioned, Block left GM, although all the other LAW leaders mentioned here still work in the plant today. Aware that the union had limited room to maneuver and increasingly worried about job security, many workers came to support a more cautious, moderate union approach. Jack Giordano deeply admired Douglas Stevens but came to feel that LAW's strategy was "a played-out approach—not a realistic approach, because it was dynamite: it could blow up in your face at any time." Eddie Soares, whose father was one of the older local union leaders opposing LAW, recalled:

A lot of those [LAW] guys just always wanted to push. They'd just push and tell the people in the plant what they wanted to hear. That's what they basically did, you know. And my father would always tell them, "Listen, that ain't the way it is. [If] you keep pushing them, you know what's going to happen. They're going to leave. It's simple." And you know, they closed plants everywhere. Ford closed one in Mahwah [, New Jersey]. "You got problems with us? We'll leave. We'll go to Bumblescrew or wherever. We'll go out to Kentucky and get a bunch of rednecks who haven't worked for a year, and they'll do whatever we want." Doug Stevens would promise you the world, and then when GM leaves, what are you going to do? Are you going to put your faith in Doug Stevens? And the younger guys finally said, "This is bull. We're here to work. We're not here to soak GM. We want to work. Let's make cars."

In May 1984, several members of the old guard were reelected to important positions in the local union. Later that year, the UAW national leadership launched selective strikes at thirteen GM plants, including Linden, to put pressure on GM in the national contract negotiations. Workers were still bitter about the givebacks they had been forced to accept two years before. "If we had taken a harder line against G.M. when they asked for all those concessions, we wouldn't be in the position we are now," a worker who had worked at Linden for twenty years told the *New York Times* during the strike. "I feel we threw G.M. a piece of steak and they're giving us peanuts back."[65] Indeed, the 1984 national GM-UAW agreement failed to reverse the concessions made by the union two years earlier, although it did include a new $1 billion job-security program, including the buyout program that would later prove extremely popular at Linden.

By this time, it was obvious to most workers—regardless of their opinions on the concessions or about LAW—that the union's glory days were over. "I was kind of disenchanted with the union, especially after 1984 when we went on strike," Edward Salerno recalled. "Because in the last [1982] contract, they took a lot away from us when they were crying poverty. So the union's hollering, 'We're getting everything back.' They were going to go on strike for it. Well, we went on strike for one week, and then all of a sudden, we settled and we got nothing. I said, 'The heck with that.' They were losing all their power." Patrick Nolan, who like Salerno took the buyout a few years later, agreed: "One of the reasons I quit was, the union was going downhill. They lost all their power. Reagan, he killed our union. He killed the unions, destroyed them."

Everyone understood that the options open to the local union had fundamentally changed by the mid-1980s. "When we built the Cadillacs, the Rivieras, and Oldsmobiles, we were the only plant that built that car," Jonathan Fox recalled. "They were the hottest-selling car in America; we were working every other Saturday, nine hours a day. We got anything we wanted. The union would ask for this, they'd hem and haw, and we'd get it. We had them. We had the power." Jack Giordano echoed this view: "In the old days, guys sat down inside the plant for a few days to make a point. And they would usually win. And the reason they would win was that the industry was growing. So a manager would say, 'Well, why not?' Now it's the other way around. Management's saying, 'I want this from you.' And the union's going over, and their stance is a little more jellyfish-like. They're willing to look at both sides of the coin. The union used to be very obstinate; they were very strong in what they believed. Like: 'No way! These are my people!' They don't take that stance anymore."

By all accounts, fewer grievances were filed in the plant during the 1980s, and those that were filed were pursued far less vigorously than in earlier years. If this was partly due to the demise of the LAW leadership, it also reflected the broader power shift in favor of management that was rooted in national developments. As Ben Kowalski put it, "The union's in the position where GM basically can tell them what to do. Because they [GM] can eliminate a plant whenever they want. You know, they have control. It's their court and it's their ball. So you play by their rules, or you don't play."

It was against this background that, in late 1984, GM announced long-rumored plans for a $300 million modernization of the Linden plant, introducing robotics and other new microprocessor-based technologies. As if to symbolize that an era had ended, the factory would no longer build Cadillacs and other luxury cars but instead new Chevrolet models. This put an end (at least for the time being) to worries that the plant would be closed altogether, but the announcement also included the less welcome news that GM would permanently eliminate 1,000 to 1,200 jobs at Linden. Then in April 1985, Tony Fernandez left the Local 595 presidency for a job in the UAW's regional office, so that LAW's already slim chances of returning to power vanished completely.[66]

Moderation was the order of the day not only in the UAW's Linden local but also at the national level. The union's General Motors Department, headed by Donald F. Ephlin from 1983 to 1989, advocated cooperation with management in efforts to cut costs and reorganize work to streamline the production process. The rationale for discarding the union's traditional adversarial posture was to enhance the competitiveness of the U.S. auto firms in the world market and thus preserve jobs for UAW members. "Today, we want to make the companies more competitive so as to see them regain their market share," Ephlin stated in early 1988. "It's our jobs that are at stake."[67] Despite substantial opposition within the union, Ephlinism was the dominant influence on UAW policy throughout the 1980s.[68]

The other main thrust of UAW policy in this period was to press for new income- and job-security programs to protect union members. The 1982 contract had already established the Guaranteed Income Stream, and the GM-UAW contract signed two years later included a new package of job-security measures. As it happened, GM-Linden was among the first plants to utilize the programs established in 1984, since job losses linked to the introduction of new technology was one of the conditions that they were designed to address. Rather than job cutbacks at Linden taking the form of layoffs, as had been the case so often in the past, this time they triggered the activation of a jobs bank at the plant, as well as the massive buyout program that led about a thousand GM-Linden workers to leave the auto industry for good. The next chapter tells their story.

Chapter Four

Farewell to the Factory

The Buyout Experience

In the 1970s and early 1980s, deindustrialization ravaged the U.S. economic landscape as millions of workers lost their jobs to plant closings or permanent layoffs. Among the causes were increased imports, corporate decisions to relocate production outside the nation's borders, new labor-saving technologies, and work reorganization. Nearly half of all workers dislocated between 1979 and 1984 had been employed in manufacturing, although that sector accounted for only about a fifth of the nation's labor force.[1] Job losses were particularly severe in industries facing intense international competition, such as steel, textiles, apparel, and autos. Motor vehicle manufacturing employment had peaked at over one million workers in 1978; but by 1983, only about 750,000 remained. A partial recovery in the automotive industry occurred later in the 1980s, but the long-term trend has been unmistakably downward.[2] Although the GM-Linden plant was not among those that closed entirely, it lost over a thousand jobs in the mid-1980s, due to technological modernization and a shift from large to small car models.

The economic and social consequences of deindustrialization have been devastating for many individuals, families, and communities. As an extensive literature now documents, dislocated workers often suffer long periods of unemployment, steep declines in income and living standards, loss of health insurance and pension benefits, deteriorating physical and mental health, and increased family tensions. Communities impacted by mass layoffs or plant closings suffer as the ripple effects of decreased worker income on other local businesses produce further unemployment, and tax revenues decline (even as demand for social services increases).[3] A study of Michigan auto workers who were laid off between 1979 and 1984 illustrates these problems. These workers' longest unemployment spell (some experienced multiple lay-offs) averaged 66 weeks. Their personal income fell 61 percent, on average, and 28 percent of them lost their health insurance coverage due to the layoffs.[4] Similarly, another study of the Ford auto assembly plant in Mahwah, New Jersey—whose permanent shutdown in 1980 did not go unnoticed by workers at nearby GM-Linden—found that nearly half of the affected workers responding were still unemployed two years after the plant closed. Their median family income was cut in half, one-fourth reported health problems, and two-thirds reported emotional problems.[5]

Most laid-off industrial workers eventually do find new employ-ment, but they typically end up in jobs that are highly inferior, at least in economic terms, to those they lost.[6] In industries like auto and steel, the jobs that have been disappearing so rapidly provided high wages, excellent fringe benefits, and union protection; by contrast, most of the new positions created in the recent period of economic restruc-turing offer far lower pay, fewer benefits, and no union coverage. This is especially true of jobs available to workers without any college edu-cation—who made up more than half the nation's workforce through-out the 1980s, despite rapidly rising levels of education over the postwar decades.[7] Whereas less educated women have long earned low wages, this is increasingly the case for men as well. Non-college-educated males like those who historically supplied the core work-force for GM-Linden and other factories like it suddenly confronted radically diminished opportunities in the 1980s, and their real wages plummeted in both absolute and relative terms—more than for any other group in the population. The gap between the earnings of col-lege-educated young male workers and young male workers with a high school degree widened dramatically: the median real earnings of 25 to 34-year-old male high school graduates fell 12 percent between 1979 and 1987, whereas median real earnings of 25 to 34-year-old male college graduates *rose* 8 percent over this period.[8] Once among the most privileged section of the working class, non-college-educated men have borne a disproportionate share of the costs of economic restructuring.

Understandably, deindustrialization has generated a surge of nostalgia among many observers for the bygone glory days of industrial America. One might expect the workers who have been directly affected to share in that sentiment—and surely many do.[9] But, as this chapter recounts, drawing on survey and interview data, the production workers who left GM-Linden in the mid-1980s in response to the buyout offer that accompanied the plant modernization—to be sure, a group far from representative of the larger population of displaced industrial workers—have a more complicated, more ambivalent perspective. They do miss the high pay, excellent fringe benefits, and union protection they enjoyed at GM. However, like Edward Salerno and Dan Cooper, introduced in chapter 1, the vast majority of the Linden buyout takers surveyed say that they are glad to have escaped the plant, with its alienating work and authoritarian social relations— glad, in short, to be no longer prisoners of prosperity.

Most of these buyout takers landed on their feet, and only a handful were involuntarily unemployed. An unusually large proportion were self-employed, and many in this group claimed to earn as much or more than they had at GM. Despite the fact that most buyout takers *did* experience some downward mobility, finding new jobs that paid significantly less than they had earned at GM, surprisingly few (about 20 percent) regret their decision. Significantly, those that do are disproportionately African American. At GM, African-American buyout takers received the same pay and benefits as whites, but those who left are now subject to the race-based inequities of the external labor market. (White women fared worse in the external labor market too, but they were *less* likely to regret taking the buyout than white men.)

Even considering the fact that the outcome was more problematic for African Americans, overall the GM-Linden buyout takers were far better able to reposition themselves in the labor market than most other dislocated industrial workers. One reason was that these were relatively young workers (typically in their early thirties) at the time they accepted the buyout offer, a status that greatly enhanced their prospects of securing new employment quickly. In addition, when they took the buyout in late 1986 or early 1987, the New Jersey economy was relatively strong, with an unemployment rate well below national levels. The state's economy is also highly diversified, unlike the monoindustrial communities devastated by plant closings where so many less fortunate dislocated workers have begun their search for new jobs. New Jersey is one of the most unionized states in the United States, and indeed, a surprisingly high proportion of buyout takers found new jobs in the unionized sector. The buyout takers were also self-selected to a degree, as none was forced to take the buyout, although, as I will show, low seniority was an important factor pushing many of them out the door. Finally, in contrast to most cases of involuntary job loss, here the buyout money itself served as a cushion.

Although these special conditions distinguish the buyout takers from the larger population of displaced workers, their stories are revealing nonetheless. In some ways they may be more indicative of the future prospects of non-college-educated workers than the more dramatic stories of emiseration among those who bore the brunt of deindustrialization in the 1970s and 1980s. The Linden buyout takers' perspective helps illuminate the differences between the old world of traditional manufacturing employment and the new postindustrial labor market in which future working-class generations must find a niche. Precisely because they left the factory under such favorable conditions, the buyout takers' stories offer a lesson obscured in the more familiar accounts of deprivation caused by deindustrialization: namely, that many features of the factory jobs they left behind fully *deserve* to be dead and buried. This is not true of the pay, benefits, or union protection these jobs carried, but few workers are nostalgic about the routinized, boring work or about the draconian supervisory regime that so deeply poisoned social relations on the shop floor.

The buyout takers' experience also suggests that under some conditions—conditions all too rare in the contemporary United States—the transition from industrial employment can be relatively painless and even beneficial in some cases. With appropriate policies in place—either public policies or, as in this instance, private ones achieved through collective bargaining—the inevitable shrinkage of the nation's industrial base might be achieved with far less pain to its potential victims than has typically been the case. Although the success of the Linden buyout depended as much on fortuitous local conditions as on the design of the national program of which it was a part, the buyout takers' experiences must be understood against the background of the GM buyout program as a whole, along with the larger set of job-security provisions that were established in the 1984 UAW-GM contract.

The JOBS Program at GM-Linden

The UAW has a long history of concern with job security, starting from its early, depression-era demands that layoffs be done on the basis of seniority. Because the auto industry has always been especially sensitive to economic cycles, layoffs remained an issue long after the depression's end. At the height of national prosperity in the 1950s, the UAW won (starting in 1955) Supplemental Unemployment Benefits (SUB) to tide workers over during long-term layoffs. By 1967, the SUB program, combined with state unemployment insurance payments, provided 95 percent of take-home pay to laid-off auto workers for up to a year.[10] As layoffs skyrocketed in the late 1970s and early 1980s, however, the funds allocated for SUB (designed for cyclical layoffs rather than the structural shifts of these years) increasingly fell short. This was among the concerns the UAW sought to address in its historic 1982 contract negotiations with GM, which brought significant improvements in job security as a quid pro quo for the massive concessions the union made in other areas. Among other things, GM made new lump-sum contributions to the SUB funds, and agreed to provide up to two years of SUB pay for high-seniority workers affected by layoffs.[11]

In the 1984 UAW-GM National Agreement, job- and income-security programs were extended once again. The most important innovation was the Job Opportunity Bank–Security (JOBS) program, which included the buyout option later introduced at Linden. The JOBS program was designed to protect all GM workers with one or more years of seniority from layoffs resulting from four specific causes: outsourcing, negotiated productivity improvements, a change in the product being made at a particular plant, and the introduction of new technology. Layoffs or plant closings due to other contingencies were not covered by the program, and layoffs due to adverse market conditions were specifically excluded.[12]

The JOBS program provides full wages and benefits to eligible workers, who are placed in an Employee Development Bank, more often known as a jobs bank. While in the bank, they may receive training, fill in temporarily for more senior plant workers who are undergoing training, perform nontraditional jobs in the plant or in the local community, or be placed in a job opening at their home plant or another GM location. The JOBS program also includes an early retirement program for eligible workers and a Voluntary Termination of Employment Program (VTEP), known at Linden as the golden handshake or simply the buyout. Workers who opt for the buyout cease to be GM employees and receive a lump-sum payment ranging from $10,000 to $55,000, depending on seniority.[13] Since the program's establishment in 1984, about 24,000 GM hourly workers have accepted buyouts, most of them in the late 1980s.[14]

Prior UAW-negotiated programs had protected workers' *incomes* without providing them with new work or training opportunities. The key breakthrough in 1984 was *job* security, in the shape of a no-layoff guarantee for covered workers, designed to encourage GM's unionized workforce to cooperate with management's restructuring efforts without fear of job loss. As the UAW's Donald F. Ephlin put it at the time, the program signaled "that management finally understands that there is very little incentive for workers to help improve productivity if the end result is that they are laid off as their reward."[15] The JOBS program, in which participants receive the same income as regularly employed GM workers for up to six years, also offers more income security than the SUB program, which provides a maximum of 95 percent income coverage for up to two years. JOBS also went far beyond the Guaranteed Income Stream program introduced in 1982, which applied only to workers with ten or more years' seniority and provided far less income coverage (50 to 75 percent, depending on seniority). The only limitation is a spending cap (set at $1 billion in the 1984 contract).[16]

GM-Linden was among the first plants to implement the JOBS program.[17] The 1985–1986 modernization introduced extensive new technology along with a change in product (the plant switched from making Cadillacs and other large cars to small Chevrolets) and was unambiguously a "qualifying event" under the contract.[18] Indeed, plans for Linden's modernization were already under way when the JOBS program was negotiated. As a GM official who helped draft the contract language later recalled, "We were aware of the fact that we would be saddling Linden with a bank that could be as large as 1,800 employees." He went on to explain that the buyout was also designed with Linden in mind: "We wanted something that we could use to stimulate attrition where we had large banks. We knew about Linden. . . . And so we talked about accelerating attrition, talked about where the bank is of such size [that if] you can't be placed in the next twelve months, not only do you go into Attachment B [buyouts and early retirement], you transfer them to other locations, spread the hurt." In the 1984–1987 period, Linden accounted for nearly half of all buyouts at GM nationally.[19] Linden also had one of the nation's largest jobs banks—although thanks to the buyout's popularity there, the bank's life turned out to be brief.

Most of Linden's production workers were laid off in September 1985, when the plant closed for its year-long technological overhaul. However, the JOBS program was not yet activated at that point, since the plant shutdown coincided with a model changeover, and model changeovers were explicitly excluded from coverage under JOBS. From September 1985 until August 1986, when the plant resumed building cars, laid-off workers received unemployment insurance and SUB benefits (although low-seniority workers had no income benefits after that year). Starting in August 1986, as they were gradually recalled into the plant in line with the acceleration of production, the jobs bank began to function, and by early December, all laid-off workers had been recalled into either the bank or the plant.[20]

Initially, the Linden jobs bank functioned, as one plant manager put it, as a "flow-through bank." As workers were recalled from layoff, they could enter the jobs bank, transfer voluntarily to another GM plant, or take the buyout (or retire early if they had enough seniority). Most of those who chose to enter the jobs bank stayed there only a few weeks before being put to work in the plant, at which point a new group of workers were recalled into the bank. "It was off the street, into the bank, into the plant," UAW Local 595's Tom Barbarro re-

called. "It was like a revolving door." The jobs bank population fluctuated rapidly: it had over 600 workers in November 1986 but shrunk
to less than 100 in December, when all the available jobs in the plant
had been filled. By May 1987, only nine months after the bank had
opened, so many Linden workers had accepted buyouts or other options that none remained in the program.

Although some jobs-bank workers received outside assignments
(including the extremely unpopular one of filling in on jobs in the
plant while more senior workers were deployed on nontraditional assignments in the union hall or in the plant's offices), most attended
classes for eight hours a day while in the bank.[21] However, the small
size of the Linden jobs-bank population, combined with its high turn-
over rate (the revolving door), set limits on the training that could be
provided. Arrangements were made with a local community college
to offer courses in English as a second language (ESL), basic skills
(English, math, and, reading), as well as General Equivalency Degree
(GED) preparation for those who had not completed high school.
Workers who already had high school diplomas were offered college-
level courses for credit in English, math, business, and psychology, as
well as noncredit seminars on such topics as real estate, stress management, time management, and starting a business. There were also
classes in basic computer skills.

Some workers were skeptical about the educational offerings. As
the GM-Linden manager who helped run the jobs bank recalled, "You
had people who were automatically turned off, maybe primarily because most of their school experience was pretty negative to begin
with, and the idea of being forced to go back into that was not all that
attractive to them." There were also logistical problems due to the
constant uncertainty as to how long any individual could expect to
remain in the bank. As one participant put it, "What's the sense of
going into classes and studying if you're not going to be here for the
final exam anyway?" Despite these problems, the ESL and GED programs were quite well received, especially by the thirty-six workers
who passed the GED exam as a result.

Some workers wanted vocational training to help prepare them for
new jobs outside GM, something that was discussed extensively but
never implemented. "I was really disappointed," local unionist Tom

Barbarro said. "They were promised all kinds of vocational training—
auto mechanics, radio and appliance repair—so they would be able
to go out of the automobile industry and get a job. In my opinion,
that's what the jobs-bank program was all about. But they never did
that, because it's too much money." In a similar spirit, workers scoffed
at the college courses provided. "They gave me three credits for math
and three for psychology," one complained. "They stuck me in a room
with teachers, and they gave me six college credits. What the hell do
I do with them? If they gave me a diploma, what would I do with it?
I've been in the factory all my life. I'm a factory worker. I want the
trades, I want the skill." On the whole, most participants appreciated
the bank more for the income security it provided than for the educational opportunities.

The Linden Buyout

The Linden jobs bank was a short-lived venture, primarily because
the buyout proved so popular there. To the surprise of both management and union representatives, almost a fourth of the Linden workers eligible for the buyout accepted it during 1986 and 1987—a far
higher proportion than in other plants where it was offered at the
time. In this initial period, 905 Linden workers took the buyout, while
another 99 opted for early retirement; and about 300 voluntarily transferred to other GM plants.[22] Most of those who took the buyout (84
percent) received lump-sum payments (before taxes) of $25,000 or
$35,000, depending on seniority—roughly a year's pay for a GM pro-
duction worker at that time.[23]

In April 1986, GM and the UAW surveyed all eligible Linden workers about their interest in the buyout, and in July, the 660 who expressed a desire for more information were invited to attend meetings about the buyout and the jobs bank, with joint presentations by
management and union representatives. Later, in the fall of 1986, as
workers were being recalled, another series of meetings was held to
explain the options and to answer questions. Once workers were recalled, they had forty-eight hours to decide whether to take the buyout (or, for a few workers, early retirement) or go into the jobs bank,
so the later meetings were particularly critical.

At these meetings, workers were told that if they lacked sufficient seniority to work in the plant, they could go into the jobs bank. However, many who attended came away with a skeptical view of the JOBS program. The presentations emphasized that workers in the bank might be forced to relocate to another GM plant, as this excerpt from a list of anticipated questions and answers, used in connection with the fall 1986 meetings, reveals:

Q.   What will happen to me if I don't accept the VTEP [buyout] payment?

A.   You will be recalled to work or to the jobs bank. If recalled to the bank you will be assigned to work as agreed to by the local JOBS committee. You may be assigned to a job in Indiana and if refused would go on layoff status.

As UAW Local 595's Tom Barbarro explained, "Say you had 1979 or 1980 seniority. You're like in limbo. The buyout looks good because we're telling them, 'You may wind up in Indiana.'" Another concern was the $1 billion funding cap on the program. "They'd ask, 'How long do you think that money will last?'" Barbarro recalled. "How could we honestly answer? I thought [at the time] that a billion dollars ain't nothing for the whole country. No way!" (In 1993, the program's funding did indeed run out, although this did not occur during the Linden jobs bank's brief lifetime.)[24]

Many workers' decisions were influenced by the projections that management provided at the meetings as to how much seniority a worker would need to be reasonably assured of permanent employment at Linden. Although these projections were tentative, and both union and management officials avoided making recommendations as to what any individual should do, the vast majority of workers who took the buyout had relatively low seniority. Management's initial projection was that a worker had to have been hired before June 22, 1977, in order to be assured of a job. As Barbarro recalled: "The cutoff date was 6/22/77, that was the last person who was going to work in Linden, on any shift in production; 6/22/77, his name was Ortiz—I see it in my sleep! That was one big thing that made them do that [take the buyout], in my opinion. At that time, when we were giving the presentations, the 6/22/77, that looked like it was in concrete, really. It didn't appear like it was going to change much."

As it turned out, workers with seniority dates as low as 1982 ultimately would be recalled, partly *because* so many people had accepted buyouts. But no one anticipated this at the time. Sixty-one percent of the buyout takers (but only 28 percent of workers who declined buyouts) had been hired after the June 22, 1977, cutoff date. Fully 94 percent of the buyout takers (but only 57 percent of those who declined it) had been hired during or after 1976, when the plant had gone back to two-shift operation and hired many new workers. Thus nearly all the buyout takers were drawn from the "Lordstown" generation of relatively young and restless workers, mostly working on the night shift, the same group that had been the stronghold of the militant LAW faction in the local union in the 1970s, as described in chapter 3.[25]

In the long run, low-seniority workers who took the buyout because they feared they would have neither a permanent job in the plant nor long-term income security may have gauged the situation accurately. In the short run, however, their fears proved unwarranted. All those who declined buyouts were recalled to the plant by mid-1987 (with the jobs bank providing interim protection); only a handful of workers ended up relocating, and those did so on a voluntary basis. But then in February 1990, GM-Linden laid off its entire second shift, and in the fall of 1991, the entire plant closed for a two-year conversion to light-truck production, resuming operations only in late 1993. Because the 1990 layoff was due to poor car sales, and the 1991–1993 shutdown was for a model changeover, neither was covered by the JOBS program. Workers did receive unemployment compensation and SUB, however, for two years or more, and these payments equaled or exceeded the amount they would have received had they taken the 1986 buyout. However, for many of those laid off in February 1990, the benefits were insufficient to cover the entire layoff period; and by then, it was obvious that no one could count on permanent employment at GM, validating the logic of those low-seniority workers who were motivated by job insecurity to take the buyout.

Indeed, lower seniority (and age, which is highly correlated with seniority) was the main factor distinguishing buyout takers from workers who chose to remain in the plant. Indeed, as table 3 shows, 32 percent of buyout-eligible workers hired in 1976 or later chose to take the buyout, compared to only 4 percent of those with higher seniority status—a statistically significant difference.[26] The June 22, 1977, date to which Tom Barbarro ascribed so much importance was also a major factor: 43 percent of eligible workers hired on or after that date chose to take the buyout, compared with 12 percent of those hired earlier. (Among eligible workers hired between January 1, 1976, and June 22, 1977, inclusive, 21 percent accepted buyouts.) In view of the deepening uncertainty about the auto industry's future, the critical role of seniority in these workers' choices is hardly surprising. "There's no guarantee that your job will be there in five years. This was just what we thought was the first wave of automation," one union official pointed out. "A lot of people didn't know if they'd have jobs in the future, except the high-seniority ones who could see something was going on with all the new machinery—they knew the plant wouldn't close. But who knew about the second shift?" Many of the younger workers may have accepted the buyout not only because of the greater uncertainty they faced at GM, but also because of their youth. They may have been more confident about their ability to find other work than their older counterparts.

The gender and racial composition of the two groups also differed, as table 3 shows. Thirty-nine percent of eligible female workers took the buyout, nearly twice the proportion (19 percent) among eligible men. This is partly an artifact of women workers' relatively low seniority at GM-Linden, due to the fact that relatively few (only 5 of the 590 women eligible for buyouts) were hired prior to 1976.[27] However, even if analysis is limited to those workers hired in 1976 or later (table 4), a significantly higher proportion (39 percent) of eligible women accepted buyouts than eligible men (30 percent). Within this low-seniority group, white women were especially likely to accept the buyout, with nearly half (47 percent) of those eligible accepting it, a far higher rate than for white men (30 percent) and, indeed, higher than for any other demographic group.

Race was another influential factor: African Americans were underrepresented among buyout takers, even though their seniority status was similar to that of whites. Only 19 percent of eligible African

TABLE 3. Buyout Acceptance Rates at GM-Linden, by Selected
Worker Characteristics

Worker Characteristic	N	Percentage of Eligible[a] Workers Accepting Buyout
Seniority		
Hired 1/1/76 or later	2,683	31.5[b]
Hired before 1/1/76	1,421	4.1[b]
Hired 6/22/77 or later	1,303	42.8[b]
Hired before 6/22/77	2,801	12.4[b]
Age (in 1986)		
Less than 30 years old	539	48.4[b]
30 years old or more but less than 40	1,470	28.3[b]
40 years old or more but less than 50	1,331	14.0[b]
51 years old or more	764	5.4[b]
Gender		
Female	590	38.8[b]
Male	3,514	19.2[b]
Race/Ethnicity		
White	2,550	22.6[b]
African American	1,038	18.7[b]
Latino	501	25.5[b]
Race/Ethnicity and Gender		
White male	2,295	19.9[c]
White female	255	47.1[c]
African-American male	765	14.6[c]
African-American female	273	30.0[c]
Latino	442	23.3[c]
Latina	59	42.4[c]
Education[d]		
Less than high school education	1,553	22.3
High school graduate	2,165	22.0
More than high school education	384	23.3
All Workers	4,104	22.0

SOURCE: Computed from data supplied by GM-Linden plant management.
[a]Does not include workers who accepted early retirement or transfers to other GM plants.
[b]Chi-square test on underlying 3-way cross-tabulation of worker characteristic shown (in each panel) by buyout decision, significant at $p < .05$.
[c]Chi-square test on underlying 3-way cross-tabulation of gender by race by buyout decision, significant at $p < .05$.
[d]Total does not add due to missing data for 2 cases.

TABLE 4. Buyout Acceptance Rates at GM-Linden, by Selected Worker Characteristics, for Workers Hired 1/1/76 or Later Only

Worker Characteristic	N	Percentage of Eligible[a] Workers Accepting Buyout
Seniority		
Hired on 6/22/77 or later	1,303	42.8[b]
Hired before 6/22/77	1,380	20.9[b]
Age (in 1986)		
Less than 30 years old	539	48.4[b]
30 years old or more but less than 40	1,262	31.3[b]
40 years old or more but less than 50	668	23.4[b]
50 years old or more	214	15.9[b]
Gender		
Female	585	38.8[b]
Male	2,098	29.5[b]
Race/Ethnicity		
White	1,684	32.4[b]
African American	652	28.2[b]
Latino	332	33.4[b]
Race/Ethnicity and Gender		
White male	1,433	29.7[c]
White female	251	47.4[c]
African-American male	379	26.9[c]
African-American female	273	30.0[c]
Latino	274	31.8[c]
Latina	58	41.4[c]
Education[d]		
Less than high school education	917	35.2[b]
High school graduate	1,502	28.9[b]
More than high school education	262	33.2[b]
All Workers	2,683	31.5

SOURCE: Computed from data supplied by GM-Linden plant management.
[a]Does not include workers who accepted early retirement or transfers to other GM plants.
[b]Chi-square test on underlying cross-tabulation of worker characteristic shown (in each panel) by buyout decision, significant at $p < .05$.
[c]Chi-square test on underlying 3-way cross-tabulation of gender by race by buyout decision, significant at $p < .05$.
[d]Total does not add due to missing data for 2 cases.

Americans chose to take the buyout, compared with 26 percent of eligible Latinos and 23 percent of eligible white workers.[28] (See table 3.) The acceptance rate for African Americans remains similarly low when the analysis is limited to workers hired in or after 1976, as can be seen in table 4. African Americans may have been less optimistic than their white and Latino counterparts about alternatives to employment at GM. If so, this view was well founded, for those African Americans who did take the buyout proved more likely to regret it than other buyout takers. In contrast, Latinos—most of them immigrants—were overrepresented among buyout takers. There were no significant differences in buyout acceptance rates by educational level for the overall group. However, for workers hired in 1976 or later, both the least and the most educated workers had significantly higher acceptance rates than did high school graduates (table 4).

Multivariate analysis of the effects of gender, race, and education on the buyout decision reveals the independent effect of each factor while taking the others into account. This analysis yields results similar to the simpler (univariate) analysis presented above.[29] Because the workers hired before and after January 1, 1976, have such distinctive relationships to the buyout and differ greatly in demographic composition as well, they are treated separately here.[30] There is relatively little to say about the group hired before 1976. As table 3 shows, this group is highly unlikely to take the buyout, irrespective of race, education, or age. (Gender cannot be analyzed for this group since only 5 of its 1,421 members are female.) The sole exception is that the odds that a Latino worker hired before 1976 will take the buyout are 3.5 times higher than for other workers hired before 1976. This effect is strongly statistically significant. The only other significant effect is for age: the odds of acceptance fall about 10 percent with each year of age.[31]

For the group hired during or after 1976, gender produces by far the strongest effect: the odds that an eligible woman will accept the buyout are 2 times those for an eligible man.[32] However, this effect is modified by that of race: whereas the odds of acceptance for white women are nearly 3 times as high as for white men, African-American women have odds only 1.6 times[33] as high as white men (though African-American women are more likely than African-American men to accept the buyout). Among men, however, African Americans are not significantly more likely than whites to accept. The odds of acceptance for Latino men, on the other hand, are more than 1.5 times as high as those for white men. The June 22, 1977, date that figured so prominently in management's job security projections also has significant effects, even for this low-seniority group: the odds of acceptance for workers hired after that date are 2.5 times higher than for those hired earlier. Age also has a significant effect: there is a 10 percent decline in the odds of acceptance with each year of age (as for the pre-1976 cohort, this effect is cumulative).

The data analyzed above reveal the demographic composition of the buyout takers but are silent on the reasons workers chose to take the buyout, how they felt about it, or how they fared in its aftermath. These issues were explored in a series of three telephone surveys of buyout takers conducted over a five-year period. The first survey was taken in late 1987, using a random sample of the 905 GM-Linden workers who accepted buyouts in late 1986 or early 1987. Ninety-one buyout takers were interviewed in this initial phase; most were reinterviewed in 1989 and again in 1991.[34] The survey results, along with in-depth interviews with about a dozen buyout takers, show that most made a smooth transition to some alternative form of employment. Only a minority—roughly 20 percent across the three surveys—expressed regret about taking the buyout. This group is disproportionately made up of African Americans, who fared far worse in the labor market after leaving GM than did whites. Paradoxically, white women also fared badly economically, yet they were no more likely than white men to regret leaving GM in response to the buyout offer. Overall, the most striking finding is the highly positive view that so many buyout takers (with the key exception of African Americans) expressed about their decision. The vast majority of respondents were deeply relieved to leave the factory that had provided them with employment for nearly a decade.

Why Workers Took the Buyout

When asked in the initial 1987 survey what led them to take the buyout, workers cited several factors. Two were mentioned especially frequently: job security concerns and a dislike for working at GM. While the survey interviewers explicitly asked about job security, negative feelings about the work only surfaced when workers themselves volunteered such feelings as a reason for taking the buyout. Even so, dislike for GM as a workplace was cited nearly as often as job security when workers were asked to name the most important reason that they took the buyout: both were cited by about 30 percent of those answering the question. Another factor, which 13 percent of respondents gave as their main reason for taking the buyout, was a desire to start or continue a small business.

In view of the unexpected prominence of negative views about GM in motivating workers to take the buyout, it is worth examining the telephone survey script directly. Interviewers read the following questions to respondents:

I have a list of reasons here that some people have told us were important factors in their decision to take the buyout. I'd like to read you the list, and ask you if any of these factors were also reasons for you. Did you take the buyout because:
   a. you wanted to go back to school?
   b. you wanted to start or continue your own business?
   c. you didn't have enough seniority to be sure of a permanent job at Linden?
   d. you wanted the lump sum of money to pay off bills?
   e. you had another job that you preferred to GM?
   f. you didn't want to transfer to another GM plant?
   g. your spouse worked and the family income was enough without your Linden job?
   h. you wanted to spend more time with your family?
   Were there any other reasons that I haven't mentioned that contributed to your decision to take the buyout?

It was this last query that elicited so many responses involving a dislike for working at GM. Here are a few of the "other reasons" survey respondents offered in this vein:

I was always aggravated working on the line: overtime, hard work, layoffs. . . . A lot of times working there, people didn't show up, but there was no relief; we just had to work harder; and sometimes we couldn't go to the bathroom.

I was disenchanted with working on the line at GM.

It was a hellhole to work in. GM's promises are a bunch of bullshit.

I hated working for GM, the way they were running the plant.

I was unhappy with the job; they were constantly jerking you around, turning you into a cog, putting you on worse jobs. I was burnt out.

I was sick of working at GM. It's tedious, boring—not a job for a woman. The ladies' room was twenty-eight steps up, with no chairs, benches, or stools. We used to sit on the sinks. And the GM bosses were nasty; they treated us like a master [does] slaves.

I was tired of breathing exhaust fumes; I got bronchitis. There was not enough respect from the foremen.

My foreman tried to make me look bad, tried to make it look like I wasn't a good worker.

I wanted to be free and get out from GM. I felt like I was in jail there!

I didn't like working the second [night] shift; some foremen treated you like shit, and then there was the favoritism.

Since many respondents indicated that they had more than one reason for taking the buyout, they were asked next whether each factor they had identified was a "major" or "minor" influence on their decision (all the above examples were labeled major). Finally, they were asked, "Of all the reasons you've just identified as contributing to your decision to take the buyout, which was the most important?"

Of the 90 individuals who answered this last question, 22 indicated that lack of "enough seniority to be sure of a permanent job at Linden" was the most important factor; another 4 cited fear of being "transfer[red] to another GM plant"; while 1 individual volunteered that he "saw no future in the auto industry." Thus a total of 27 respondents (30 percent) cited job security concerns as the key factor in their decision, hardly surprising in view of the employment projections provided to buyout takers prior to their decisions. Jack Giordano expressed the common worry many shared: "Basically, I didn't want to put my family in jeopardy. I feel that General Motors, as far as Linden is concerned, is doomed. I don't think they're going to be there too many more years, and I didn't think they could carry my family where I wanted them to carry us, into the year 2000 and beyond. To have to sit by the phone and wait for them to call me to say, 'Yes, your future is not in jeopardy any longer'—I didn't want that. I tossed the dice when I was younger; I didn't want to toss the dice as I got older. I can't wait any longer for GM to get their shit together." John Pierce's decision to take the buyout was also motivated by uncertainty. "We had just bought this home," he recalled. "And at that point it was a new product coming into the plant, and they weren't really sure—you never know how the public is going to accept a product. I felt I was vulnerable. And that is mainly why I went ahead and took the buyout."

The other key factor that propelled many workers to take the buyout, whose importance is difficult to exaggerate, is that they disliked working at GM so intensely. Although job security ranked first as a motive for taking the buyout, nearly as many respondents (26 people, or 29 percent) said that the main reason they took the buyout was their frustration with working at GM. One can only speculate as to how many more might have identified this as a reason had the interviewers directly asked about it! Mike Evans, who had been hired in 1978, was one buyout taker for whom this was the key motivation: "I'd had it with this place. I just wanted to get out. I remember the first night I started working there. I knew right away I didn't like it. I was miserable there. I was just looking for an excuse to get out. [During the 1985–1986 layoff] I had been looking around for a new job, and I was trying to find something that would pay close to what I was making, because I was getting used to that income, and I wasn't having too much success. So when I found out about the buyout, I decided I might as well leave with some money in my pocket. Yeah!" Similarly, when asked why he took the buyout, Patrick Nolan responded, "I wasn't happy there. Forget about it. Drugs were everywhere; it was drug city! I didn't like it. It was a big decision to take the buyout, because I'd just gotten married; we'd bought a new house. But I just hated working there!"

It is possible that the buyout takers hated working at GM even more than those who remained.[35] Unfortunately, the available data offer no systematic way of comparing the two groups, but as chapter

2 shows, workers from both groups routinely compared GM to the military, prison, slavery, or even a concentration camp. Some of those who declined the buyout expressed envy for those who left. "It was my family that kept me there," Jeffrey Goetz told me. "I would've left in a heartbeat. I wanted to leave." Similarly, Zachary Smith confessed, "I considered the buyout just for the aggravation that I've been getting for this past so many years at the plant." And when I called a household where, unbeknownst to me, both father and son shared the same given name, which was on my list of buyout takers, the father started to respond to the first survey. After a few minutes, he realized that my questions were for buyout takers and exclaimed, "Oh, you want my son. I still work in that hellhole!"

The third major reason workers cited for taking the buyout was that they wanted to start or continue their own businesses. This was a factor for fully 36 percent of respondents and was the primary reason for taking the buyout for 13 percent. Twice this proportion, nearly a third of those respondents who were employed, were in small business of some sort at the time of the first survey, and another group had wage and salary jobs and ran their own businesses on the side as a second job. If the latter are included, 34 percent of all respondents and 41 percent of those who were employed were in business on their own at the time of the first survey. Most of these businesses had been started before the buyout was offered, which may be why relatively few respondents cited the desire to run such a business as their main reason for accepting the buyout.

For many of the self-employed, a combination of factors shaped their decision to take the buyout. "I was making more money in my own business [than at GM]," one respondent explained, "and I couldn't do both. Plus I hated working for GM." Some mentioned the limited opportunities for advancement in the factory, especially compared to the small business world. For example, Dan Cooper, the chimney sweep introduced in chapter 1, truly thought that anyone willing to work hard could get ahead in the world—except at GM: "I'm a firm believer that you couldn't bury me, because I think I could start flipping hamburgers at McDonald's and be a manager in no time. If you're willing to go out there and put the hours in and show that you care about it, any business you're going to advance in—except

GM where you can get lost in the sauce. . . . I took the buyout because I had the business started already, and I never went there [GM] with the intent to stay."

Job security concerns, a dislike for working at GM, and self-employment, then, accounted for the vast majority of buyout decisions. No other factor was cited as the key reason for taking the buyout by more than 6 of the 91 respondents, but a few indicated that they wanted to go back to school, needed the money to pay off bills, or wanted to spend more time with their families. Family issues were particularly important among the women buyout takers. A few were pregnant at the time the buyout was offered or had small children; others had grown children and no longer felt the need for a second income, or were approaching retirement age.

Although most respondents were glad they had taken the buyout, about 1 in 5 did regret his or her decision, and an even greater proportion—rising from 29 percent to 38 percent over the survey period—said that they would return to GM given the opportunity (assuming they could keep the buyout money). Workers with regrets were much more likely than others to report that they had received inadequate information about the buyout before accepting it. Indeed, of the 48 workers who said "yes" when asked, "Do you feel that you were given all the information you needed to decide whether to accept the buyout, or not?" only 1 regretted taking the buyout; whereas among the 31 workers who said "no," 19 (or 61 percent) had regrets, a statistically significant finding.[36] Some respondents felt they had been misled or manipulated. "We were led to believe it was a one-time deal," one complained. "That was a farce! They are still offering it now [in 1987], with more money." Others were angry about the employment projections management had made, which had turned out to be unduly pessimistic. "They said I couldn't count on being rehired, but then they started hiring everybody back," one worker recalled. "I would have stayed if I had known." Another confessed, "I took it out of a panicky situation. We should have had better figures about seniority and job security." A few were also unhappy that taking the buyout meant they were permanently ineligible to be rehired by GM—a concern that sparked a lawsuit from workers at another plant where the buyout program was implemented.[37]

Many workers who declined the buyout had seriously considered taking it. As for the buyout takers, age and seniority were often key factors in the decision for this group. "I never considered taking the buyout," Jonathan Fox recalled, "because I'm older, and I always knew where I stood. I go to the seniority board and count the names—I'm up to page 26 now. You have to see the handwriting on the wall." For Ben Kowalski too, age and seniority were crucial. "If they told me that I could retire tomorrow, I'd be gone, believe me," he said. "But see, the thing is, I'm 40 years old, and I got fourteen and a half years in there now. Which means, the way things are going, I'll probably be able to retire at, maybe twenty-five years. Now if I go start another job at 40 . . . " Similarly, Richard Scott said, "Take the buyout, you sign your life away from General Motors, your time served. Right now, I have fifteen years, half my working life. You can't just give up fifteen years! It's really tough because I'm 43 years old, real close to it. What am I going to do with a high school education?"

Many of those who decided not to take the buyout had a relatively optimistic view of the Linden plant's future. "There's quite a few that are taking the buyout that have just given up on the plant," Matthew Larson explained. "But I don't think they'll close the plant down. It's in a good location, the best location they could have, and I don't think with all the money that they put into it, that they're going to close." For still others, family considerations—and a generally cautious outlook—prevailed. "My brother took the buyout, and he went to school for two years," Sean O'Brien recounted, not without envy:

He's doing well now. He fixes heart machines, blood splitters; he's in the medical field. He's got it made now. He had ten years. And the other thing, he was single and under thirty. He was living with somebody, he was divorced from his wife, and he could do what he pleased. For me, it wasn't worth it. I got a house and everything to lose—and I didn't have a business. I knew one guy, he took the buyout, but he had a business already—he'd had it for a year, so that guy I could see taking a buyout. . . . The people that have businesses, you knew they were going to make it because they could expand. But a lot of them just took the buyout and tried a new business. I didn't think that was the way to go, even though we thought about it. [He pauses.] You know what our problem is? We're not going to take nothing but a sure thing. Other people took a chance, and some are doing okay.

Winners and Losers: The Buyout Takers'
Employment Trajectories

The vast majority of buyout takers easily found new employment. A year after the buyout, 76 of the 91 respondents to the first survey (84 percent) were employed, and of the 15 who were not, only 5 were actively seeking work. (The other 10, 9 of whom were female, were going to school, raising young children, physically ill, or the like.) The proportion of respondents who wanted a job but could not find one remained at this low level (5 percent) across all three surveys, even in the recession year 1991. Already this pattern contrasts sharply with the massive unemployment typically associated with plant closings and layoffs. It helped that New Jersey had a very low unemployment rate when these workers took the buyout in late 1986 or early 1987—about one-third less than the national average. Among large states, only Massachusetts had a lower rate at the time.[38] And whereas many displaced workers live in monoindustrial communities devastated by large plant closings, the GM-Linden plant continued to operate, albeit with a reduced workforce, in a diversified local economy. It is probably no accident that 26 percent of the buyout takers who relocated to another state, but only 17 percent of those who stayed in New Jersey, regretted their decision to take the buyout five years later, although this difference is not statistically significant.

Not only were relatively few buyout takers unemployed but also a surprisingly large proportion found attractive alternatives to GM. Almost a third went into some form of self-employment (although the proportion declined over time), and a majority of respondents in this group claimed to have earnings higher than at GM. Those buyout takers (the majority) who turned to wage and salary jobs generally fared worse economically than if they had stayed at GM, but a surprisingly high proportion found positions with union protection and relatively good pay and benefits. White male buyout takers were especially fortunate; indeed they were generally glad that they took the buyout. African Americans (of both genders) fared worse than whites and Latinos in the labor market, and were the one demographic group in which as many as half of the respondents regretted taking the buyout. White women also fared badly economically, but were no more likely than men to regret their choice to accept buyouts.

The Self-Employed

At the time of the first survey, nearly a third of the employed respondents (24 of 76) had a primary occupation involving self-employment, although by 1991, the level had fallen to less than one-fourth (15 of the 66 employed respondents), as figure 1 shows.[39] Even this latter proportion is substantially higher than that of self-employed people in the workforce as a whole—by a factor of 2 or 3, depending on which estimates of overall self-employment one prefers.[40] Even in an era when small business and informal economic activity generally are on the increase, the extent of self-employment among these former auto workers seems extraordinary.[41] Like the chimney sweep Dan Cooper, most of them were very pleased with their new lives. Almost none of the self-employed regretted taking the buyout, and as a group, they were by far the happiest and most successful respondents.

Marco Furtado came to the United States from Portugal in 1975, and after working in a series of low-wage factory jobs, he was hired at GM in 1978. He got the job through the Portuguese "buddy system," an immigrant network well established at Linden by that time. "I made good money at GM but worked hard for it," Furtado recalled. His brother still works there, and Marco Furtado probably would have stayed a lot longer too if not for the plant modernization. In late 1985, during the long layoff that preceded the buyout, he started working part-time at a gas station for $4 an hour in "cash under the table," while collecting SUB and other benefits. He was also going to a technical school during this period, at GM's expense (under a union-negotiated Tuition Assistance Program), hoping to learn some computer skills and then go back to Portugal.

What began as a casual gas-pumping job soon pushed Marco in a different direction. A few weeks after he was hired, the station owner "just gave me the keys and took off," and Marco quickly learned how to run the business. "I figured I might as well do this for myself," he recalled, and he drew on his savings, along with help from his in-laws, to buy his own gas station franchise. Then the buyout came along, and

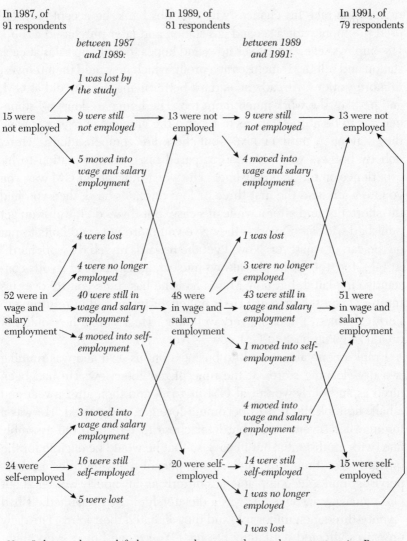

In 1987, of
91 respondents

In 1989, of
81 respondents

In 1991, of
79 respondents

*between 1987
and 1989:*

*between 1989
and 1991:*

*1 was lost by
the study*

15 were
not employed

*9 were still
not employed*

13 were not
employed

*9 were still
not employed*

13 were not
employed

*5 moved into
wage and salary
employment*

*4 moved into
wage and salary
employment*

4 were lost

1 was lost

*4 were no longer
employed*

*3 were no longer
employed*

52 were in
wage and
salary
employment

*40 were still in
wage and salary
employment*

48 were
in wage and
salary
employment

*43 were still in
wage and salary
employment*

51 were
in wage and
salary
employment

*4 moved into self-
employment*

*1 moved into self-
employment*

*3 moved into
wage and salary
employment*

*4 moved into
wage and salary
employment*

24 were
self-employed

*16 were still
self-employed*

20 were self-
employed

*14 were still
self-employed*

15 were self-
employed

5 were lost

*1 was no longer
employed*

1 was lost

Note: Italic type denotes shifts between employment and unemployment categories. Roman type denotes status of respondents in each survey year.

[a]Includes both those actively seeking work (5 in 1987, 4 in 1989, and 4 in 1991), as well as those who had voluntarily left the workforce, temporarily or permanently.

Figure 1. Trajectories of Linden-GM Buyout Takers, 1987–1991

rather than take his chances with the jobs bank, he accepted it. He used the money for a second gas station and later purchased a third. He employs several relatives now, and hopes to build up sales at each station and sell the franchises at a profit, which he would then reinvest in more stations. Already he earns a better living than he did at GM, and he likes the work much more too. The hours are longer—someone has to be at the stations to receive the gasoline at 6:30 A.M., and they stay open until 11 P.M.—but there are compensations: "Here, nobody bothers you!" Marco compared his current situation to his experience on the assembly line: "The worst thing about GM was, you go into a job, and the first three or four days, it's hard; then you find the shortcuts, and after a while, it's easy. But if you do it well, you get punished with *more* work—they give you more nuts and bolts to put on the car, or whatever. Now, I get the rewards myself if I work hard." At GM, too, the future was always unclear, and rumors of layoffs constantly circulated, but now Marco feels he has some control over his future: "I can sell or stay." He is no longer interested in returning to Portugal, since "I'm doing very well now." He says that he would not dream of going back to GM now—"No way!"

Frank Leone also went into business on his own and was running two dry-cleaning stores at the time of our interview. He had been hired as an hourly worker at GM in 1978, and then after a year and a half, he took the test to become a foreman and passed. He was a foreman for several years but later chose to return to the assembly line (with a substantial cut in pay), so that he would be eligible for the buyout. Even though he himself was part of the widely despised supervisory ranks, he complained as bitterly as any hourly worker about GM's managerial style. "It was a dictatorship!" he exclaimed. "I had seventy-three men under me, and they all hated their jobs." The daily pressures affected his family life too. "You come home every night feeling bad, because the guy above you is making you discipline the people under you," he recalled. Leone became increasingly alienated and was thinking of quitting anyway when he learned about the buyout. He immediately resolved to pursue it. "When you get to the point where you hate your supervisor so much you want to hit him, it's time to move on," he explained. Since he knew that only hourly workers were eligible for the buyout, he returned to the production worker ranks shortly before the 1985–1986 layoff. He collected SUB during the layoff period and then eagerly accepted the buyout.

Leone's plan all along was to invest the money in a small business. Years before, his father had owned several dry-cleaning stores, and when he retired, he offered Leone the chance to take them over. At the time, Leone was happy at GM, having just become a foreman, and so he turned down this opportunity. But now he is grateful for his family's knowledge of the business, to which he gives much of the credit for his current success. His income has already risen above the salary he earned as a foreman at GM, and he says he's much more relaxed now. After only a few years in business, he has raised his standard of living considerably, moving to a larger house in a better neighborhood and buying a European luxury car, as well as a boat.

He feels that his business has "unlimited potential" and is thinking of buying two additional stores. Leone has only two complaints about his current situation: One is that he hates having to pay so much for the fringe benefits he enjoyed cost-free at GM. The other involves recruiting reliable workers: "At GM, my biggest problem was the people above me; here it's inadequate help." Still, he tries hard to treat his employees fairly (when I visited one of his stores he invited me to ask them if he was a good employer). And he has no regrets about leaving GM. "I hated it! When I worked there, I came home worrying all the time. I had no control over anything; my hands were tied," he recalled bitterly. "It's so different now. People who come in to have their clothes cleaned are usually in a good mood, and if I'm in a good mood too, things are rosy. At GM, everyone was always edgy. I wouldn't go back there even if they offered me the same money I make now!"

Patrick Nolan is also happily self-employed as a dump-truck owner-operator. Unlike Furtado and Leone, however, he had a difficult time in the period immediately after he took the buyout. "When I left there [GM], I went into [illegal] bookmaking," he explained. "I've got a friend whose family is in the business. And it panned out, but then I started doing drugs because I had too much money. I almost got divorced over it." With help from someone he knew at GM, he was admitted to a drug treatment clinic: "I was there for forty days, and that was it. After that, I got on the right track, and I got out of bookmaking completely." At that point, Nolan fell back on truck driving, which he had done as a teenager and also "under the table" while he was laid off from GM.

So, I started driving for this guy. He was paying me $9 an hour, with no benefits. I'd tell him every couple of weeks, "I'm going broke; I need more money." So I went up to like $15 an hour. My wife had benefits, that's the only reason I could do it in the first place. He was a nice guy, but he didn't know anything about the business, and I knew all the people in it. I helped him build it up. He'd never made so much money before. See, in dump trucks, you have to know people. So then I turned around, I tell myself, "Here I'm making this guy $100,000 a year, while I could be doing this myself." So I went up to him and said, "Look we have to go partners, or else I got to get out and I'm going to go on my own."

After about a year as his former employer's partner, Nolan took over the business: "I bought him out, and I've been on my own ever since." With three trucks, he earns much more than he did at GM, has bought a new home, and overall is much happier now. "It's not like working, driving a truck. At General Motors, you make good money, but you can't even go to the bathroom when you want to. You're doing a job every minute, you know. This here, you're more or less on your own. It's a good business. You make your own hours. If I don't feel like getting up tomorrow for work, I make a phone call and I put a guy on the truck. I love it!" He is well aware that his business—which depends on roadwork and construction—is vulnerable to the ups and downs of the economy. "In the last recession, it got so bad that people would burn their trucks to collect the insurance," he explained. "If the economy goes well, I'll be in it; if it falls out, I don't know what I'll do." His wife earns a good salary as a supervisor at an insurance company, which is also the source of his health insurance and other benefits. "It's shaky, but my wife works, you know; she makes almost $40,000 a year now." Despite his sense of uncertainty, Nolan is glad he left GM. "I'm not sorry I took the buyout," he said. "I was for a while, but I just hung around and everything fell into place."

The desire to start small businesses has long been associated with factory workers. Former manual workers, and especially males, have always been overrepresented among the self-employed, and self-employment is a well-documented mobility strategy for blue-collar workers who lose their waged jobs.[42] Small business has an understandably powerful appeal to workers who have experienced the extremely bureaucratic, authoritarian industrial regime that GM-Linden exemplified. "Man, I want my kid to work for himself," said longtime Linden worker Charlie Ferraro, articulating a sentiment shared by many of his co-workers. "Never want to work for nobody if you can help it. I've worked in small places, big places—it's all the same bullshit." Ely Chinoy analyzed this aspiration toward independence in his classic study *Automobile Workers and the American Dream* (based on fieldwork at GM's Oldsmobile plant in Lansing, Michigan), published in 1955, when the U.S. economy was in its heyday: "The generalized attributes of life in a large mass-production plant constantly stimulated the desire to leave the factory among workers. . . . Paradoxically, the very process of alienation which Marx thought would transform industrial workers into class-conscious proletarians has instead stimulated their interest in small business and in small-scale private farming, institutions of capitalist society which Marx asserted were doomed to extinction."[43] But in the 1950s, these aspirations were seldom realized. Of the workers Chinoy studied, only a handful actively pursued their "utopian daydreams" of going into business on their own. They clung instead to the security and high pay that automobile industry employment provided at the time, and the fantasy of "being your own boss" was a safety valve. "Even though hopes crumble when put to the test of reality," Chinoy noted, "the talk and the daydreams they generate may soften the irritations and aggravations of the moment."[44]

Four decades later, however, with job security increasingly tenuous for American auto workers in the face of intensified international competition, and with self-employment and informal economic activity burgeoning all over the globe, the phenomenon Chinoy identified has become a reality, rather than merely a dream, for a significant number of former auto workers. The GM buyout program helped facilitate this, and indeed, at least one other such program (at the French auto firm Renault) yielded similar results.[45] While their economic rewards have been modest by the standards of the business world, on the whole the self-employed buyout takers claimed to have improved their incomes after leaving GM. At least half of the self-employed buyout takers reported earnings higher than at GM across all three surveys, compared to only about one-fifth of those employed in wage or salary jobs, a statistically significant result (for all three years).[46] The one thing that many of the self-employed missed about their jobs at GM was the fringe benefits, which are very expensive for individuals to obtain (although some, like Patrick Nolan, received benefits through their spouses' jobs).

The self-employed expressed extremely high levels of satisfaction with their work, typically because they liked "being their own boss." In all three survey years, over 90 percent of self-employed respondents said they preferred their present job to working at GM, compared with about two-thirds of the respondents in wage or salary jobs—a statistically significant difference.[47] The self-employed were also far less likely than the wage and salary respondents to regret taking the buyout. Over 90 percent (and in the third survey, 100 percent!) of the self-employed respondents said they would still take the buyout if they could make the decision over again, compared with about three-fourths of the wage and salary workers—a statistically significant difference for two of the three survey years.[48]

Survival rates for the businesses these former auto workers owned were fairly high, in part because many of them had been established long before, as second jobs while their owners were employed at GM or during the long layoff immediately preceding the buyout, and had already survived the difficult start-up period when so many new enterprises fail. Of the 16 businesses, first identified in 1987, that were still the primary occupation of the respondents two years later, 13 had been founded prior to the buyout; and this was the case for 10 of the 13 businesses in this group that were still operating in 1991.[49] Another factor that may have made it easier for these businesses to survive is that most had extremely low capital requirements. None had more than a handful of employees, and most were unincorporated. Between a third and half (over the three surveys) were in the construction sector, either at the business-to-business level, like Patrick Nolan's dump-truck business, or doing retail home repair or remodeling. Most of the rest were small service or retail operations, like Frank Leone's dry-cleaning stores, Marco Furtado's gas stations, and Dan Cooper's chimney sweep business. Other businesses owned by respondents included a bar, a jewelry store, a pizzeria, and a video rental outlet. Some were run directly out of the owner's home, and many operated on an "all-cash" basis. Such informal microenterprises may have a higher success rate than the larger "small businesses" tracked in most previous research.[50]

Wage and Salary Workers

Self-employed workers are among the happiest and most successful buyout takers, and they make up a surprisingly large proportion of the total. But they are not entirely typical. Most buyout takers ended up in ordinary wage or salary jobs, and economically, this group had much more in common than the self-employed with the larger population of downwardly mobile displaced industrial workers, except that only a handful could not find work at all. Respondents in wage and salary jobs were spread across a wide range of occupations and industries. Although many were engaged in blue-collar work, relatively few found new employment in manufacturing: this sector accounted for only 10 percent of the buyout takers in wage and salary employment in the first survey, although the proportion doubled by 1991.

Unlike the self-employed, most buyout takers in wage or salary employment were worse off financially than they had been as auto workers—typically working in service sector jobs with relatively low pay and inferior benefits, and often lacking union protection. However, even in this group a surprisingly large number found relatively good jobs. Around 40 to 50 percent were unionized, an even higher proportion than one might expect in heavily unionized New Jersey, where 26 percent of the workforce was covered by union contracts in 1988 (only 3 of the 48 contiguous states had higher union density).[51]

Despite the fact that many suffered downward mobility economically, only a minority of these wage and salary respondents expressed nostalgia for their old jobs at GM. In the recession year 1991, five years after they took the buyout, only 28 percent of respondents in wage and salary employment regretted their decision.[52] A majority of the wage and salary respondents expressed very positive sentiments about the buyout, although their feelings were more varied than among the self-employed. Edward Salerno, the insurance company employee whose story is told in chapter 1, is among the wage and salary workers who is delighted to have left GM. Another is Mike Evans, who told me, "I'm real happy to be out. Even if they didn't have the buyout, I wouldn't have went back anyway after the shutdown, because I would've taken that time to look for another job, which is what I did." He worked for a while as a messenger, earning only $6.50 an hour, with no benefits, and then he saw an ad in the newspaper for a job at AT&T's Bell Laboratories. "So I went and took the test. I got lucky—I just happened to be in the right place at the right time."

Evans has been happy at AT&T, where he was hired as a systems technician. "I don't climb telephone poles or anything like that. They call us dedicated technicians because we're assigned to one building. We maintain and install the telephone lines and data lines, and that's pretty much all we do." He might have stayed at GM if he could have gotten a skilled-trades job, but when that aspiration was blocked, he decided to take the buyout. He worked at Linden for almost eight years, but he always disliked it, mainly because of the working conditions and the fact that there were no possibilities for advancement. Although he still earns less than he did at GM, the AT&T job is unionized, and there is a system of pay progression. Although he started at $8 an hour, Evans figures that in five years "I'll probably be making more than I would have if I had stayed at General Motors." In any case, he said, some things are more important than money. "One thing I found out is that the money doesn't matter to me that much. I have to be doing something that I like. I've always been a health-conscious person. I don't smoke. I jog. I cycle. I try to take care of myself. And at GM, the job that I had was welding. I would have been willing to forego certain raises just to get decent working conditions, because to me, my health is more important than actual money." In this regard, the AT&T job is a huge improvement.

Compared to General Motors, it's just like night and day. Because it's a nice, air-conditioned building. It's quiet, with hanging plants all over the place. It's just totally different from what I had at General Motors. It's peaceful there, and I like it. It's not like working on the line. Like you come in in the morning, and if you want to sit down and have a cup of coffee and relax for a couple of minutes before you go to work, you can. At General Motors, when that whistle blew at six-thirty, that line's moving, and if you're not ready to work, that's just too bad. And [at GM] you're working every minute of the day, just about. You get your breaks and you get your lunch period, but lunch was the same thing. The whistle would blow, and you'd get exactly thirty minutes. The end of thirty minutes, boom! You're right back on the line.

Evans is also taking college courses at night, with AT&T paying his tuition. He dreams of a career in theater and travels regularly to New York City for acting classes. He's not sure how long he'll stay at AT&T: "One problem I've always had is, I'm not good at long-term planning. Right now I'm playing it by ear, to see what happens with the acting and with the job. I've only been at AT&T a year and a half, so I don't have a lot of time invested there. But I am single, and I feel as long as I stay single, I have more options. Right now, I'm just taking it as it comes."

Eddie Soares also has been happier since taking the buyout. He has two young children, and although he had a relatively good, off-line job as a utility worker at GM, filling in for people on a wide variety of jobs, he hated working the night shift. "You leave for work at three o'clock or three-thirty. You come home, and everyone's sleeping. You get up; everyone's been up half a day. You're around for a couple of hours; then you go." Soares thought that after the plant modernization his chances of working days at GM were slim. "They were putting the robots in and all that good stuff. I was already on nights for five years, and I figured there's another five years on nights at least, because I knew guys with ten years. It was just too much and I just decided to get out." Soares's wife, who was home during our interview, recalled, "Working nights, that was really the pits. He was so unhappy coming home from work!" During the layoff, Soares explained, "I tried a few things and liked working days a lot better, and that was basically it. But I was a little jumpy at first. I was on pins and needles, wondering, 'Was this the right move?'"

He now works as a carpenter for a small firm that builds and installs boilers and cooling towers. He found the job almost by chance: "What happened is, my wife was babysitting for the guy who became my boss, and I was just talking to him. This was right before I took the buyout. I hung around with him a couple times, went to the jobs, and watched what he did. And it was cool, because I'd never heard of a cooling tower before I started, even though I'd worked in construction before. Basically, any big building would have a cooling tower for air-conditioning. All it does is cool the water down a little before it goes back through the chillers and the Freon." Another big plus is that the work is mostly done outside. "It's carpenter's work—heavy construction. It's an outdoor kind of thing. And that's what I like. In the plant, it was always hot in the summer, cold in the winter. Plus it's a lot freer, you know, than in GM. Every day you're on another job—you're here, you're uptown, you're downtown, you're in, you're out" Soares earns more now—about $25 an hour, with full benefits—as a unionized carpenter than he did at GM. He has moved to a large house in a better neighborhood and is optimistic about the future: "I like what I'm doing; I like the guys I'm working for. I'd like to stay with the company."

Tim Murphy also feels he is better off now. He works as a laborer for an oil and chemical company, "transferring oil and chemical products to trucks, railroad cars, and ships and barges." Like Soares, he prefers working outside and appreciates the fact that his new job is less routinized. "At General Motors, they are very hard lined, and it was more—I don't like to use the word *stagnant,* but it was the same work every day, day in and day out. Where I'm at now, I get a variety of work. The monotony of doing the same task day in and day out isn't there." The pay is about the same as at GM, and often more, if he works overtime. He has a union and fairly good benefits, and the job seems more secure: "I'm better off now than at General Motors as far as my position, because it's a smaller company, and there's not that much foreign competition."

Murphy said he would not have chosen to take the buyout if the job he has now had not been available. "I made the decision to take the buyout because at the time I had the opportunity to go into something I always wanted to go into. I felt I was young enough to find something better, and I did. Also, there [were] monetary gains there, from the [buyout] money that they were presenting to me, and I made the decision." He feels very lucky to have his current job: "If I didn't get this job, I would have stayed at General Motors. If I had to go to work for Burger King for $4 an hour, I'd still be at GM. But I'm in a position where I'm just doing something that I like a lot better."

Mike Polansky is also glad he took the buyout. "I got real lucky," he said. He now works at a warehouse for a supermarket chain, is a member of the Teamsters' union, and earns a slightly higher wage than at GM. "I can work twenty hours a week in overtime if I want it. So that makes a big difference. And there's no layoffs—unless something dramatic happens where they go out of business, but I don't see that happening, because right now, they're building new stores like crazy. Obviously, they plan on being around for a while." Like many buyout takers, he finds his current job far less onerous than working at GM: "GM is working on the line; you're doing the same exact thing over and over. Whereas over here, you're stacking the cases onto the pallet and putting them into the trailer. Even though that is a little monotonous, it's not the same stuff over and over. You're always doing cases, but every case is different. It's almost like you have to be creative to build your pallet right. It's not as boring. Plus they always need extra people to do easier jobs, so they go by seniority, down the list, and they find out if you want to do this for that day. Right now, I do an easy job almost every day. I'm not doing the really backbreaking work."

Polansky has no illusions about the warehouse, however. "It's really just a job. I look at it as a job. There's no room for advancement and that, as far as I can see. But as long as they want me around, I'll be there. If something else comes up again, that's even better—but I mean I don't really look for a job." He has absolutely no interest in moving into white-collar work: "I don't want no pressures. When I'm done with my eight hours, I want to go home. I don't want to know nothing, you know. I have friends that are white collars. It's like, most of them, they have got to come home with work. I want to come home and sit in the backyard and cook a burger. I don't want to be doing more work. That's how I look at it. I like to work with my hands anyhow and be physical. I don't think I could sit around for eight hours. It would drive me crazy, looking at four walls. That's not for me."

Of course, not everyone who took the buyout was as pleased with the outcome as these four individuals. As white males who had found new jobs that paid nearly as much as GM, with union protection and good benefits, they were among the most fortunate in the wage and salary group. By contrast, roughly half of the wage and salary respondents were no longer working in unionized workplaces, and a sig-

nificant minority now lacked health insurance (20–25 percent) and
pension benefits (40–50 percent). In most cases their earnings declined significantly relative to what they had earned at GM. In 1987,
the median hourly pay for the wage and salary respondents was only
$9.00, although it rose to $11.50 in 1989 and to $12.00 in 1991.[53] In
1987, about two-thirds (64 percent) of the wage and salary respondents earned less than at GM, although this fell to half (52 percent)
by 1991. As one might expect, those with lower earnings were more
likely to regret taking the buyout. Over one-third (38 percent) of those
wage and salary respondents earning less than at GM in 1991 regretted their choice, compared with only 13 percent of those wage and
salary respondents earning the same or more than at GM, a statistically significant difference.[54]

Tom Peterman had the strongest feelings of regret of any respondent among those white men surveyed who wish they had stayed at
GM. Asked if he would go back to Linden, given the chance, if he
could keep the buyout money, he not only said yes but added that
he'd even be willing to give back the money. At one point, after hearing that everyone who didn't take the buyout was recalled to work, he
had even telephoned the plant's employment office to inquire about
whether this might be possible. He had had a relatively good job at
GM, as a metal finisher in the body shop. But during the long layoff
in 1985–1986, he moved back to his native Kentucky, and when the
buyout offer came along, he decided to stay for good. He worked
"under the table" painting cars in his garage for a while. Then, thinking his GM experience might be an asset, he applied for a job at
the new Toyota auto assembly plant in Georgetown, Kentucky, even
though it was a three-hour drive from his home: "They sent me a letter
wanting me to come up there and everything, but I was gone somewhere and I missed the interview." He also applied for a job closer to
home at a chemical-waste disposal facility but was immediately rejected:

> Through a friend I found out they had a few openings. So I went up
> there and put an application in. Well, the first guy I talked to said he
> wanted me to come back and all this stuff. So I went back up there,
> and this other guy, he had the application, and he started asking me
> things about General Motors. Then he goes, "Was that unionized?" I

said, "Yes." I don't think he liked that. I don't want to say what he said on the tape.

[RM: That's okay, I don't care.]

He told me, "Get the fuck out of here; we don't want your kind here." I felt like kicking that guy's ass right there—he had me so mad! Since then I don't mention that I worked for General Motors anymore. Around here, you get fired if you even mention unions.

Peterman eventually found a sales job with a company called Combined Insurance.[55] He was assigned to cover about half the state, so he spent a lot of time and money driving (with no reimbursement for expenses), and because he was paid strictly on a commission basis, his net earnings were very low—at most $200 a week for 50 hours of work. He quit after about six months. "I always heard the same complaint from the customers, 'Oh, man, don't they ever send us the same guy?' After a few months, I realized nobody stayed." He said his family (he has two children) would have starved during this period if his wife hadn't gone out to work, cleaning houses. His family also got some financial help from relatives.

After quitting the insurance job, he found some part-time work in a local body shop, but soon he starting looking around for something else.

I decided to go to trucking school. That was a big mistake, too. I wish I'd never done that! The school was one of these real expensive ones—they promised all this and never delivered. They said they'd get me a local driving job, and they never did. And I finally went and got one going over road [long-distance trucking]. I did that for three months. It paid pretty well, about $600 a week. But then I had an accident, turned the truck over in New York, and that's when I busted my leg and my shoulder. I was laid up for a year and a half. I had two different doctors looking at me, and they said I wasn't going to walk again. But I went to physical therapy, and that pretty well got me back into shape. Though if I stand on concrete too long, it gets to hurting.

Now Peterman drives a taxi, earning about $50 to $75 a day—about half his GM pay. Even though he works as much as 60 hours a week, he is employed as an independent contractor, so he gets no benefits. He also occasionally works as a bartender at a nearby hotel, mainly for private parties. In addition, sometimes he works for an old friend in a local body shop. His wife has a part-time job at a nearby Wal-Mart, earning just over the minimum wage, and is hoping to get a full-time job there, so the family can have health insurance and other benefits: "One girl that's ahead of her, she's going to leave in June, and she's up next for full-time." Tom's injury was covered by workers' compensation, but the family has no other medical coverage. He is resigned to the situation: "It was kind of rough at first, but now things seem to be working out." He still thinks wistfully about trying to get a job at Toyota, at the GM plant in Bowling Green, or at the Nissan plant in nearby Tennessee: "I'll be thirty-five soon; maybe if I could get in there and maybe stay ten years, long enough to get a pension . . ."

John Pierce, an African American who worked on the final line at Linden for nine years, is also sorry that he took the buyout. He had bought a house shortly before the offer came, and based on the information he had at the time, he thought his job at Linden was too insecure, and that the buyout was his best option. "I took it out of a panicky situation," he recalled. "I was led to believe you'd be hung out to dry if you didn't take the buyout." Pierce became angry later, though, when he learned that the buyout was offered again several more times, and that workers at his seniority level turned out to have fairly secure jobs at GM after all. He worked in a series of low-wage jobs immediately after the buyout, but then "I lucked up" and found a job as a unionized driver for New Jersey Transit. Even this involved a substantial pay cut relative to GM, at least initially, and inferior benefits: "Eventually, I'll get back to the salary I had, but I figure I've lost maybe three years of earning that type of money. It takes three years to reach the top rate, which is about $13.96 right now [1989]."

Though he is bitter about his economic losses, and wishes he had stayed at GM, Pierce does prefer some things about his new job: "The job itself is better. It's stressful because you're driving and you're dealing with the public, but other than that, I like it. I have good days; I like dealing with people sometimes—I really do. I drive different lines—I'm not on the same line all the time—and I have an opportunity to pick the hours that I wish to work. It's a lot less physical than working on the line. It's less of a toll on my body—it's stressful but not physical. At GM, you have a lot of stress *and* it's physical." He was hardly fond of working at GM, but he still regrets taking the buyout and feels that he would have been better off staying. He considers himself very lucky to have found his present job.

Joyce Cowley is also sorry that she took the buyout, although at the time she made the decision, it seemed to make sense. She is older and more senior that most of the buyout takers, and had worked at GM since 1972. When she first got the job, she was a single mother, supporting her two children alone, which she continued to do for over ten years until she remarried. By the time the buyout came along, she felt ready to leave: "My kids were grown and they had their own jobs; they had their own insurances. I said, 'I'm getting old for this; I'm just going to take it easy now and find something to keep me busy.' I figured I didn't really have to be up at four-thirty every morning and out the door at five-thirty—there was no need for it. So, I said, 'Well, I'm going to take the buyout.' I thought I could start taking it easy and slow my pace—but it turned out all backwards."

Not wanting to stop working completely, Cowley found a new job as a cutter in a small nonunion factory that makes scuba-diving equipment. The pay is less than half what she earned at GM, although the work is easier too: "As long as your work gets done, you can go; they don't care how many breaks you take." She doesn't like it very much, but as things turned out, she feels she has no alternative but to stay. Soon after she took the buyout, her family's luck turned bad. Her second husband, a construction worker, lost his full-time job and with it his health insurance coverage. (The family cannot afford the $1,100 quarterly payments it would take for them to maintain the old insurance policy.) Cowley has health insurance benefits at her new job, but since her husband has emphysema, the company refused to add him to her policy. Her son, who had also worked in construction, lost his job too and moved back into her house. Meanwhile, her daughter got divorced and also moved back in, along with Cowley's small grandson. This is actually a big help, because "we can't afford the house on my little salary."

Cowley doesn't like her new job, but she said, "I have to stay there now, because my husband might work one day a week, if he's lucky. This is not really what I want to do, but I'm in a bind, financially."

She is looking for something better, but as a woman in her forties with only a high school education, her options are severely limited. She desperately wishes she could turn the clock back and get her old GM job back. "There's always that hope at the back of my head that if it came to the point where they really got booming, and they needed people, that instead of hiring off the street, they might get in touch with the people that took the buyout. If that happened, I'd jump on it—I really would. I'd go back tomorrow!"

Race and Gender

To a great extent, the winners and losers among buyout takers were differentiated by gender and race. As table 5 shows, white male buyout takers reported average earnings 3 times those of women (all races) in 1987, falling to 1.5 times in both 1989 and 1991. And white male respondents reported mean earnings more than 2 times those of African-American (both sexes) buyout takers in 1987, although the gap narrowed later. The small number of Latinos in the sample— most of them male immigrants like Marco Furtado—fared better than either the African Americans or the women, though not as well as the white males.[56] (As table 5 indicates, the differences in reported earnings between Latinos and white men were not statistically significant in two of the three survey years; despite the small number of female and African-American respondents, statistically significant differences were found for these groups relative to white men.) This systematic inequality contrasts dramatically to what these individuals had experienced at GM-Linden, where regardless of gender or race, wage rates for production workers seldom varied by more than $.50 an hour, and where in 1987 the lowest rate was $13.51 per hour (for sweepers and janitors), while the highest was $14.69 (for metal repair workers in the body shop).[57] For those who took the buyout, the normal differentials of the external labor market, stratified by race and gender, now prevailed.

African-American male respondents were not significantly less likely to be self-employed than their white male counterparts, yet the earnings of African Americans were dramatically lower. In all three survey years, not one African-American respondent of either gender (there were 12 in the sample) reported earning more than at GM, even though about one-third of the whites and a substantial minority of Latinos did so. In all three years, at least three-quarters of the African-American respondents reported that they earned less than at GM, a much higher rate than for either whites or Latinos.[58] This supports William J. Wilson's claim that African Americans are particularly hard hit by the effects of deindustrialization, although unemployment was rare in the case of the buyout takers, and not one appears to have joined the underclass.[59] Still, in light of the downward mobility that virtually all the African-American respondents experienced, it is not surprising that African Americans were less likely to take the buyout in the first place, nor that they were more than twice as likely as respondents generally to regret doing so. In two of the three survey years, fully half of the African-American respondents said that if they could make the decision over again, they would not accept the buyout—a far higher rate of regret than for any other group of respondents.[60]

The gender gap in earnings was even wider than the gap between

TABLE 5. Average Hourly Wages Self-Reported by GM-Linden Buyout Takers, 1987–1991, by Race and Gender

	Mean Hourly Wages ($)		
	1987	1989	1991
White males	17.47	15.34	14.99
N	(54)	(45)	(43)
Females, (all races)	5.94°°	9.61°°	9.69°
N	(20)	(20)	(19)
African Americans, both genders	8.08	9.74°°	9.52°
N	(12)	(12)	(12)
Latinos, both genders	12.28	12.57	9.94°
N	(15)	(15)	(14)

SOURCE: Author's surveys.
°Significantly different from white men at p ≤ .10, using two-tailed t-test, pooled variance.
°°Significantly different from white men at p < .05 using two-tailed t-test, pooled variance.

white men and African Americans, as table 5 shows. One contributing factor was that there were almost no women among the self-employed buyout takers. In the first survey, every single one of the
self-employed respondents was male (a statistically significant difference).[61] Since the self-employed generally had higher earnings than
the other buyout takers, this negatively affected women's earnings.
Even among the wage and salary workers, however, women's earnings
lagged far behind men's. For 1987, women averaged $5.94 an hour,
compared with $11.10 for male wage and salary workers; the differ-
ence is smaller for the later years but still statistically significant.[62]

In general, women buyout takers shared a pattern of sharp downward mobility with African Americans, but despite this brutal economic reality, women were not significantly more likely to regret taking the buyout than men. Perhaps women workers were even more
disenchanted than their male counterparts with the experience of
working at GM. As described in chapter 2, women in the plant had
to contend not only with poor treatment from supervision but also
with a lack of acceptance on the part of their co-workers. Although a
fairly large proportion of the white female and Latina buyout takers
voluntarily withdrew from the workforce after taking the buyout,
mostly—as in Joyce Cowley's case—for family-related reasons, there
was no significant relationship between leaving the labor force and
expressing regret about the buyout.[63]

Conclusion

"Nothing I'd read before starting my fieldwork on the Chrysler shutdown quite prepared me for the fact that a lot of people in and around
Kenosha were *happy* to see the plant close," the social anthropologist
Kathryn Dudley comments in her case study of the Chrysler auto-
plant closing in Kenosha, Wisconsin.[64] In her study, this view is limited
to the middle-class professionals in the community, but the experience of the GM-Linden buyout takers suggests that workers themselves may also, at least under certain conditions, see the shrinkage of
the nation's manufacturing sector in a positive light. Overall the buyout takers expressed little nostalgia for the days they had worked at

GM-Linden, with the important exception of the African-American respondents.

Many did miss the high pay and excellent benefits that they had enjoyed at GM, but most felt that escaping from the plant's daily humiliations was adequate compensation for their losses in those areas. Interestingly, many buyout takers did express some nostalgia for the UAW. In the 1991 survey, over 40 percent (11 of the 27 who answered this question) of the wage and salary respondents who were no longer union members said they missed being in a union, compared to only 15 percent (4 respondents) who were glad they were no longer unionized (the other 44 percent, or 12 respondents, were indifferent). Moreover, among the wage and salary respondents who were in unionized jobs in 1991, over two-thirds (13 of the 19 answering the question) said the UAW was a better union than their current one, while only 1 in 10 (2 of the 19) said his or her current union was superior (the other 21 percent, or 4 respondents, rated the two unions about the same).

Indeed, what motivated most of these workers to remain at GM as long as they did was the fact that, for people with limited education and few marketable skills, this work offered a middle-class income, excellent fringe benefits, union representation, and historically at least a high degree of job security. Of course, this is precisely why so many observers have portrayed the decline of this type of employment in tragic terms. Such commentators would probably also point out that the self-employment phenomenon uncovered here has its negative side. Even if it offers some individuals the opportunity to earn higher incomes, the shift to small business ownership from traditional corporate employment is a type of workforce casualization, with all the disabilities that implies: economic precariousness, lack of fringe benefits, and so forth.

Why then do so few of these former GM workers express any regrets? The technique of asking individuals how they feel about a decision they have already made may produce some bias against their acknowledging that they have made a mistake and perhaps lead them to exaggerate their well-being as well. Also, it is possible that a disproportionate number of the workers who could not be located or who declined to participate in the study were in serious distress, although our response rate was reasonably good. Still, the overwhelmingly positive assessment by the respondents of their postbuyout experience cannot be discounted entirely. A large majority seemed genuinely relieved to have left the automobile industry.

The explanation for this seemingly paradoxical finding may lie less in the research methodology than in the characteristics of this particular group of workers, who, as I have shown, were in so many ways atypical members of the growing population of displaced industrial workers. Not only did they receive a substantial payment when they left GM, but they were also a relatively young group, typically in their early thirties at the time. It was far easier for them to make a new start than it would have been for workers twenty or thirty years older. Equally critical, they were a self-selected group, and many who chose to take the buyout did so with a clear alternative in mind. And unemployment was minimal in New Jersey in the period just after the buyout.

It would be wrong to conclude that deindustrialization is not as socially devastating as many others have argued, or is perhaps even a positive thing. Rather, the lesson of these workers' experiences is that under certain conditions, the transition away from industrial employment *can* be relatively painless, and for some, perhaps even beneficial—at least for white males. Continued shrinkage of the manufacturing sector is inevitable, and the buyout experience suggests that nostalgia for the industrial past is deeply misguided. The real issue is how to protect workers from the impact of this massive economic shift, and how to restore high wages, decent benefits, and union protection to those who have lost them.

Chapter Five

The "New Linden"

Rhetoric and Reality

Like their counterparts who left in response to the buyout offer, those workers who remained at GM-Linden after the plant's massive 1985–1986 modernization nourished hopes that their working lives would change for the better. Their optimism was inspired by a radical shift in managerial thinking that swept the United States in the 1980s, away from the long-established, authoritarian Fordist model and toward an emphasis on workers' participation in decision making. At the same time (and helping to spark the change in management philosophy), new microprocessor-based technologies were transforming the physical infrastructure of the nation's factories. Even GM, an industrial behemoth that is usually a laggard in managerial innovation, felt the effects of these changes.

When GM-Linden reopened in the fall of 1986 after its $300 million, year-long technological overhaul, workers were encouraged to expect improvements in daily life at the plant. Upon returning from their year-long layoff, they spent two full weeks in a special training program (jointly run by the UAW and GM) introducing the "new Linden." By all accounts, most workers liked what they heard. Not only had the new technology eliminated some of the most arduous production jobs, they were told, but also supervision would be more humane, and workers themselves would be expected to take greater responsibility for productivity and quality. Although the "team concept" introduced in several other GM plants during this period was not part of the "new Linden," workers left the training program filled with expectations of major changes on the factory floor.

As it turned out, however, GM-Linden management failed to deliver many of the organizational reforms announced with such fanfare during the training program. The impetus for change had come from GM corporate planners in Detroit, but they offered few incentives to the plant's hands-on managers to change their behavior. As a result, many first-line supervisors ultimately resisted the reform process. Many foremen reverted to the demeaning behavior that had generated such bitterness among the workforce in past years, and other promised improvements were subverted or distorted by shop-floor managers under pressure from above to ensure uninterrupted production in the face of chronic technological glitches. Even when it functioned properly, the new technology was a mixed blessing for workers, eliminating some of the worst jobs but also many of the most desirable ones. In the end, the daily reality of work in the plant changed far less than workers had been led to expect, and the widespread sense of disappointment obscured those improvements that did occur. Workers readily embraced the new managerial rhetoric of participation, but its woefully incomplete implementation at GM-Linden led to unanticipated results. Rather than enhancing productivity and commitment as intended, the (largely unrealized) principle of participation became a tool of critique that workers appropriated to attack managerial practices.

New Technology, New Industrial Relations

The changes in managerial thinking and the massive retooling that occurred in the U.S. auto industry during the 1980s came in response to developments in the 1970s, when fundamental shifts in the international economy began to undermine the once-legendary power of the U.S. automakers. Skyrocketing oil prices led to dramatic growth in demand for imported cars from the economically resurgent nations of western Europe and, most important, from Japan. For the first time in their history, the U.S. auto producers faced a serious challenge in their home market.[1] After initially ignoring these developments, in the 1980s the Big Three began to confront their international competition seriously. They invested heavily in computerization and robotization, constructing new high-tech plants and modernizing their existing facilities. GM alone spent over $40 billion during the 1980s, renovating old plants and building new ones.[2]

At the same time, inspired by both their Japanese rivals and the nonunion manufacturing sector in the United States, the auto firms began to experiment with "employee involvement" programs and other kinds of worker participation, while seeking to reduce the number of job classifications and work rules in their plants.[3] By the end of the 1980s, virtually every auto assembly plant in the United States had institutionalized some form of participation, and the impetus toward workplace transformation had diffused widely through the U.S. economy.[4] The changes ranged from suggestion programs to quality circles and other small group schemes that actively solicit workers' ideas about how to improve production processes to team concept systems, which organize workers into small groups that rotate jobs and work together to improve productivity and quality on an ongoing basis. All these initiatives were designed to promote trust and improve communication between management and labor, in the name of efficiency and enhanced international competitiveness.

One of the most dramatic experiments occurred at a GM-Toyota joint venture in Fremont, California, called New United Motors Manufacturing, Inc. (NUMMI), which attracted enormous attention throughout the industry in the mid-1980s when it achieved productivity and quality ratings comparable to those of Toyota plants in Japan. Under the terms of the joint venture, which began operating in 1984, Toyota managers were responsible for running the factory, but the production workforce was drawn entirely from the ranks of former GM employees (and UAW members) who had worked at the same plant before GM closed it in 1982. NUMMI demonstrated unequivocally that the team-concept-based Toyota production system could be successfully transplanted to the United States, and the plant rapidly became a showcase within the industry, inspiring widespread imitation among auto producers throughout the United States (and, eventually, worldwide). NUMMI's success also led to a shift in emphasis within GM, whose efforts at internal transformation earlier in the 1980s had primarily involved massive capital investment in robotics and other new technologies. NUMMI was actually relatively low tech, and its spectacular debut led to growing recognition of the importance of worker participation for raising productivity.[5]

GM's second success story is the Saturn plant in Spring Hill, Tennessee, which began building cars in 1990 as an independent subsidiary (wholly owned by GM) with worker participation at all levels of decision making. Saturn emerged from a special agreement between the UAW and GM, signed in 1985, to launch an experiment in extensive labor-management cooperation. Saturn uses self-directed work teams like NUMMI's but extends the idea of "jointness" (GM-UAW lingo for labor-management cooperation) even further, involving worker representatives in long-range corporate planning, as well as relations with dealers, suppliers, and stockholders. Saturn teams do their own hiring and develop their own policies for such matters as absenteeism. Team leaders are elected, and traditional supervisors are nonexistent.[6]

Such organizational innovations signaled a historic break with previous industrial practices. Both the Taylorist organization of work in the auto industry and the system of labor relations that developed around it were predicated on the idea that the interests of management and those of workers were fundamentally in conflict. However, at plants like NUMMI and Saturn, management discarded this assumption, redefining its interests as best served by *cooperation* with the workforce. The motivation here, of course, was far from altruistic: for management, the goal of worker participation is precisely to increase productivity and quality by mobilizing workers' own knowledge of the labor process and by increasing their motivation to work and thus their commitment to the firm.

Despite the UAW's long tradition of adversarialism, the union's national leadership, faced with unprecedented job losses in the industry and the threat of more to come, has been an enthusiastic partner in both the NUMMI and Saturn efforts, as well as in more modest participatory programs elsewhere. The union leaders justify their cooperative stance to an often skeptical rank and file by arguing that resistance to change would merely prevent the domestic auto industry from becoming internationally competitive, which in turn would mean further job losses. Once the union leadership won job security provisions protecting those members affected by technological change—like the jobs bank and the buyout program discussed in the last chapter—it also welcomed management's investment in technological modernization, hoping the resulting changes would help the Big Three meet the challenge of foreign competition. Local unionists applied the same logic to their individual plants, each of which was struggling to survive in the face of the domestic industry's massive overcapacity. "The new technology was a necessary evil," a UAW officer at GM-Linden asserted. "Those plants that do not have technology today are in fear of losing their plants altogether, because of GM's excess capacity." Classification mergers, teams, and worker participation schemes were more controversial among local unionists, but the national UAW leadership has embraced these too, again in the name of enhancing the domestic industry's competitiveness.

Many academic commentators portray the innovations in technology and industrial relations that the auto industry (among others) undertook in the 1980s in extremely positive terms. The most extravagant claims come from a team at the Massachusetts Institute of Technology (MIT), made up of James P. Womack, Daniel T. Jones, and Daniel Roos. Their best-selling book, *The Machine That Changed the World,* popularized the term "lean production" to describe the system first perfected by Toyota in Japan and later transplanted successfully to NUMMI (as well as to several nonunion Japanese-owned auto plants established in the United States during the 1980s). "Lean producers employ teams of multiskilled workers at all levels of the organization and use highly flexible, increasingly automated machines to produce volumes of products in enormous variety," they write.[7] Although their research did not include any direct examination of the impact of this system on workers, the MIT team argues that lean production is a vast improvement on traditional Fordist mass production:

While the mass-production plant is often filled with mind-numbing stress, as workers struggle to assemble unmanufacturable products and have no way to improve their working environment, lean production offers a creative tension in which workers have many ways to address challenges. This creative tension involved in solving complex problems is precisely what has separated manual factory work from professional "think" work in the age of mass production. . . . Lean production is a superior way for humans to make things.

It provides better products in wider variety at lower cost. Equally important, it provides more challenging and fulfilling work for employees at every level, from the factory to headquarters. It follows that the whole world should adopt lean production, and as quickly as possible.[8]

While few have matched the hyperbole of the MIT team, many other commentators have expressed optimism about the potential for improvement in the experience of routine work offered by new technologies and reorganized work systems that institutionalize employee participation. New production technologies, they argue, hold the promise of eliminating the most boring and dangerous jobs, while upgrading the skill levels of those that remain. In this view, new technology potentially offers auto workers something the UAW has never been able to provide: an end to the deadening monotony of repetitive, de-skilled work. Similarly, participative programs like Japanese-style quality circles, employee involvement, and teams are widely depicted as a means of work humanization, complementing the new technology. By building on workers' own knowledge of the production process, the argument goes, participation enhances both efficiency and the quality of work experience.

Computer-based technologies, in this view, are fundamentally different from earlier waves of industrial innovation. Whereas in the past, automation involved the use of "dedicated" (special-purpose) machinery to perform specific functions previously done manually, the new information-based technologies are flexible, allowing a single machine to be adapted to a variety of specific tasks. As Shoshana Zuboff points out, these new technologies often require workers to use "intellective" skills. Workers no longer simply manipulate tools and other tangible objects but also must respond to abstract, electronically presented information. For this reason, Zuboff suggests, computer technology offers the possibility of a radical break with the Taylorist tradition of work organization that industries like auto manufacturing perfected long ago, moving instead toward more skilled and rewarding jobs, and toward workplaces where learning is encouraged and rewarded. "Learning is the new form of labor," she declares.[9] Larry Hirschhorn, another influential commentator on new technology, has a similar view. In the computerized factory, he writes, "the deskilling process is reversed. Machines extend workers' skill rather than replace it."[10]

Like the new technologies with which they are often associated, worker participation programs offer the potential for a new era of work humanization and industrial democracy. Michael Piore and Charles Sabel, in a highly influential book published over a decade ago, *The Second Industrial Divide,* argue that the Fordist mass production system has become less and less viable, thanks to the growth of increasingly specialized markets and new information technologies. They point to an emergent system of "flexible specialization" that "opens up long-term prospects for improvement in the condition of working life." While admitting that the transition to this new system may involve a severe loss in union power, they claim that workers would still gain: "Mass production is least attractive on the shop floor. . . . [It] invites an adversarial, hierarchical relation between workers and managers, and among the different units of an organization. Mass production's extreme division of labor routinizes and thereby trivializes work to a degree that often degrades the people who perform it. By contrast, flexible specialization is predicated on collaboration. And the frequent changes in the production process put a premium on craft skills. Thus the production worker's intellectual participation in the work process is enhanced—and his or her role revitalized."[11] Piore and Sabel are hopeful that these changes will help to humanize and democratize work, and they urge organized labor to "shake its attachment to increasingly indefensible forms of shop-floor control," so as not to impede such progress. They specifically applaud the UAW for its willingness to experiment with classification mergers and worker participation.[12]

As computer-based technology and organizational reform have transformed more and more workplaces, claims like these have won widespread public acceptance. They are, indeed, the basis for labor market projections that suggest a technologically driven decline in demand for unskilled labor and the need for educational upgrading to produce future generations of workers capable of functioning in the factory and office of the computer age. Yet it is far from clear that the reality of industrial work—outside of a few highly visible showcases like NUMMI and Saturn—is actually changing in the ways that this optimistic scenario suggests. Robert Thomas's more agnostic view seems closer to the mark: "New technologies may appear (and be perceived) as exogenous drivers of organizational change, but there is nothing automatic about the effects of technology on organization."

This perspective is supported by the evidence from GM-Linden, which exposes formidable obstacles to the far-reaching change that commentators like Zuboff, Hirschhorn, or Piore and Sabel project. As Thomas observes from his own case studies, "[M]any of the 'new age' ideas about participatory work structures, flexible specialization, and the like have yet to reach those who are supposed to be designing 'new age' technology."[13] Indeed, despite the diffusion of new technologies and participatory rhetoric, many workplaces have changed their internal organizational structures only marginally, if at all. As Eileen Appelbaum and Rosemary Batt report in their exhaustive 1994 study of workplace reforms, "Despite the reported gains in performance and the apparent acceleration of experiments with innovative practices, the overwhelming majority of U.S. workplaces are traditionally managed."[14]

Several critics have pointed out that even at NUMMI, Saturn, and other workplaces where participation has been institutionalized in a serious way, the rhetoric of worker control masks the fact that employee involvement, classification reductions, and team systems are first and foremost *management* control strategies. Rejecting the equation of participation with workplace democracy, for example, Guillermo Grenier suggests that workers participate in the work process "much as slaves participated in slavery—as captives of an economic and social structure beyond their control."[15] Similarly, Mike Parker and Jane Slaughter's influential critique of the team concept in the auto industry argues that, far from offering a humane alternative to Taylorism, "whether through team meetings, quality circles, or suggestion plans . . . the little influence workers do have over their jobs is that in effect they are organized to time-study themselves in a kind of super-Taylorism."[16] They condemn the UAW's cooperation with the team concept and other forms of worker participation as a betrayal of the union membership. For these authors, if such a system benefits management and "the bottom line," the idea that it might also be good for workers is anathema.

Workers themselves, however, are remarkably enthusiastic about the idea of participating in decision-making processes historically monopolized by management. For many, this prospect has intrinsic appeal, especially compared to traditional American managerial methods—even when participation is restricted to a narrow arena, such as helping to streamline the production process or otherwise raise productivity. Although Parker and Slaughter downplay it, even they acknowledge that at NUMMI "nobody says they want to return to the days when GM ran the plant."[17] Similarly, at plants like GM-Linden, workers often complain about management's failure to live up to its own stated principles, but they explicitly endorse the *concept* of participation. Unless one believes that auto workers are simply naive victims of managerial manipulation, the team concept's enormous popularity with the NUMMI workforce and the appeal of participatory rhetoric elsewhere suggest that lean production and other workplace reforms—even though their main purpose is to serve the needs of management—do offer some positive benefits to labor.

Indeed, the boundless alienation auto workers have long felt meant that when the postwar capital-labor accord finally collapsed under the weight of international competition in the 1980s, and GM began to experiment with new ways of organizing work and with participatory forms of management, the workforce was willing and eager to go along. The initiative for change had to come from above, however, since under the terms of the accord forged so many years before, management alone had the right to organize production. As it became apparent that the system that had served GM so well for decades was no longer viable, there was no question that *workers* could be induced to accept the idea of change—they hated the status quo so desperately that they could be persuaded to try almost anything.

Paradoxically, however, despite its potential for improving productivity and for enhancing worker satisfaction, workplace transformation has proved an elusive goal in many U.S. auto plants. The NUMMI and Saturn success stories have not been easily reproduced elsewhere. More common is a situation like the one at GM-Linden, where top management makes the decision to move toward a reformed workplace organization without much input from the key players. Changing the behavior of shop-floor management, and especially of first-line supervisors—behavior that is deeply embedded both in individuals and in the organizational traditions they have built up over the years—has proved extremely difficult.

Organizational changes like the team concept or merging job classifications do not achieve their intended effects if they are imposed in a mechanical fashion, without genuine commitment from shop-floor managers and without winning the trust of the workforce. This is the likely explanation for the findings from a study of 53 plants in one of the largest U.S. auto companies, which uncovered—to the researchers' surprise—an *inverse* relationship between the use of teams and productivity: "Greater use of team systems in this company has led to substantially *higher* labor hours and more supervisors. We found no evidence that plants with fewer production worker job classifications performed better. The absence of positive results from adopting work teams and reducing production worker job classifications was particularly striking in light of the fact that a number of auto and other companies have recently invested so much effort in shifting to these kinds of work practices" (emphasis added).[18]

All too often, as at GM-Linden, the rhetoric of participation has been introduced without adequate measures to assure its actual implementation. While no one plant is entirely typical of the industry, the experience of GM-Linden workers with new technology and workplace reform is far more representative of GM, and of the Big Three generally, than the NUMMI or Saturn cases, which have attracted such disproportionate attention. We now turn to a detailed discussion of the changes, both technological and organizational, that were introduced at Linden in the mid-1980s, and the obstacles they encountered.[19]

The Linden Changeover, 1985–1986

During the year-long shutdown that began in September 1985, nearly half a century after the plant first opened, the Linden plant was transformed into a showcase of GM's progress toward state-of-the-art manufacturing technology. At a cost of over $300 million, the plant was completely overhauled, with computer technology installed to monitor and integrate all production operations. When the plant reopened, it had 219 robots, 113 automated guided vehicles (AGVs) to carry the car bodies through the assembly process, and 186 programmable logic controllers (PLCs) to program the robots. Before the modernization, Linden had only 1 robot, no AGVs, and 8 PLCs.[20]

The most extensive changes occurred in the body shop, where almost 90 percent of the robots and all the AGVs were located. Whereas before the changeover, workers had used handheld welding guns to join the car bodies together, now nearly all the welding was done by robots or other automatic equipment. Workers watched from a distance as the AGVs and the robots interacted electronically; a host computer monitored the process and alerted operators to problems. Linden also was the first GM plant to use lasers in the body shop, both for checking alignments and for welding. The laser inspection system increased precision and allowed for more rigorous quality control.

The paint shop was also modernized, with 12 new robots to seal the cars against exhaust or water leaks, a process previously done manually. New automatic sprayers were installed to paint the car bodies (although this process had been automated before, the equipment was updated), and robots were added for installing and sealing the windshield and back window. In the trim and chassis departments, there were no robots, and the changes were less dramatic; but some of the least desirable jobs were eliminated with the changeover. For example, in the past, many chassis workers had been stationed in hot, uncomfortable "pits" underneath the assembly line; now these extremely unpopular positions were done away with, and the line itself was elevated instead. Other changes made some of the trim and chassis jobs less arduous. For example, on several operations, computer-controlled torque guns were installed, held by articulating arms, reducing the physical effort required.

Some analysts have criticized GM's investment in new technology during the 1980s as a quick fix, throwing vast sums of money at the crisis of international competitiveness without seriously revamping the firm's organizational structure or its management strategies to make the most efficient possible use of the new equipment. As Maryann Keller put it in 1986, "The goal of all the technology push has been to get rid of hourly workers. GM thought in terms of automation rather than replacing the current system with a better system."[21] The technology was meant to replace workers, not to transform work. This criticism seems justified in that often the technology was introduced without much thought given to job redesign. But, contrary to the fear of massive job displacement that is so often associated with new technology, it eliminated a surprisingly small number of jobs.

Certainly at GM-Linden, there were many fewer jobs after the 1985–1986 changeover than before, as table 6 shows. But the employment losses directly linked to the new technology were relatively modest. Even without the plant modernization, a drastic reduction in jobs would have occurred with the change in product: the Chevrolet Corsicas and Berettas made at Linden after 1986 were much smaller than the Cadillacs and other large luxury-car models built at the plant earlier, and had only about one-third the number of parts.[22] The number of skilled-trades workers actually *rose* after the changeover, reflecting

TABLE 6.   Employment at GM-Linden before and after the 1985–1986 Changeover, by Category

	Before[a]	*After*[b]	*Percent Change*
Production workers	4,629	3,110	-33
Body shop	568	385	-32
Paint shop	681	520	-24
Trim department	1,385	779	-44
Chassis department	1,020	755	-26
Inspection	425	177	-58
Other	550	494	-10
Skilled-trades workers	235	425	+81
First-line supervisors[c]	156	90	-42
Other salaried workers	608	437	-28

SOURCE: Data supplied by GM-Linden plant management.
[a]For production workers and salaried workers, August 1985; for first-line supervisors, July 1985; for skilled-trades workers, September 1984.
[b]For production workers and skilled-trades workers, December 1987; for first-line supervisors, July 1988; for salaried workers, August 1987.
[c]Includes foremen, but not superintendents, production coordinators, or other shop-floor managers.

the greater maintenance demands of the new technology. Nonetheless, there were sharp employment declines for production workers, first-line supervisors, and salaried workers.

In the body and paint shops combined, there were about 350 fewer jobs after the changeover than before. It is probably safe to assume that these employment losses were due primarily to the new technology, which was highly concentrated in those two departments. But these 350 jobs account for less than one-fourth of the total employment decline (1,519 jobs) among GM-Linden production workers. The bulk of the job losses were in the plant's trim and chassis departments, where nearly 900 jobs were eliminated. While the new technology played some role here, in these departments the main job killer was the dramatic reduction in the number of parts used in the Chevrolets relative to the previous car models built at Linden. Another important factor was the shift from producing some components in-house to purchasing them from outside vendors, what industry insiders call outsourcing. For example, until 1985, the plant built seats for use in the luxury cars it assembled; after the changeover, GM closed the "cushion room" where this operation had been located, and the seats were trucked in by an outside supplier.

The changing employment levels shown in table 6 also reflect organizational reforms introduced at Linden after the changeover. Although far more modest than the lean production system used at NUMMI and some other plants, the Linden reforms did depart from traditional practices in several respects. Perhaps most important, now GM-Linden workers were instructed to consistently complete their assigned tasks in their own work station. Just before the plant reopened, the local union and management agreed that: "[T]he new process is aimed at world class quality. The new process also results in changes in some traditional processes. Under this concept operators will be expected to push the Stop-the-line button whenever they are unable to meet the job requirements of their operation. After having pushed the button the operator is expected to effectuate the proper completion of his job assignment. . . . At the same time, it is intended that a utility operator . . . [will] respond to the line stop with the supervisor and aid in the resolution of the problem."[23] This was the build-in-station concept: that quality is enhanced when a job is done properly the first time by the person who routinely performs it. Now any worker could stop the line to address a production problem on the spot; in the past, this had been strictly forbidden, and problems had been tagged for later attention from repair workers. The idea underlying this change was that if production workers were given greater responsibility, both quality and productivity would increase.

Although as I will show, the practical effectiveness of these innovations was limited by the actions of first-line supervisors, their introduction probably does explain the sharp decline in the number of inspection workers shown in table 6, as well as the more modest decline in the supervisor-worker ratio (from about 1 supervisor for every 32 hourly workers before the changeover to 1 for every 40 afterward). Other innovations associated with the changeover also contributed to job losses. The introduction of the just-in-time parts delivery systems eliminated many jobs involved in handling and distributing parts from the plant's internal inventory, although many of these jobs would have disappeared in any event due to the dramatic reduction in the number of parts used in the smaller car models. (Such inventory-related work accounts for the bulk of the production workers categorized as "Other" in table 6.) Also, whereas before the changeover, production workers were often assigned to repair defective parts, the new practice was to return such parts to the suppliers, so that far fewer repair workers were needed in-house. And the plant shifted from "tag relief," a system in which workers take their breaks sequentially and are temporarily replaced by a floating relief worker while they do so, to "mass relief," in which everyone takes breaks at the same time. The advantage of the latter is that it ensures consistency in the worker who performs any given operation, presumably enhancing the quality of the end product. But this change also led to the wholesale elimination of the relief classifications, which employed hundreds of workers before the changeover.

The number of contractual job classifications was also reduced following the plant modernization. The three-year agreement between the local union and GM that took effect in October 1984 (which was negotiated after plans for the changeover had been announced) listed 167 job classifications: 137 for production workers and 30 for the skilled trades. Such complex systems are often seen as an obstacle to flexibility and are anathema to advocates of lean production. Even in 1984, however, over a third of the GM-Linden classifications existed only on paper: that is, no workers were actually employed in the listed jobs. By 1987, only 62 production and 15 skilled-trades classifications were populated. The new local union agreement that took effect in October of that year reflected this reality, listing only 82 classifications: 60 for production workers and 22 for skilled-trades workers.[24]

Compared with NUMMI, which has 1 production classification and 2 for skilled trades, the 1987 Linden contract is relatively traditional. However, by late 1987, nearly three-fourths of GM-Linden production workers (72 percent) were concentrated in only 8 classifications, and fully a third were in the 2 largest classifications. This is a substantial change from the prechangeover situation, when the 8 largest classifications accounted for less than half (48 percent) of all production workers, and the 2 largest, for less than a fourth.[25] Such consolidation did not take place in the skilled trades, although there was a dramatic increase in the number of skilled electricians, since this classification was used for nearly all the newly hired robot-repair workers and related personnel.

New Technology and the Skill Question

Although Zuboff, Hirschhorn, and others have argued that new technologies of the sort introduced at Linden should lead to a general upgrading of the workforce skill levels, the lack of any effort to alter the long-standing division of labor between skilled-trades and production workers made such an outcome unlikely. With the introduction of robotics and other computer-based technologies, the relative size of the skilled-trades workforce did increase: from 5 percent of the total hourly workforce before the changeover to 12 percent afterward. In that sense, one might say that technological modernization led to upgrading in the skill levels of the plant's workforce.[26] But for the 88 percent of GM-Linden's hourly employees classified as production workers after the changeover, skill levels had either stayed the same or decreased. Indeed, at this plant, the new technology magnified existing skill differentials among workers, leading to skill *polarization* rather than the sort of across-the-board upgrading Zuboff or Hirschhorn would have predicted.[27] After the modernization, the skilled-trades workers did enjoy massive skill upgrading and gained higher levels of responsibility. But the much larger group of production workers, whose jobs had always been extremely routinized, experienced still further de-skilling and found themselves increasingly subordinated to and controlled by the new technology.

The skilled tradespeople were enthusiastic about the plant modernization. "They were anxiously awaiting the new technology," electrician Richard Raguso recalled. "It was like a kid with a new toy. Everyone wanted to know what was going to happen." Charlie Ferraro agreed: "The robotics, it's something to behold! Like if you went to Epcot in Florida—it's that awesome." In the course of the changeover, the skilled-trades workforce learned how to maintain and repair the robots, AGVs, and other new equipment. Since the new technology was far more complex than what it replaced, these already highly trained individuals acquired many new skills. They received extensive new training, especially in robotics and in the use of computers. To become intimately familiar with the maintenance needs of the new equipment, some of them traveled to the plants where the robots and other computerized machinery were built. GM-Linden's skilled-trades workers reported a median of 48 days of technical training in connection with the changeover, and some received far more.[28] Many came away from the training feeling confident about their employment security. "If this plant closed tomorrow and I was forced to go out into the job market, I have something special to offer that I didn't have five years ago," machine repairman John Adams said. "The products might vary, but there are many other industries that are going into robotics, PLCs, automation, so my lifestyle will be able to be maintained."

With all the new technical knowledge skilled workers acquired came a heightened sense of responsibility. "You push the wrong button, you make a big fat mistake, you can cause a disaster!" exclaimed toolmaker Lou Franklin. In addition, there were daunting safety hazards associated with the new equipment. "If you don't take the right precautions, you can get seriously hurt," union committeeman Ben Prindle said. "A robot has no conscience. If it goes into working mode and you're there, it's going to hurt you." One of the victims was Max Funk:

I got three stitches in my head. A robot came down on top of me. And I almost lost a finger another time. Some other people really got hurt badly; they were out maybe six, seven weeks. We had one guy in there who got fifty-two stitches in his hands. But nobody got killed.

There's one machine, the lay-down side frame, that has twenty-eight robots on it. It lifts up the car bodies and transfers them from one station to the next, and automatically, all the robots will come in. The computer, the PLC, has a switch that's called STATION HOLD. If you put that switch on, it shuts the robots off; the robots can't come in. So this guy that I was working with, when it said STATION HOLD, he thought that nothing was going to happen. But when he went inside the line, the track started moving, traveling like fifty feet a second. He's lucky to be alive!

That machine is the most feared piece of equipment in the plant. Anytime they want somebody to do something, they threaten to transfer them to the side frame. We've thought about bringing in a live chicken, maybe once a week, and just throwing it into the machine, you know, to satisfy the side-frame god.

Despite their heightened consciousness of danger, most of the skilled-trades workers were pleased by the results of the changeover. They described their work as more challenging and intellectually demanding than before. "When the robots came," electrician Christopher Kuczynski explained, "it was a little more interesting. Before, you'd repair things, but you didn't have to use your head; you'd just change a fuse. You were like a robot yourself. Later on, you were a little more in control because they had to come to you. It took more knowledge." Peter Finney, another electrician, was more enthusiastic: "We're responsible for programming the robots, troubleshooting the robots, wiping their noses, cleaning them, whatever. It's interesting work. We're doing something that very few people in the world are doing, troubleshooting and repairing robots. It's terrific! I don't think this can be boring, because there are so many things involved. There are things happening right now that we haven't ever seen before. Every day there's something different. We're always learning about the program, always changing things to make them better—every single day." Moreover, some skilled workers found that the traditional boundaries of their trade had been made obsolete by the new technology, leading them to learn some of the skills traditionally monopolized by others. As John Adams explained:

With high technology, skilled tradespeople are being forced to learn other peoples' trades in order to do their trade better. Like with me, I have to understand that controller and how it works in order to make sure the robot will work the way it's supposed to. You have to know the whole system. You can't just say, "I work on that one little gear box. I don't give a damn about what the rest of the machine does." You have to have a knowledge of everything you work with and everything that is related to it, whether you want to or not. You got to know pneumatics, hydraulics—all the trades. Everything is so interrelated and connected. You can't be narrow minded anymore.

However, the situation was quite different for production workers. Their jobs continued to involve extremely repetitive, machine-paced, unskilled or semiskilled work. Far from being required to learn new skills, many found their jobs simplified or further de-skilled by the new technology. As Tom Miller, a trim department worker with nineteen years' seniority, commented in 1988: "It does make it easier to an extent, but at the same time, they figure, 'Well, I'm giving you a computer and it's going to make your job faster, so instead of you doing this, this, and this, I'm going to have you do this and eight other things, because the time I'm saving you on the first three, you're going to make it up on the last.' Right now I'm doing more work in less time, the company's benefiting, and I am bored to death—more bored than before!" Many others agreed that while the work was physically less strenuous, they were expected to work at a more rapid pace than before the new technology was introduced. "It makes me work faster," Alan Stanley complained. "Let's face it, General Motors didn't spend $300 million to make it easier for me. They wanted to make me more productive. That's what it comes down to." Indeed, the perception of increased efficiency was widespread. In a 1988 in-plant survey, 67 percent of GM-Linden production workers responding said the plant was run more efficiently after the changeover, while only 7 percent said it was run less efficiently.[29] "Before, there was a lot more waste in the plant, you got away with a lot more, and there were a lot of extra people running around," Matthew Larson said. "Now there's less people not doing anything. They mostly utilize everybody that's in the plant."

In the body shop, where most of the robots and other new technology were located, there was a sharp increase in injury rates immediately following the changeover.[30] "A lot of guys are getting whacked up; a lot of guys are getting caught and banged up pretty good," Jack Giordano reported. But in every other respect, working conditions in the body shop improved dramatically with the changeover. "Before it was terrible; it was the dirtiest place," Matthew Larson recalled. "It was filthy over there. Now they have to keep it real clean 'cause of the computers." Max Funk agreed: "The old body shop was filthy. There's one section they called the jungle; it had all these welding guns hanging down, and the pollution was horrible with the fumes. It was really bad. Now with the new setup, it's a tremendous improvement." And Jeffrey Goetz exclaimed, "It's like a total turnaround. We used to wear a helmet like Diver Dan, have air piped in; we'd have gloves on up to here. The conditions have drastically improved. It's like night and day. Now everybody's looking to get into the body shop."

Despite the improvement in working conditions, however, most production workers in the high-tech body shop did not experience skill upgrading. On the contrary, de-skilling was widely reported. "The jobs are real easy over there now," Matthew Larson said. "Most of the guys just have buttons to push for loading up stuff, and robots do it." And George Karas, who had worked in the body shop for a total of sixteen years at the time he was interviewed, reported that his job was de-skilled:

I'm working in assembly. I'm feeding the line, the right-side panel, the whole right side of the car. Myself and a fellow worker, in the same spot. Now all we do, actually, is put pieces in, push the buttons, and what they call a shuttle picks up whatever we put on and takes it down the line to be welded. Before the changeover, my job was completely different. I was a torch solderer. And I had to solder the roof, you know, the joint of the roof with the side panel. I could use my head more. I liked it more. Because, you know, when you have your mind in it also, it's more interesting. And not too many fellow workers could do the job. You had to be precise, because you had to put only so much material, lead, on the job.

Despite this, few workers mourned these changes in the body shop, which was easily the plant's most unpleasant department before the plant modernization. Mike Evans strongly favored the introduction of robots there: "I don't think human beings should have to do this work," he said, "because of the health effects." Most workers seemed to agree with this.

In other departments, where the technological change was less dramatic, production workers also reported stable or declining levels of skill, rather than the skill upgrading predicted by Hirschhorn and Zuboff. Even when they used computers—a rarity for production workers—they typically did so in a highly routinized way. "There is nothing that really takes any skill to operate a computer," Tom Wasson, a production worker in the plant's final inspection area, reported. "You just punch in the numbers; the screen will tell you what to do: it will tell you when to race the engine, and when to turn the air-conditioner off, when to do everything. Everything comes right up on the screen. It's very simple."

Not only were some of the more demanding and relatively skilled production jobs—like soldering, welding, and painting car bodies—automated out of existence, but also many relatively desirable off-the-line jobs were eliminated by organizational changes other than the new technology itself. The shift to a smaller, less complex car model destroyed many subassembly jobs, always considered good jobs because their pace was not controlled by the assembly line. Outsourcing also eliminated subassembly jobs. "Before, there was more people working subassembly, assembling parts," Tom Wasson remarked. "Now they just come—the radiators come in, and you just put them on the car." In addition, the shift from tag to mass relief eliminated at one stroke the relief classification, which had demanded the ability to perform a large number of different jobs, and was thus inherently more skilled. The number of production workers assigned to inspection and repair jobs also fell with the new policy of sending defective components back to the vendor rather than repairing them in the plant as was done before. As Tom Miller explained: "On my particular job, they took a skill away from me. I used to do electrical repair, which I'm still basically doing. But now they don't want us to find the problem; they want us to 'isolate the problem.' If a part is bad, remove and replace it, and we'll send it back to the vendor and let him rectify it. So if I have a bad wire harness in my dashboard, I have to scrap the whole thing and send it back to the vendor. The computer says it's not good; ship it back to where it came from, the vendor, and put a new one on. It's better I guess for quality, but they're basically taking my skill away from me. I'm not a repair man or a specialist; I'm just a parts changer." On the whole, most production workers agreed with Tony Stefano, a trim department veteran, who commented sadly, "In the last model [Cadillac], I had the feeling it was more craftsmanship than building this kind of car. This is all impersonal machines, you know, very little hands-on craftsmanship. These units are flying down the line real fast."

Not only was the number of desirable jobs reduced as a result of the various technological and organizational changes introduced in the plant, but because so many low-seniority workers took the buyout and no new production workers were being hired, it took much longer than before to work one's way up the seniority ladder to a better job. "You have some of the old-timers working on the line right now," lamented trim worker Steve Pawlowski. "Before, if you had more se-niority, you were, let's say, in subassembly, off the line. Now you need forty years' seniority to get off the line, with fewer people working and some of the better jobs eliminated." Jonathan Fox was among those who were effectively demoted. "For me, it was worse [after the changeover] because I'd had that off-the-line repair job, and you couldn't do any better than that," he recalled. "So I wound up on the line again." Again, the production workers' situation in this respect contrasts sharply to that of the skilled trades. Many new trades work-ers were hired as a result of the changeover, and relatively young skilled workers gained access to extremely desirable jobs working with the most modern industrial technology in the world.

These impressions of skill polarization between the skilled-trades and production workers are verified by the findings of an in-plant sur-vey conducted at GM-Linden in 1988. Skilled-trades workers, asked about the importance of 12 specific on-the-job skills to their jobs before and after the plant was modernized, reported that all but 1 (physical strength) increased in importance. Despite the small sample size ($N = 52$), the reported increases were statistically significant for

5 of the skills measured, as table 7 shows. In contrast, a simultaneous survey of the plant's production workers, asking about the importance of a similar list of skills found that all 12 declined in importance after the introduction of the new technology. As table 7 shows, the decline was statistically significant for 8 of the 12 skills measured.[31] The survey also found that boredom levels had increased significantly for production workers: 45 percent stated that their work after the changeover was boring and monotonous "often" or "all the time," compared to 35 percent who indicated that this was the case before the changeover. Similarly, 96 percent of production workers said that they now do the same task over and over again "often" or "all the time," up from 79 percent who said they did so before.[32]

TABLE 7. Percentage of Skilled-Trades and Production Workers for Whom Skills Shown Were "Very Important" to Their Jobs, before and after the Changeover

Skill	Skilled-Trades Workers (N = 52)		Production Workers (N = 217)	
	Before	After	Before	After
Knowing about tools and machines	79	85	47	35***
Memory	56	81***	63	42***
Accuracy/precision	46	73***	71	63*
Problem solving	52	73***	51	36***
Judgment	69	71	57	47***
Ability to communicate clearly	48	60*	46	38**
Concentration	42	60**	58	48***
Speed	31	37	59	57
Reading/spelling	23	31	17	14
Knowledge of math	17	19	8	6
Physical strength	21	15	41	34*
Creativity	31	40	na	na
Knowing how your department works	na	na	51	36***

SOURCE: In-plant surveys conducted by the author and Cydney Pullman.
*p < .10; **p < .05; ***p < .01; using one-tailed paired t-tests.

The GM-Linden modernization, then, had opposite effects on skilled-trades and production workers. Underlying this pattern of polarization was the crucial fact that no significant job redesign was attempted in tandem with the introduction of robotics and other new computerized equipment. Most important, the boundary between skilled trades and production work was maintained, despite the radical technological change. While management could have chosen (and the union might have agreed) to transfer some tasks from the skilled trades to production workers, such as minor machine maintenance, or to redesign jobs more extensively in keeping with the potential of the new technology, this was never seriously attempted at Linden. Engineers limited their efforts to conventional "line balancing," which simply involves packaging tasks among individual production jobs to minimize the idle time of any given worker. In this respect, the engineers treated the new technology very much like older forms of machinery. As production worker Joyce Cowley, who took the buyout in a later round, remarked, "It was new jobs—it was all new—but it was still the same way of working." The fundamental division of labor between production workers and those in skilled trades persisted despite the massive infusion of new technology, and this organizational continuity led to the intensification of the existing skill polarization within the plant.

GM-Linden appears to be typical of U.S. auto assembly plants in that new technology has been introduced without jobs being fundamentally redesigned or the traditional division of labor altered between production and skilled-trades workers. Even where significant changes in the organization of labor—such as flexible teams—have been introduced, as at NUMMI or the new Japanese transplants, they typically involve rotating workers over a series of conventionally deskilled production jobs, rather than changing the basic nature of the work. While being able to perform eight or ten unskilled jobs, rather than only one, might be considered skill upgrading in some narrow technical sense, it hardly fits the glowing accounts of commentators who claim that with new technology, in Hirschhorn's words, "the deskilling process is reversed." Rather it might be characterized best as "flexible Taylorism" or "Toyotism."[33] Perhaps work in the auto industry *could* be reorganized in the ways Zuboff and Hirschhorn envision if not for the enormous bureaucratic inertia on the management side, for which GM in particular is legendary. This proved a problem at Linden not only in regard to the skill effects of the new technology but also in the human relations arena, despite some serious efforts to introduce change.

Jointness and the "New Linden"

If GM-Linden production workers did not gain (and in many cases lost) skills after the changeover, they might still have benefited from the opportunity to be more involved in areas of decision making traditionally reserved for management. Indeed, several explicitly participatory programs were introduced at the plant in the course of the changeover. A few years earlier, a quality of work life program that briefly existed in the plant had been abandoned in the face of widespread criticism from the local union, and UAW Local 595 had expressed strong opposition to the team concept introduced at other GM plants during this period. Perhaps this is why GM did not attempt to introduce teamwork at Linden, choosing instead to put in place more modest participatory structures. Elsewhere, however, GM did impose the team concept on reluctant workers, using the threat that it would simply close plants whose local unions refused to go along. These threats were highly credible, since the vast overcapacity in the industry meant that some plants would inevitably close, as every worker was keenly aware.

The impending modernization of the GM-Linden plant would appear to have made the 1984 local negotiations there a perfect opportunity for exactly this sort of managerial blackmail, yet GM made no serious effort to introduce teams at that time. GM-Linden unionists attributed this to Local 595's tradition of militancy and to the fact that, as one union official put it, "we were the only plant that was building the Cadillacs and Eldorados and Rivieras at the time [1984,] and we were in a better bargaining posture." A high-level GM-Linden management official confirmed that fear of union resistance was one factor in the decision not to force the plant to adopt the team concept. "Our management organization is not ready for it either," he stated. The team concept is "unquestionably the most efficient way to run a plant, but only *if* you can get the organization to buy into it." He went on to point out that traditionally organized plants could also be highly productive, a point that academic researchers have also documented.[34]

GM did, however, cultivate "jointness" at Linden. For example, the preface and introduction to the 1984 local union contract include the following language:

In our effort to make our work and workplace an example of the finest joint relationship we fully intend to:
   —establish effective lines of communication among all Linden employes [*sic*]

   —encourage participation of all employes [*sic*] who desire to become involved

   —strive for expeditious resolution of mutual problems

   —treat all employes [*sic*] with dignity and respect

   —stress courtesy and consideration in all business transactions

   —recognize the contributions of each individual . . .

Linden management and the Local Union sincerely believe that the interests of the employer and the employe [*sic*] are basically alike.[35]

A more substantive effort to cultivate jointness was the week-long, off-site ride-and-drive program involving members of the local union shop committee and a group of top plant managers in October 1985, shortly after the plant closed for the changeover. The group drove various cars—both GM models and those of the competition—and "looked within," as a management participant put it, to jointly identify problems in the plant and develop strategies to solve them. Later, the off-site experience was offered to lower-level managers and union officials. "They played games, Tinkertoys and everything, to work on their minds and explain the new philosophy. They also fed them, and they even went as far as having an open bar at the end," unionist Tom Barbarro explained. The program lasted for a week, and participants received full pay. "You'd hear everyone bragging, 'Hey, that's all right, getting paid,' " Barbarro recalled.

During the initial, top-level off-site program, the union and management officials present began planning a jointly sponsored 80-hour orientation for the hourly workforce as they returned to the plant after the modernization. They also agreed to introduce Employee Involvement Groups (EIGs) for production workers at the end of the changeover period, for a half hour during the lunch break once a week. Participation was voluntary, but workers who attended were paid overtime rates, and by 1988, about two-thirds of workers were coming regularly. Here workers were encouraged to express their ideas about how their work area could be made more efficient and to highlight production problems. Sometimes other types of problem-solving meetings were held in the postchangeover period as well. Management also increased its efforts to communicate with hourly workers, regularly distributing information to them about the auto industry and how Linden's performance compared with that of other plants. In another gesture toward hourly workers, the former cushion room (where car seats had once been assembled) was turned into a fitness center for workers to use at lunchtime and during breaks.

The more radical experiments in worker participation at NUMMI and Saturn included extensive efforts to eradicate the traditional distinction between management and worker—such managerial perquisites as a separate dining room and preferential parking spots were eliminated, everyone wore the same clothes, and foremen were replaced by team and group "leaders." At GM-Linden, there was little effort along these lines. A small number of desirable parking spots were opened up to workers who arrived early (a gesture facilitated by the substantial reduction in the size of the salaried workforce). But otherwise, supervision remained a world apart from blue-collar workers, with virtually all the traditional symbolic and material distinctions—from white shirts to separate dining facilities—preserved intact.

Still, the changes that did occur at Linden—the build-in-station concept, the shift to mass relief, the just-in-time inventory system, the consolidation of job classifications, the move toward jointness, and the EIG program, as well as the new technology itself—introduced key elements of lean production. Although far more modest than what occurred at NUMMI or Saturn, these reforms did constitute a real effort toward a more efficient and participatory system. This was the "new Linden" that workers who declined the buyout were told about in the 80-hour training program starting in the fall of 1986.

The 80-Hour Training Program

As they returned to the plant after the year-long changeover layoff, all production workers spent two forty-hour weeks in a special orientation program, developed by a group of hourly workers who had been jointly selected by the local union and management. Salaried managers attended a similar program for twenty hours a week for up to six weeks. (A few skilled-trades workers also went through the training, though most were not permitted to do so, because of the intense demand for their services in the immediate postchangeover period, when the new machinery needed constant attention.) The training curriculum included various components, ranging from a plant tour showcasing the robots and other new technology to a presentation on sexual harassment and equal opportunity to safety and fire-prevention sessions. Time was also spent familiarizing participants with such features of the "new Linden" as just-in-time, statistical process control, "problem-solving decision analysis," and quality issues. The entire last day for workers (and for managers the last twenty-hour week) focused on the build-in-station concept.

The single largest component of the training, and by far the most memorable for workers, dealt with the psychology of motivation. More than twenty of the eighty hours were devoted to a prepackaged motivational program from Louis E. Tice's Pacific Institute in Seattle, Washington; in addition, an entire day was devoted to interpersonal skills. The Tice program, called *Investment in Excellence,* was dedicated to the proposition that "human beings have an unlimited potential for growth." The local union shop chairman and a top-level plant manager had seen some of the Tice material on a visit to GM's Doraville, Georgia, plant, and they jointly suggested that it be presented at Linden. Two of the twelve hourly workers selected to run the 80-hour training program traveled to Seattle to become familiar with Tice's teachings in detail. At Linden, the Tice material was presented in the form of videotapes, followed by discussions facilitated by the trainers. Workers also were provided with a set of Tice audiocassette tapes to take home, with titles like *Relaxation and Stress Reduction, Staying on Track,* and *Motivating Yourself and Others.*

The program was designed to improve individuals' self-esteem through role-playing and other techniques. It included units titled *Possibility Thinking, Your Self-Image, Adjusting Attitudes to Reach Goals, How Self-Talk Builds the Self-Image, Change without Stress, Self-Esteem and Performance, Elevating Self-Esteem, Constructive and Restrictive Motivation*, and the like. Most of the material dealt with self-improvement and personal life issues, as these excerpts from one of the audiotapes illustrate:

All meaningful and lasting change starts first on the inside, and works its way out. You can get temporary change by controlling and forcing it from the outside in, but it isn't lasting change. . . .

You must look forward with warmth, or look forward with joy, or look forward with a feeling of accomplishment. Look forward safely, and as you look forward safely often enough, over and over, this time deliberately and intentionally, you're going to change your self-image. . . .

You can go out and creatively and innovatively change things and still keep what you have. But no longer will you be happy with the old status quo. As you visualize the new, you become discontent [ed] with the old. And that's what imagery does for you.[36]

"The people enjoyed it because it had nothing to do with the corporation," Brendan Cook, one of the hourly trainers who had visited Tice's Seattle institute, explained, adding: "It's strictly a personal thing. The whole point is that you can use it outside [GM] as well as inside. You know, if you've been here twenty or thirty years, you've gone through every training program conceivable, and this is the only one where you actually get something out of it. Not for the company, but for you. It's more like a self-realization program. It gets the potential that's underneath out, and instead of saying, 'I can't,' basically getting people to say, 'I can if I want to.' For a lot of people, Tice raised their self-respect."

Few GM-Linden workers had any previous exposure to the therapeutic culture that the Tice materials drew on, albeit in a somewhat crude form. "Everything that is in Tice is nothing new; it's been written in many books," Cook noted. "What Tice has done is put it together in a nice little package. Instead of reading fifteen books on psychology and motivation and all this, it's all in one place." Although the video and audio programs were not designed specifically for GM-

Linden, some portions did speak directly to the issue of management style. Tice sharply criticized the coercive approach to motivating people that GM had practiced for the previous half century:

That was an easy, easy way of motivating people. It's a way of getting people shaped up and lined up, to do the things I want them to do. See, what I'll do is, I'll show 'em what's going to happen if you don't. . . . So what we're really saying is, theologically, "Be good!" Not for goodness' sake, not for the glory, the possession of God, for doing right, but because if you don't, you're going to go to hell. . . . Now some of you run your companies that way. Fun, isn't it? Some of you run your whole life that way. Fun, isn't it? . . .

You interested in productivity in this outfit? How many supervisors, managers and leaders have you got pushing, coercing and trying to shove people into better performance? And do you know what you do? What? You get a countereffect. They slow down! An advantage of having this information is, you stop shoving people around and things go better. You can push 'em into absenteeism and being late if you want. . . . Procrastination, then slovenly work, is another reflex action. Coercive motivation. Slovenly work means, I will do work to the minimal requirement of this outfit and no better. How much do I need to do to get you to shut up? That's all I will do. . . . So if somebody has to come here, they will show up in body, but not in spirit or mind. . . .

So your employees who feel, your subordinates who feel pushed into a job or a goal, they not only take their own time, break the equipment down, sabotage so you need to redo over and over and over. "Well, I got this other thing I need to do, I got these other tasks I need to do, I got to get to the paperwork, I've got to make these phone calls, I—" Creative avoidance! . . .

Look around you. What kind of leadership do you have? Do you need new equipment? Do you need to dump more money into it? All you got to do is change the mentality of the leadership. But hey, don't fix the blame on the leaders. That's the way they were led. In the military, theologically, in schools, most of us were led, "shape up or else ship out." We don't have another style. How you going to get people to do things? You got people who want to, choose to, like it, love it. You've got to become an empathetic kind of a leader now. . . . You don't kick 'em in the rear end anymore. . . .

By the way, those of you that still have pushership in your companies, you're so out of date. With human rights legislation, with unions protecting the rights of men, where is your hammer? You tell people, do it or else, and they tell you, "Tell me a little more about the 'or else.' " And you get to thinking, "or else I got to do it myself." There aren't any "or elses" hardly anymore, are there? So what are we going to do? Gotta motivate them on a want to—and that doesn't mean that you've got to let people walk over the top of you.[37]

In case the connection wasn't sufficiently obvious, the training program explicitly linked Tice's idea of "constructive motivation" to specific concerns in the plant. Much was made of the "new Linden" philosophy that workers and foremen should behave respectfully toward one another to maximize everyone's motivation, performance, and thus the plant's competitiveness. As it was memorialized in the local union contract, "Good employer-employee relations depend on mutual respect and proper treatment of all concerned. It is Management's policy to extend to employes [*sic*] a working environment [where] they will be treated with dignity and respect."[38] Brendan Cook explained the underlying logic: "In the past, management had the impression that once you walk through the door, you leave your brains there, you come in, and you do what you're told. But they've come to a realization that they probably have more brain power out on the floor than they do up in the front office. So now they're working together, because they realize there's a lot of untapped potential out there."

The trainers were aware that converting first-line supervisors to this way of thinking was particularly crucial. In addition to the Tice materials, which were presented to both hourly and salaried workers in identical form, there was a twenty-hour program for the salaried group focused specifically on problem-solving decision analysis. As one manager involved in administering the program explained, "You had to demonstrate through role-playing and little exercises that group decision making usually came up with a better solution to a problem than an individual trying to figure it out on his own. You had to demonstrate that it would be to their advantage to involve the hourly workforce in things that were traditionally considered management functions." There was a general consensus that the older supervisors were particularly resistant to the new approach. Again, Brendan Cook:

See, supervisors have the problem because when they first got into supervision, how were they trained, and by what method? It was the 1935 style of

confrontation management: "Do as I say or else." More like coercive motivation. Now the younger supervisors are more open minded. They have not
been, quote-unquote, indoctrinated into the old style of management, and
they haven't been doing it as long. The older ones are what I would call
stubborn, set in their ways. Or that's what they like to believe. No one is ever
set in their ways. One of the examples that we bring up in class is the fact
that nobody likes change, but change is the universal way: it happens every
day, slowly, slowly, slowly. . . .

In a sense I feel sorry for some of the production foremen because, really,
they're in the front-line trenches. One of the biggest complaints we had in
the salaried people when they're going through classes was "Well, okay, I
believe in this, but what about *my* boss? Is he going to go through this?"
That was their thing, and it was exactly what the hourly people were saying:
"Is my boss going to go through this?"

Some of the supervisors changed and are better people for it today. If you
go into their sections and ask the people, "How was this person three years
ago as versus today?" "Oh, he did a 180." There are other people that for a
period improved, but as the pressures and stress on the floor production-wise
increased, they backslid to their old habits. I mean, there's a lot of success
stories out there, and there are a lot of nasty people out there too. The thing
is, I think, the percentage of nasties has been reduced.

By all accounts, the 80-hour program generally and the Tice component particularly were very well received by GM-Linden workers.
According to the local union president, "A lot of people wanted to go
through the classes a second time." Brendan Cook described reactions
to the Tice materials this way:

A lot of the people in salary, and some of the old-time hourly people, the
first day or two of the class, had an attitude like, "Well, I'm from Missouri,
show me." You can just tell from their body language, you know. But getting
into the third and fourth day, when you really got into the meat of the program, these people will go, "Damn, they're not trying to pull anything over
on me. They're speaking the truth here." That's when even the hard-core
ones opened up, you know, and they go, "Well, damn, he's not threatening
me with anything; he's trying to show me an easier way to handle it," and
even the hard-core ones started really getting into it. Usually for the real
hard core, it took about two days, but by the third day, they were like an
ex-smoker, a zealot; they were leading the charge.

Most reactions I got from people after the class is: one, I wish I would have known this twenty years ago; and two, I can't wait to show this to my kids. As a matter of fact, I had people cry in the class, saying, "If I knew this, this wouldn't have happened between me and my son," or, you know, "If I only knew this then." Even the supervisors were impressed by Tice.

In addition to finding personal value in the classes, most workers, as well as many managers, welcomed the official recognition that the status quo ante at GM was deeply problematic, and came out of the program hopeful that better days were in store. The difficulties began when the training program ended, and workers returned to their jobs on the line. "I think by and large we were effective in the classroom," a plant manager who was himself deeply committed to the "new Linden" philosophy explained.

Now the difficulty is always making that transition from the classroom back to the floor. In certain areas of the plant, you still had more of the old-style supervisors. And change is a lot tougher for them, a lot slower. You're up in the classroom for a couple of weeks, and suddenly, you're a changed person? In many instances, it happened, and we had supervisors at the end of a Tice class come up with tears in their eyes and say, "I understand what you're talking about as far as how you motivate people, and how you nurture and get the best in terms of the work situation, but I also understand what you said about raising kids. My life has been such a mess, my wife and my kids— they left home and they all hate me—and I can see exactly why, because I treated them at home the same way I treated the workers in the plant. And had I known this then, my family would have been so much better. What I did to my boys"—actually with tears in their eyes. So it was for many people very dramatic and powerful. In many other cases, they understood, and they said, "Yeah, that makes a lot of sense, and that's really the way I should conduct my business." They'd go back down to the floor, and if they were in an area that didn't support that, they'd get a superintendent who said, "That stuff you learned up there in that ivory tower, leave it up there, because this is the real world down here"—that watered it down in a lot of areas. You'd have some supervisors who were never really happy about the new style of management. By and large our supervisors come from the hourly ranks. And sometimes, the cliché goes, as soon as a guy puts on a tie, it must stop the circulation or something, because suddenly they get brain damaged, and they don't treat people right. There were some people who would have liked to operate with the new style of management, but the support to do that wasn't there. There's other supervisors who say, "It's the same old way, and I've got to go back to the old style of management." You've got the whole continuum.

Middle managers had limited incentives to change their own behavior, since their treatment at the hands of upper management remained extremely authoritarian. That not only hourly workers but also supervisors were being offered buyouts and lived in continual fear of layoffs did not help matters. In any case, the incomplete conversion process among middle managers meant that workers who emerged from the training program expecting things to change for the better were deeply disappointed. Their initially high hopes were quickly transmuted into cynicism, as Charlie Ferraro recalled:

They're running people through a two-week training—it's costing millions of dollars, a full two weeks when you come back to work. You are sent to a two-week, eighty-hour course, and *paid,* for Louis Tice. The Louis Tice course, it's an excellent course. It tells you how to be a positive thinker. . . . If things go wrong on a daily basis, you try to give yourself some inner strength. And there's nothing wrong with the course. They give you tapes. Then they go back to work. And the foreman goes over there and acts like an asshole. And they're still stupid, and they still don't listen to people! This bullshit about working together! I mean, there is more anger in that plant now, you know. Now it's supposed to change, and that's what's offending people. In the old days, you knew you were going to get screwed by your foreman, so you always came in prepared for it, and you almost accepted it. Like this one guy who—years back, this guy went through hell with General Motors. He almost got his arm ripped off, and when he came back to work, they just jerked him around. Now that was common in there. He came up to me two weeks ago, and we start talking. He said, "It's getting bad, man; it's really getting bad. I mean, it's terrible. You ain't going to believe this, but when they sent me through that school, I came out," he said, "I even told my wife, 'They spent a lot of money on this thing, and I had a real bad time with these people. I've been here about ten, eleven years, and they really kill me. But maybe they're serious. So you know what? I'm going to rest up this weekend; I'm going to go in there Monday, and I want to start all over again. I'm going to pretend like I just got hired.' " He said, "I'm telling you God's honest truth, I came in, got my tools out, and I said, 'Let me start fresh like I never worked here.' " He said, "Then they screwed me just like in the old days, and they're busting my chops because I took three minutes extra for a cup of coffee." That's it. They got the benefit of the doubt, and that's what is going on now.

Seduced and Abandoned?

Just as the skill effects of the changeover were different for skilled-
trades and production workers, so too were their impressions of the
"new Linden." Although most skilled-trades workers did not even attend the 80-hour training program, many reported an improved relationship with management—largely because their enhanced technical
knowledge often rendered supervision superfluous. "There's a foreman somewhere," said electrician Peter Finney, interviewed on the
job in 1988. "Tomorrow we'll see him—payday. They [supervisors]
are scared. They don't know anything about the area. They can't assist us; all they can do is get us parts if we need anything." In the
1988 in-plant survey, skilled-trades respondents indicated that they
were under less pressure from supervisors to work harder than before
the changeover, although in other respects they reported no significant change in their relationship with supervision.[39] Some skilled-
trades workers, however, felt things had improved. As machine repairman George Baran put it: "I see more cohesiveness between
management and the worker. They don't take this confrontational
viewpoint. They listen to each other, at least in this department. As
far as my foreman—he's in the shop. I call him when I need him. In
the twenty-three years I've been here, I haven't seen a cooperative
effort put forth as much as I've seen it in the last year here. The old
concept was that management was always right. Now they don't do
that."

Production workers tended to be more critical of the "new Linden." In the 1988 survey, 66 percent of respondents reported no
change in their relationship with supervision since the changeover,
and another 9 percent said the relationship was worse than before.
For many, the initial focus of disappointment involved the *stop-the-
line* concept. They had come away from the 80-hour training with
the sense that if they were unable to complete their assigned task in
their own work station, they could and indeed *should* stop the line.
However, as production of the new model began to accelerate, and
shop-floor management—experiencing the usual difficulties involved
in getting the bugs out of the new machinery—came under pressure
to increase output, workers who stopped the line were immediately

reprimanded. In the 1988 survey, 39 percent of respondents said "yes" or "sometimes" to the question, "Do you ever hesitate to stop the line?"; and 60 percent of this group indicated that this was because they feared it would anger their supervisor. "They really didn't want you to stop the line," reported Ben Kowalski. He explained: "Officially, you were allowed to do it, but when you did, they came down real quick: 'Don't worry about the problem yet. Let's get the line running; then we'll talk about it.' It was supposed to be, like, if you didn't have your parts or anything, you could stop the line. But they'd rather have a repair man go down there and put the parts on than you stop the line, 'cause every minute they're down, to them, all they see is dollar signs. So, they put it [the stop-the-line button] there, but they really didn't want you to use it all."

Fred Lawton's experience was similar: "They don't want that line to stop for any reason! When I'd stop the line, they got real mad and everything, started the line, and said, 'Don't do it again.'" And union official Tom Barbarro commented: "The 80-hour training was great. All that jazz, telling all the people we're going to have 'stop the line' and we're going to fix the car. And they did all that for a little while. But the little while didn't last too long. Some places, people are not allowed to stop the line, even though they said they were going to be. They got it set up so that when you press it, nothing happens—it's like bypassed. When they don't get the count, all the good talking stuff goes down the tube, and that's one of our problems in America."

Supervisors themselves confirmed that it was very difficult for them to adjust to the stop-the-line idea. "It took a while for us to get used to, as managers, because we always wanted the line to continue running," one supervisor explained. "For twenty years that was what was always bred into us. Production was first!" The conflict between workers who felt empowered to stop the line as a result of the training program and managers who resisted their efforts ultimately became a topic of local union bargaining. Managerial hegemony in determining the effective limits of the stop-the-line concept was officially acknowledged in the 1987 local union contract: "It was mutually recognized that certain circumstances could arise wherein it would not be necessary in all cases for operators to stop the line every time they are unable to meet the job requirements of their operation. In this respect, recognized examples could include situations where a supervisory determination is made not to stop the line but to effectuate the necessary correction at some other point in the production process."[40]

Some workers were also disappointed by the flip-flops in parking policy. For a brief period after the plant first reopened following the changeover, parking spaces formerly reserved for foremen had been opened up to workers on a first-come, first-served basis. Later, for reasons that are unclear, this policy was reversed. Charlie Ferraro was bitter:

That parking lot, it used to be salaried; then with the big kissing affair going on, to show we're all equal, they opened it up. I get to work forty minutes before I have to be there, and so then I could park right up front. But now, I can't park there. The lot's empty, but I can't park there, because I'm not a foreman, I'm not supervision. I said, "What happened to all this kissy-kiss shit?" I says, "Is it back to the old way?" He [a manager] says, "Nobody else is complaining." I says, "I don't know about that." I said, "I get here forty minutes ahead of work, and I got to park all the way over there, and then some shithead foreman can get here two minutes before the whistle blows and gets a prime spot." I said, "That sounds a little prejudicial to me."

The same theme of broken promises resounded in workers' comments on the Employee Involvement Groups (EIGs) that were institutionalized after the changeover. The idea was appealing to many, but in practice many problems emerged; and after three years, management effectively dropped the program by ending the previous policy of paying workers (at overtime rates) who attended the half-hour weekly meetings. By the early 1990s, some GM-Linden workers were nostalgic for the EIGs. "We used to meet at lunchtime and discuss all the problems, and supervision would come and you would talk things out," Raymond Perry recalled. "They cut that out! It was great: I had a situation I discussed there, and it was worked out." Dennis Tucker agreed: "EIG was a very good program, other than getting paid for just sitting and eating lunch. Even if one problem got resolved in your area, it was worth it." Jack Giordano also had a positive view: "Nine times out of ten, we would walk away and have nothing accomplished. But when something was accomplished, it was a big deal, because it had to do with the people who were busting their ass, people on the line working. When we finally got something done, people were happy. And if you keep people happy on the line, you know, they produce a better job."

Others were more cynical about the program. "So, once a week you have a meeting," George Karas said. "It's like psychiatry: you tell them your problems, you go home. That's the way I see it." And Ron Clark commented, "It's just to pacify you, so you don't write up grievances. It's a half-hour's pay for sitting there and eating your lunch. It takes forever to get anything done. Like just to get a water fountain, it takes months of screaming and yelling and bringing it up. To get a fan, it's the same thing." Ben Kowalski had a similar view:

It would have been a good system if management did what they said. But they didn't bother themselves as much as they should have. You were allowed to air your complaints, voice your opinion, and supposedly, they would do something for you. Say one of your machines—one of the clamps isn't working right. Or you need a table, so you can set up your work. "Okay, we'll get you the table next week." So you go to this meeting on Tuesday at lunchtime. You don't go out to lunch, you eat your lunch there, and you tell them, "I need a table." "We're working on it." That's generally what it comes to. A lot of times, you'd be there, and it's the same every week, the same people complaining about the same things, and it got ridiculous.

Sometimes workers were unwilling to voice their complaints in the first place. "In my group, nobody would say anything," Sean O'Brien reported. "They'd eat their lunch. Because we had a pain-in-the-ass foreman, nobody would say anything against him—they didn't want him riding their back. You could get little things done, but it was only there for the company. Workers got nothing out of it but the half-hour pay." And in areas where the program did get off the ground, sometimes workers themselves balked. "If there was a problem, like if one of the lug nuts kept chipping or being stripped, they wanted us to go back to the operator and find out why," Fred Lawton explained. "I'm not getting paid for that—that's supervision's job. If you do it, you're more or less ratting on your fellow workers. I couldn't do that. I'm not going to point the finger, and that's what they wanted." Jeffrey Goetz made a similar point: "To a point, it would work, but then sometimes the people would get power hungry. They'd start acting like a foreman and stuff like that. They would actually go and try—they'd go to the root of the problem and say to the employee, 'Yo! This is the way it should be done.' And [the worker would reply] 'Who the hell are you? You're not a foreman. We don't listen to the foreman as it is, let alone to a damn employee! Fuck you,' you know. 'Go get the foreman, and he'll tell me to do it.'"

Underlying the failure of both the stop-the-line and the EIG programs was a pervasive belief among production workers—suspended briefly during the 80-hour training but soon revived—that management simply could not be trusted. Although most workers emerged from the training hopeful that the "new Linden" would truly be different from the old, they quickly found that supervisors failed to live up to the principles set forth in the Tice program. "Louis Tice told me that the job should be built in the station!" Louis Lambert exclaimed. (Actually, Tice was not physically present but was seen on video in the training program.) "That's all bullshit. They're not doing it the way they said they were going to do it." Indeed, after the training program raised workers' expectations, foremen—faced with the usual pressure to get production out—seemed quickly to revert to type. The result was predictable: "The 'new Linden,'" Jeffrey Goetz intoned with disgust, "it got lost in the wash." As Ellen Thomas explained: "You still have the management that has the mentality of the top down, like they're right—they don't listen to the exchange from the workers—like the old school. So that's why when you ask about the 'new Linden,' people say it's a farce. Because you still do not feel mutual respect; you feel the big thing is to get the jobs out. This is a manufacturing plant; they do have to produce. But you can't just [. . .] give me this big hype, and then [. . .] have the same old attitude."

Ron Clark was equally disillusioned: "It sounded good at the time, but it turned out to be a big joke. Management's attitude is still the same. It hasn't changed at all. Foremens [*sic*] who treated you like a fellow human being are still the same. No problems with them. The ones who are arrogant bastards are still the same, with the exception of a few who are a little bit scared, a little bit afraid that it might go to the top man and, you know, make some trouble. Everyone has pretty much the same attitude." Raymond Perry agreed. "They just went back to their old ways. A lot of the things Tice was talking about were good. But I think a lot of people didn't want it to work."

Ultimately, workers appropriated the ideas they heard in the 80-

hour program to bolster their long-standing critique of management behavior. Tom Miller, for example, said:

If management was to get a grade score on that Louis Tice course, if I were to grade them, I'd give 99 percent of them an F. With management, they don't have the security that we have. Because if a foreman doesn't do his job, he can be replaced tomorrow, and he's got nobody to back him up. So everybody's a little bit afraid of their jobs. So if you have a problem, you complain to your foreman; he tries to take care of it without bringing it to his general foreman; or the general foreman, he don't want to bring it to his superintendent, because neither of them can control it. So they all try to keep it down, low level and under the rug, and [they say,] "Don't bother me about it—just fix it and let it slide." And that is not the teachings that we went through in that 80-hour course!

Oscar Hansen had a somewhat different view, but like Miller, he couched his critique in the language of the 80-hour program:

The Tyson [Tice] program, as far as I was concerned, it was very interesting if people would go by the program of it. We have a half-hour [EIG] meeting once a week, and that's a help. If you tell me I missed something, I feel that I must have missed it; because if I didn't, you wouldn't tell me. But if the foreman tells me, then I get an attitude. Because I know he doesn't know as much about the job as I do. And see, that's the whole problem. That's what's wrong with this place today. The foremen don't really know anything. But if the men would learn to work together, it wouldn't be as big a problem. And this was the idea that Tyson [Tice] was trying to get over to the people. I mean, working together. . . . See, we are not children; we are men. I used to work upstairs, and I had a problem, no water anywhere around. I called the foreman, and he told me, "When you have a break, you can get water, and after that, you don't have to have no water till the next break." But I didn't do that. When I got ready for water, I just made it my business, went out, and got the water. I intend to do a good job as long as I'm here, but I don't intend to be pushed around. I mean, we are not slaves! And you're supposed to be able to go get a drink of water. The reason they don't do no more for us than they do, is because we're doing without it. But if you know you need it, then it's up to you. That's what Tyson [Tice] told me!

Sean O'Brien was one of many who felt that the older foremen— the dinosaurs—were particularly resistant to change: "You talk to any foreman in there that had over twenty, twenty-five years, and they'll tell you it [the Tice training] was garbage, a waste of time and money.

Only a fool would expect them to change. It was only brainwashing to get you to do more work." Joyce Cowley, who took the buyout on the second round, echoed this view: "The older foreman, they were so set in their ways, nobody could change them—I don't care what you did. Luckily, I didn't have any of them." One older superintendent was especially notorious—some workers referred to him as a Nazi. Committeeman Ben Prindle, who dealt with him regularly, explained: "I see what management is trying to do. I know that the dinosaurs will be gone from here someday, and the union and management will probably have a better relationship. But in my department, we have a superintendent that doesn't believe in that stuff. He doesn't believe in it. He's back in the 1940s when the union and company fought constantly. It just can't work that way anymore. We have to learn to get along. But he's from the old school and doesn't believe in employee involvement and that kind of thing. He puts a fight up about it."

Some workers grudgingly acknowledged that the quality of their relationship with supervision had improved somewhat. Grievance rates did fall slightly, although this may well have reflected a continuing decline in the local union's power rather than increased satisfaction with management.[41] In any case, whatever improvements did occur in labor-management relations fell so far short of what most production workers felt they had been promised, that they still felt disappointed. Some suggested that the commitment to change was only present among upper management, with first-line supervisors going along with the program only insofar as they feared reprisals from above. Most agreed with Committeeman Ed Piccone that "with higher-up management, you can see the change, but on the line, it falls apart." Ben Kowalski reported: "I didn't see much of a change with the foremens [*sic*], but with the upper management, it seemed like you could talk to them a little more. They had an open-door policy: if you ever had a problem, just come right in. I never had the need to, but it was there. So I think it did help." Matthew Larson offered the following analysis: "[The foremen are] a little more worried because I guess they're under pressure from getting laid off themselves. Because [management is] supposed to cut 25 percent [of the foremen], and [it's] handpicking them. So they're all nervous about every little thing that goes on. They're a lot nicer now because before they used to yell a lot and scream and curse and threaten. They were warned—I think they were told that they're not allowed to do that anymore, you know, degrade a person really. Because it only ends up with sabotage or whatever afterwards. There's still a few that get hot-headed and start yelling and screaming, but then it never works out, because there's a payback for it." Many middle managers themselves agreed with this view. As one, a self-described convert from the "hard-nosed old school" to the new gospel of employee participation, complained:

Upper management is trying very hard to get involved with the local union people and the hourly people. But I think they missed a very important step in the process, and it's the first-line supervisor. I think they stepped over him completely. It's obvious that GM is trying to reduce 25 percent of its white collars. Here's upper management, and here's the union, and we're going to skip this guy in the middle. I guess upper management thinks that because we're salaried that we're automatically involved. But see, I put my pants on the same way everyone else does, and I got questions and problems. I don't think we in management have the opportunity to speak openly to our people without the fear of recrimination. Don't say anything because your boss will get mad, and if your boss gets mad at you, then you're not going to get a raise. You're not going to get a raise anyway because they're not giving any, but there's always that threat.

Conclusion

The recent history of GM-Linden casts doubt on the common pre-sumption that productivity improvements are necessarily associated with innovative labor-management relations like those pioneered at NUMMI and Saturn. Despite the many failures and disappointments recounted here, in 1990 the Linden plant was rated "GM's best" in an authoritative national study of productivity in auto-assembly plants. To be sure, with the exception of NUMMI, GM as a whole fared far worse in this survey than Ford, Chrysler, or the Japanese transplants, so that even as GM's most productive assembly plant, Linden only ranked twenty-first among all the plants studied.[42] Still, its strong showing suggests that productivity can be improved significantly even in the supposedly archaic context of classically adversarial labor-man-agement relations.

Workers laid the blame for the failure of the "new Linden" squarely on management's shoulders and for good reason. They tended to be most critical of the GM representatives with whom they had daily contact, namely the first-line supervisors. But top-level corporate management's own commitment to transforming the industrial relations regime at Linden was the root of the problem. First-line supervisors were offered no incentives to change fundamentally their own behavior; on the contrary, their own ranks were constantly being reduced, even as they were placed under continual pressure from above to get production out. All the signals they received suggested that any rewards they might garner would come from improved productivity by whatever means necessary, and they had little reason to believe that the cooperative management regime the 80-hour training had celebrated would help.

Already battered by the events of the early 1980s, the UAW lost some prestige as well with the failure of the much-touted reform effort. No one faulted the local union for its cosponsorship of the popular 80-hour training program, since most workers agreed with the principles enunciated there. But the union's initial embrace of "jointness" and its role in encouraging members to believe that the "new Linden" would really be different from the old probably cost it some credibility once management reverted to its old ways. Meanwhile, the union's power, which had declined dramatically already in the early 1980s, continued to erode. If UAW Local 595 officials ever did place any genuine trust in management, that had vanished by 1990, when in local contract negotiations they were forced to give up a long-standing ten-minute break, known in the plant as the coffee gap, unique to the Linden plant. Aside from its obvious practical value, the coffee gap had great symbolic resonance as a carryover from the glory days of the auto industry when the UAW had more clout. Its loss dispelled any lingering doubts that those days were gone for good.

The profound sense of insecurity that GM-Linden production workers felt about their future employment prospects made the always formidable task of building a new relationship of trust between labor and management nearly impossible. Whereas before the changeover, Linden had been the only plant manufacturing Cadillacs and other top-of-the-line luxury cars, now there was a twin plant (in Wilmington,

Delaware) building the same car models. The threat this arrangement implied was not lost on anyone. "Whether people want to mention it or not, we are in direct competition with the Wilmington, Delaware, plant," one union committeeman pointed out. "And whoever puts the most cars out for the cheapest price is the one that's going to stay open, so there is definitely pressure on the men here." Belaboring the obvious, large electronic signs displayed throughout the plant compared the production output for Wilmington and Linden each day.

Production workers also were worried that, even if the plant stayed open, there would be fewer jobs there in the future. "What I'm afraid of is that unskilled jobs are being eliminated and replaced by skilled workers," commented Doug Hogan. Sean O'Brien agreed: "Automation, you know. Anybody with half a brain knows [the auto industry is] just going to get smaller and smaller and smaller. There's nothing you can do about it; that's just the way it is. Eventually, I think, if you don't fix something, you'll work with a white tie, or you'll be shoveling shit. Those will be the only three things, really. That's the way it's going." That these fears were pervasive is confirmed by the 1988 survey results: 86 percent of production-worker respondents said that they expected that the number of workers in their department would decrease in the next five years, while only 3 percent expected it to rise.[43]

Their apprehension soon proved well founded. In February 1990, GM laid off Linden's entire second shift. Except for a few with unusually high seniority, most of these workers would never work in the auto industry again. In September 1991, the plant's first shift was laid off as well, while the company spent more than two years retooling the plant to produce light trucks—moving all the machinery that had been installed in the 1985–1986 changeover to another plant and bringing in new equipment once again. The first shift was eventually (more than two years after they had been laid off) recalled to work in the plant. But by then, the second shift had been laid off so long that most workers had lost their right to be recalled to the plant, and by the mid-1990s, Linden had become a location at which workers displaced from other GM plants around the country were offered jobs.

Some of the second-shift workers may now wish they had taken buyouts back in 1986. Although the income they received through unemployment benefits and SUB during the year after they were laid off was roughly comparable to what they could have collected earlier through the buyout program, the buyout was superior in some respects. It was a lump-sum payment and, unlike SUB, placed no restrictions on new employment. In addition, the workers laid off in 1990 found themselves in a more problematic situation than the buyout takers had faced a few years before. Not only were they older—a significant handicap in searching for new employment—but also, the labor market prospects for non-college-educated workers had deteriorated significantly in the intervening years.

As for those production workers who remain at GM today, they have no more illusions about a "new Linden." Their experience remains hopelessly remote from the optimistic claims of many academic commentators about upgraded skill levels, increased autonomy on the job, and improved relations with management—much as they would welcome such changes. Prisoners of still enviable wages and benefits in an era of national economic decline, they are resigned to enduring the daily humiliations of shop-floor life—humiliations made more painful by the knowledge that their union is weaker than ever. Despite their high seniority (most have at least twenty years' service at GM), like all workers in the United States today, they live with profound uncertainty about the future. They can only cling to the hope that their jobs at GM-Linden will survive another decade or so, until they are eligible for retirement. If that day comes, they too will gladly say farewell to the factory.

Appendices

APPENDIX 1. Occupational Classification and Department of Linden-GM Production Workers, by Seniority, Gender, Race, and Hourly Wage Rates, 1985

Occupational Classification, by Plant Department	Number of Workers	Median Seniority (years)	Percent Female	Percent Black	Percent Latino	Hourly Wage Rate($)
Trim						
Hang and adjust door & lids	663	9.0	28.5	27.8	12.2	12.98
All instrument panel operators	208	9.0	19.7	23.6	8.2	12.85
Trimmer A	92	15.5	5.4	22.8	15.2	13.02
Cushion makeup	74	8.5	17.6	39.2	16.2	12.85
aDoor refitting (car conditioning)	60	9.0	1.7	21.7	18.3	13.09
C.V. & sliding glass	59	9.0	3.4	22.0	15.3	13.02
Assemble seats B	56	9.0	19.6	14.3	12.5	12.96
Trim repair-new car conditioning	34	21.0	0.0	17.6	2.9	13.24
aFinal assembly	16	17.0	25.0	50.0	6.3	12.82
aWater leak check & repair	15	9.0	13.3	33.3	6.7	13.09
Trimmer B	14	17.0	0.0	14.3	21.4	12.98
Trimmer C	12	9.0	33.3	33.3	8.3	12.98
Assemble seats A	8	22.0	0.0	12.5	0.0	13.02
Seat installer	6	9.0	0.0	50.0	16.7	12.85
aSpray duco A/O Dulux	5	9.0	0.0	20.0	0.0	13.09
Assemble all glass	5	23.0	0.0	0.0	0.0	12.94

Trim (*continued*)

[a]Inspection-final car assembly line	2	11.0	50.0	50.0	0.0	13.06
Radio & electrical repair & insp.	1	32.0	0.0	0.0	0.0	13.06
Subtotal	1,330	9.0	20.5	26.2	12.0	

Chassis

[a]Final assembly	342	8.0	14.7	29.1	12.6	12.82
Frame spring & axle	171	8.0	11.7	25.7	18.7	12.82
Motor line	156	8.0	21.2	19.9	12.2	12.82
Fender & radiator	153	9.0	28.1	24.2	17.6	12.82
Car driver	112	15.0	13.4	30.4	8.0	12.82
Chassis line	111	8.0	9.9	30.6	15.3	12.82
Glazier-knife	27	17.0	0.0	37.0	11.1	12.98
Light repair	15	21.0	0.0	13.3	6.7	13.09
Hoodfit-repair	13	9.0	0.0	15.4	7.7	13.09
[a]Inspection-final car assembly line	6	14.5	0.0	66.7	0.0	13.06
Truck & misc. prod. oper.	3	9.0	33.3	0.0	66.7	12.82
Car washer	2	24.5	0.0	0.0	0.0	12.49
Driver-outside (licensed vehicles)	2	33.0	0.0	0.0	0.0	12.92
[a]Major salvage repair & inspection	1	21.0	0.0	0.0	0.0	13.06
Subtotal	1,114	8.0	15.6	26.7	13.8	

(*continued on next page*)

Occupational Classification, by Plant Department	Number of Workers	Median Seniority (years)	Percent Female	Percent Black	Percent Latino	Hourly Wage Rate($)
Paint						
Body assembly operator B	152	9.0	46.4	36.4	13.9	12.82
[a]Spray duco A/O Dulux	84	9.0	6.0	20.2	13.1	13.09
Wet sand	62	9.0	3.2	32.3	16.1	13.02
Repair between coats	62	9.0	9.8	23.0	19.7	12.98
Prime sander	31	9.0	3.2	16.1	32.3	12.98
Repair after duco	30	23.0	3.3	33.3	16.7	13.09
Machine stripe	28	17.0	17.9	35.7	7.1	12.94
[a]Water leak check & repair	26	9.0	7.7	15.4	23.1	13.09
[a]Clean equipment	25	21.0	0.0	36.0	4.0	12.56
Paint equipment maintenance	21	19.0	0.0	0.0	0.0	12.98
Insp.-metal paint & ding between coat	15	15.0	13.3	20.0	20.0	13.14
Hardware A	13	9.0	0.0	0.0	15.4	12.85
Polisher	13	17.0	0.0	61.5	15.4	13.02
[a]Spray prime glaze	12	9.0	8.3	25.0	0.0	12.98
Washer A/O cleaner	10	16.5	10.0	40.0	0.0	12.82
Elpo attendant	6	28.0	0.0	16.7	0.0	13.09
[a]Schedule-loader	4	16.0	0.0	0.0	50.0	12.82
Metal clean	4	9.0	0.0	0.0	25.0	12.82
Touch-up A	4	13.0	25.0	25.0	25.0	13.02

Paint (*continued*)

Bonderite equipment operator	4	32.0	0.0	100.0	0.0	12.92
Paint mixing & equipment cleaner	2	12.5	0.0	50.0	0.0	12.85
Subtotal	608	9.0	16.0	27.9	14.7	

Body Shop

Welder-spot	237	6.0	6.0	25.5	9.8	12.98
Metal finish	115	8.0	0.0	31.3	8.7	13.09
Welder-arc	69	9.0	1.4	24.6	10.1	13.09
Garnish molding	59	8.0	0.0	15.3	6.8	13.02
Body assembly operator A	37	6.5	22.2	25.0	19.4	12.82
Metal grind	20	6.0	0.0	10.0	20.0	12.98
Solder-torch	18	9.0	5.6	50.0	0.0	13.09
[a]Door refitting (car conditioning)	13	9.0	0.0	7.7	0.0	13.09
Metal repair & ding	8	22.0	0.0	12.5	0.0	13.48
Inspect metal finish	5	21.0	20.0	40.0	0.0	13.14
Gate loader & unloader	4	9.5	0.0	75.0	0.0	12.98
[a]Schedule-loader	4	9.0	0.0	0.0	25.0	12.82
[a]Spray prime & glaze	3	9.0	0.0	66.7	0.0	12.98
Inspect welding	3	25.0	0.0	0.0	0.0	13.14
Subtotal	595	8.0	4.2	25.5	9.5	

(*continued on next page*)

Occupational Classification, by Plant Department	Number of Workers	Median Seniority (years)	Percent Female	Percent Black	Percent Latino	Hourly Wage Rate($)
Material						
Stockman-trim	63	19.0	0.0	17.5	6.3	12.98
Stockman-chassis	59	16.0	1.7	20.3	5.1	12.98
aOperator-power equipment	58	20.0	0.0	36.2	10.3	12.82
Checker	30	16.0	0.0	26.6	13.8	12.82
aSchedule-loader	23	9.0	30.4	43.5	13.0	12.82
Checker-receiving A/O shipping	21	9.0	4.8	9.5	0.0	12.82
General	21	26.0	0.0	19.0	0.0	12.92
Stockman-body	15	15.0	0.0	6.7	33.3	12.98
Stockman-cushion	7	9.0	0.0	14.3	14.3	12.98
Stockman-car conditioning	3	32.0	0.0	66.7	0.0	12.98
Receiving inspection	3	33.0	0.0	0.0	0.0	13.09
Paint	2	29.0	0.0	50.0	0.0	12.92
Material handler	1	22.0	0.0	0.0	0.0	12.56
Subtotal	306	17.0	3.0	23.9	8.5	
Inspection						
Inspect trim & hardware	71	20.0	5.6	16.9	14.1	13.09
Inspect chassis line	37	16.0	16.2	21.6	16.2	13.06
aInspect final car assembly line	35	14.0	20.0	42.9	8.6	13.06

Inspection (*continued*)

Inspect final new car conditioning	25	30.0	4.0	24.0	4.0	13.14
Inspect final hood, doors & caps	17	16.0	11.8	5.9	5.9	13.13
Road & roll test inspection	16	18.5	6.3	25.0	12.5	13.09
Minor salvage repair & inspection	13	15.0	0.0	23.1	15.4	12.82
Electrical inspection & repair	7	19.0	28.6	57.1	0.0	13.06
Miscellaneous parts inspection	6	23.5	0.0	16.7	0.0	12.92
Inspect wire & accessories	5	21.0	20.0	60.0	0.0	13.06
Insp. repair mech.-motor, axle & trans.	2	15.0	0.0	0.0	0.0	13.13
[a]Major salvage repair & inspection	1	33.0	0.0	0.0	0.0	13.06
Subtotal	235	17.0	10.2	24.3	10.6	

Maintenance

Sweeper	82	21.0	0.0	27.2	7.4	12.33
[a]Clean equipment	20	21.0	0.0	50.0	0.0	12.56
[a]Operator-power equipment	17	24.0	0.0	17.6	5.9	12.82
Janitor	12	19.0	0.0	8.3	0.0	12.33
Yard laborer	7	23.0	0.0	28.6	0.0	12.56
Oiler	5	21.0	0.0	80.0	0.0	12.92
[a]Schedule-loader	4	29.0	0.0	50.0	0.0	12.82
Power sweeper	4	21.0	0.0	0.0	0.0	12.56

(*continued on next page*)

Occupational Classification, by Plant Department	Number of Workers	Median Seniority (years)	Percent Female	Percent Black	Percent Latino	Hourly Wage Rate($)
Maintenance (continued)						
Baler & shredder	3	21.0	0.0	33.3	0.0	12.56
Waste water treatment	1	1.0	0.0	0.0	0.0	13.45
Subtotal	155	21.0	0.0	29.2	4.5	
Total	4,343	9.0	14.6	26.6	11.9	

[a]Classifications that exist in more than one department.

APPENDIX 2. Hourly Earnings of Auto Workers and of All Production/Non-supervisory Private Sector Workers, in Current Dollars and in 1973 Dollars, 1958–1992

Year	All Workers (current $)	Auto Workers (current $)	CPI-W 1973 = 100	All Workers (1973 $)	Auto Workers (1973 $)	Ratio of Auto Workers to All Workers
1958	1.95	2.64	65.1	3.00	4.06	1.35
1959	2.02	2.80	65.5	3.08	4.27	1.39
1960	2.09	2.91	66.7	3.13	4.36	1.39
1961	2.14	2.97	67.3	3.18	4.41	1.39
1962	2.22	3.10	68.0	3.26	4.56	1.40
1963	2.28	3.22	68.9	3.31	4.67	1.41
1964	2.36	3.32	69.8	3.38	4.76	1.41
1965	2.46	3.45	70.9	3.47	4.87	1.40
1966	2.56	3.55	72.9	3.51	4.87	1.39
1967	2.68	3.66	75.2	3.56	4.87	1.37
1968	2.85	4.02	78.3	3.64	5.13	1.41
1969	3.04	4.23	82.6	3.68	5.12	1.39
1970	3.23	4.42	87.2	3.70	5.07	1.37
1971	3.45	4.95	91.1	3.79	5.43	1.43
1972	3.70	5.35	94.2	3.93	5.68	1.45
1973	3.94	5.70	100.0	3.94	5.70	1.45
1974	4.24	6.23	111.0	3.82	5.61	1.47
1975	4.53	6.82	121.0	3.74	5.64	1.51
1976	4.86	7.45	128.0	3.80	5.82	1.53
1977	5.25	8.22	136.2	3.85	6.04	1.57
1978	5.69	8.98	146.8	3.88	6.12	1.58
1979	6.16	9.74	163.5	3.77	5.96	1.58
1980	6.66	10.80	185.5	3.59	5.82	1.62
1981	7.25	12.29	204.5	3.55	6.01	1.69
1982	7.68	13.01	216.8	3.54	6.00	1.69
1983	8.02	13.36	223.3	3.59	5.98	1.67
1984	8.32	14.12	231.1	3.60	6.11	1.70
1985	8.57	14.81	239.1	3.58	6.19	1.73
1986	8.76	14.99	243.0	3.60	6.17	1.71
1987	8.98	15.33	251.7	3.57	6.09	1.71
1988	9.28	16.09	261.7	3.55	6.15	1.73
1989	9.66	16.51	274.3	3.52	6.02	1.71
1990	10.01	17.26	288.6	3.47	5.98	1.72
1991	10.33	18.34	300.4	3.44	6.11	1.78
1992	10.59	18.32	309.2	3.42	5.92	1.73

(continued on next page)

SOURCES: Computed from data appearing in U.S. Department of Labor, Bureau of Labor Statistics, *Employment, Hours and Earnings, U.S. 1909–90,* vol. 1 (Washington, D.C., 1991); U.S. Department of Labor, Bureau of Labor Statistics, *Employment and Earnings,* various issues (Washington, D.C.); U.S. Department of Labor, Bureau of Labor Statistics, *Handbook of Labor Statistics* (Washington, D.C., 1989); and U.S. Department of Labor, Bureau of Labor Statistics, *Monthly Labor Review,* various issues (Washington, D.C.).

NOTE: All Workers = Production or nonsupervisory workers, total private nonfarm establishments; Auto Workers = SIC 3711 (motor vehicles and car bodies); CPI-W = consumer price index for urban wage earners and clerical workers (1987 revision of CPI).

Appendix 3

A Note on Methodology

Recent debates about workplace transformation have been conducted largely behind the backs and over the heads of the workers most directly affected. This book seeks instead to put workers' own experiences and voices at the center. Yet this is far easier said than done. Academic research on factory workers is at best a minefield, full of opportunities for misperception and deception in all directions—all the more so when the researcher is female and the great majority of the workers, managers, and union officials are male. Since this book draws on a variety of data sources—direct observation during plant visits, focus groups, surveys, open-ended interviews, as well as written documents and archival materials—I wrestled with these issues in several different arenas.

The first challenge was simply gaining access to the field site, never an easy task in this kind of research and one that often leads to pragmatic compromise between one's ideal methodology and the available possibilities. I had first become intrigued by GM-Linden in the spring of 1982, shortly after moving to New York City to teach at Queens College. I took a group of students on a field trip to the plant, and by coincidence, our visit took place in the midst of the dramatic internal battle within the UAW over contract concessions (described in chapter 3). Having read in the *New York Times* that the local union at Linden was among those opposed to concessions, I arranged to visit the union hall after our plant tour, where we spoke with some UAW officers. Not long after this, I learned that Linden would soon be the site of a massive technological overhaul, and that it might be possible to launch a research project on the implications for the workforce. I jumped at the chance.

My first choice would have been a participant observation study, in which I would have worked in the plant myself, but this was not an option. As it was, it took more than two years of negotiation for me and Cydney Pullman of the Labor Institute in New York, with whom I collaborated on the initial phase of the research, to gain access to the plant. Each of us had good contacts with the UAW—Cydney with the regional director and I with UAW headquarters in Detroit. The union wanted an evaluation of its recently negotiated job-security programs, which the technological overhaul at Linden had triggered; at this point, Cydney and I were more interested in the impact of the new technology on the workforce. Eventually we worked out an arrangement that would allow us to study both issues. The union won the official cooperation of GM for our project and provided some funding to defray the research expenses from a joint UAW-GM fund. As a result, we enjoyed about a year of unrestricted access to interviews with management and union personnel, in both Linden and Detroit. We also were able to conduct worker focus-group discussions and a large-scale in-plant survey on company time, as well as to obtain addresses and phone numbers of the buyout takers to facilitate a telephone survey of that population.

Few researchers can obtain this kind of access to an industrial field setting, and we know how lucky we were. We also felt enormously privileged to have gained quasi-insider status, and hoped that our project's official sponsorship by the company and the union would allow us to gather information otherwise unobtainable. In many respects, this proved the case, yet for some potential informants—most of all, rank-and-file workers—the very fact that we had legitimacy with management and union rendered us eminently *un*trustworthy. In the intensely political world of the factory, academic researchers were an entirely unknown quantity and could only be understood as serving someone else's immediate interests. Thus, precisely what had opened the plant doors to us—our hard-won official acceptance by the UAW and GM—also meant that workers were often guarded and suspicious in our presence. Yet it was workers' experience that we were most interested in studying! Perhaps it was just as well that we were slow to catch on to this; we simply pushed ahead with our research plan.

The promise that we would produce "hard," quantitative data through survey research was what had secured our access to the plant. My own academic credentials played no small part here. But in fact I had no previous experience designing or conducting surveys! Cydney had some, but her expertise was also limited. We resolved to do as professional a job as possible and rapidly set about educating ourselves in survey research techniques, relying heavily on the help of expert consultants to the project. Our goal was to generate data that was as objective as possible, yet as the research progressed, we were to encounter one signal after another that this was a quixotic quest indeed.

Virtually every phase of our work was affected by the social and political context in which we were operating. Wherever we turned, we were forced to confront the reality that workers, as well as many managers and union officials, had their own agendas and their own notions about who we were and whose interests our research was meant to serve. For example, because our project was sponsored by the UAW regional and national offices (and officially by GM as well), some local union officials were suspicious from the outset. They seemed to view us essentially as spies for the national union, or maybe even for GM. After we circulated a draft of our in-plant survey to the local union officers, they demanded that we delete a series of questions about the union itself and about the employee involvement program that was in place at the time. When one local unionist who was particularly sympathetic to our project tried to argue on our behalf that the questions should be retained, rumors began to circulate that he was having an affair with one of us. In the end we were forced to delete the questions involved.

That we were women (and Cydney was visibly pregnant during much of the joint fieldwork) complicated matters further. Doubtless there were aspects of the plant's deeply male-oriented social relations that remained hidden from us. On the other hand, our gender may have offered some advantages. Although there is no way to be sure, I believe that many of the managers we interviewed (nearly all of them male) were less guarded than they would have been with male researchers, simply because they seemed to have difficulty taking relatively young, female interrogators seriously. To them, it seemed, we were just "girls."

We inspired explicitly political suspicions in some quarters, due to the past work of the Labor Institute, on whose staff Cydney had worked for many years, and which was the official sponsor of the project. Many workers remembered that in the early 1980s, when a dissident union caucus, the Linden Auto Workers (LAW), had briefly won control of the local union (see chapter 3), Cydney and others from the institute had conducted an elaborate labor education program at Linden-GM. Like LAW itself, the institute was seen as a "communist" outfit by some workers, and for them, our project presumably was suspect as well. Although I had not been involved in the institute's labor education program, after taking my class to visit the plant and union hall, I had conducted an interview with LAW leader Douglas Stevens in 1982, later published in *Socialist Review.* Probably very few workers had seen this publication, but any who remembered it might well have been concerned about my political sympathies. It is hard to know just how all this affected workers' responses to the surveys, focus groups, or individual interviews, but some did comment on our supposed "communist" leanings in the course of the research.

At the other extreme, some workers apparently believed our project was designed to benefit management. One incident that occurred early on illustrates this well. On an informal tour of the Linden-GM plant one morning in 1987, I was introduced to a worker sitting alone in a booth, where he was stationed to monitor a control panel—a plum job if there ever was one. A tape recorder slung prominently over my shoulder, I walked in with my guide—an overly friendly union official who called me "honey" and tried to touch me at every possible opportunity, but who also seemed genuinely eager to help with the research. When we arrived, the worker in the booth appeared relaxed, drinking coffee and reading the newspaper while keeping an eye on the control panel for which he was responsible. I proceeded to ask him a series of questions about his job, mostly focusing on how the new technology had changed the tasks and skills involved. As he described his job and its responsibilities in great detail, I was struck by how articulate and cooperative he was, and at first I thought I had found an ideal interviewee. After a while, I asked if his job had become harder, easier, or about the same as a result of the plant modernization, and he responded that it was "about the same." At that point my escort (the unionist with the roving hands), who had known this worker for years, burst out in protest, "What do you mean, 'about the same'? Before, you were really busy, you hardly had a minute to wipe your nose. Now, we walk in, you're reading the newspaper, you're drinking coffee, you have plenty of time to talk with us. How can you say it's 'about the same'?" My interviewee responded, outraged, "I'm not going to say that. She has a tape recorder!"

Indeed, the simple fact that we were able to wander freely through the plant, sometimes accompanied by management and other times by union staff, and to conduct our focus groups and in-plant survey on company time aroused all sorts of suspicions. "There's no trust of anybody in there," Charlie Ferraro (pseudonym) warned us in a background interview. "It's really bad. Everybody's alienated—from both the union and management." We presented the project both in informal conversations and in information sheets distributed to focus-group members and survey respondents as something that would help the union better serve its members. Such a claim was inherently ambiguous in the age of "jointness" between the UAW and GM, however (see chapter 5).

However, "jointness" was also what induced so many local management officials, and a few at GM headquarters in Detroit, to answer our questions. Here our official sponsorship by company and union was essential; that "Detroit" had ordered managers to "cooperate" with our project proved invaluable. Sometimes with Cydney and at other times on my own, I interviewed managers in a variety of different jobs throughout the fieldwork. They supplied most of the quantitative data (other than the surveys themselves) reported in the text.

We also interviewed union officials, again both in Detroit and at Linden, where we spoke with all the top local officers and most of the committeemen. In addition, we had numerous observational opportunities and informal conversations with workers in the plant, sometimes on guided tours (as in the control booth mentioned above) and other times between official interviews. In all these situations, however, we were seen as girls, management spies, commies, or whatever—and this in turn determined what sorts of information we received, what sorts were deliberately withheld from us, and what sorts were manufactured for our sole consumption.

Inevitably, such influences were also present in the more structured focus-group discussions and survey research, despite our continual efforts to circumvent any obvious sources of bias. In early 1988, we conducted three focus-group discussions—two with production workers and one with skilled-trades workers. Focus-group members were selected randomly as part of a larger sample drawn from the plant roster that we also used for our in-plant survey. (The sample is described in detail below.) Each focus-group discussion, held in a conference room inside the plant during regular working hours, lasted about two hours and was tape-recorded and later transcribed. Workers were paid their normal wage for the time they spent in these discussions. This arrangement ensured perfect attendance but also underscored the project's official status. Surely this made some participants suspicious, so that they did not speak their minds freely—though many were extremely critical of management even under these constrained conditions.[1]

Both in the focus groups and in our in-plant survey, we offered respondents the usual professional assurances of confidentiality and promised that we would only report the overall results rather than those for any individual. Still, workers' worries about our true purposes inevitably influenced their responses. As Charlie Ferraro warned, "You got to understand, if I'm working on the production line and I'm asked to leave my job to come up to some office, right off the jump I start tightening up. Right off the jump. Usually you're getting thrown out when that happens, or some other bullshit, you know. So right off the jump, you're suspicious."

One undeniable advantage of our ability to conduct the in-plant survey on company time was that we got a response rate of over 90 percent, something survey researchers rarely achieve. Workers were taken off the line and invited into a private cubicle on the factory floor to respond to the survey.[2] Among a sample of 299, only 12 people refused to be interviewed, since talking to us was invariably preferable to working on the line. (Besides those 12, we were unable to interview 18 other sample members who were on medical or personal leave at the time of the survey.) Some workers transparently sought to prolong the conversation to avoid returning to work for as long as possible, and a few volunteered that they agreed to participate only because of the opportunity to get off the line.

The survey was administered in February and March 1988 in face-to-face individual interviews, with the interviewers (Cydney, myself, and a team of

CUNY graduate students) recording each participant's response to a series of closed-ended questions on a printed form. No tape recorders were used for the survey component of the research. For workers who requested it, the interviews were conducted in Spanish. The survey respondents included 217 GM-Linden day-shift production workers in the plant's four main departments (body, paint, trim, and chassis), as well as 52 skilled-trades workers. Within each production department, a simple random sample was drawn from among all workers who had been in the same department before and after the changeover, excluding utility, repair, and relief workers. In the case of the skilled trades, we used a simple random sample of workers employed at GM-Linden both before and after the plant modernization.[3] Demographically, the samples and the populations (in the case of both the production and the skilled-trades workers) were not significantly different from one another, in regard to gender, race, education, and age.

Cydney and I also designed and conducted (again, with the help of our graduate student team) an initial telephone survey of the buyout takers in 1987.[4] Prior to the actual survey, we sent all members of the buyout sample a letter about the research, on Labor Institute letterhead, enclosing endorsements from the UAW and GM. This probably increased our response rate, but it also meant that the sponsorship problems associated with the in-plant research affected buyout takers too. In the telephone interviews, a few respondents hinted of hopes that talking to us might somehow be helpful to them in the future, should they ever want to return to GM. On the other hand, some buyout takers probably felt defensive about their decision to leave the plant, and they may well have put a more positive spin on their circumstances than they would have done in a different context.

This initial buyout survey was directed at a simple random sample of 130 members of the total population of 905 GM-Linden workers who accepted the buyout in 1986 or early 1987, drawn from a list supplied by the plant management. We had a 70 percent response rate, much lower than for the in-plant survey, mostly because of difficulties in locating sample members.[5] Available demographic information on the nonrespondents makes it possible to compare them to respondents on several dimensions. The age, sex, education, and seniority profiles are virtually identical for the two groups. However, this is not the case with race: African Americans are slightly underrepresented in the survey.[6] Since (as is discussed extensively in chapter 4), African-American buyout takers fared worse than whites and Latinos, it seems likely that the survey results are somewhat biased in favor of workers who fared well.

Cydney and I produced a project report for the UAW and GM in the summer of 1988, and that ended both the period of ready access to the plant and also our collaboration. I moved to the West Coast immediately afterward to take a job at UCLA. Cydney and I agreed that we would both be free to use the jointly collected data for our individual purposes, and she went on to write her Ph.D. dissertation drawing on the in-plant survey data. I decided to gather more materials before attempting to write this book, and in the next few years, I searched for historical documents in various archives, conducted two follow-up buyout surveys, and did several dozen interviews with individual workers—both buyout takers and those who remained in the plant.

I had two important strokes of luck in this phase of the research. One involved the individual I call here Carl Block (pseudonym), a former committeeman at Linden who had almost legendary status in the memories of many of the rank-and-file workers I interviewed. He had left the plant years before I tracked him down, but he had saved several cartons of grievances, union-meeting minutes, flyers, and other plant records. A college-educated person with whom I shared some acquaintances, he both understood what I was up to and seemed inclined to trust me. Not only did he turn over his boxes of GM-Linden memorabilia, but he also provided a candid (though necessarily retrospective) interview that bristled with insights. Many of the workers I would interview later on were visibly impressed when I mentioned that I'd tracked down Block and gotten help from him.

I was lucky once again when I sought access to the National Labor Relations Board (NLRB) archival records of the union complaints against GM-Linden management (cited extensively in chapter 3). Although most such case records are routinely destroyed, these already had been selected for preservation by the NLRB. Nonetheless, because the events were relatively recent, my initial request for the material was denied. I appealed to NLRB General Counsel Fred Feinstein to gain access to the records, and I am extremely grateful that he granted the majority of my requests—although some materials remained withheld on grounds of protecting individuals' privacy.[7]

From UCLA, I designed two follow-up surveys of the buyout takers (which modified the initial survey and introduced some new questions), again doing a portion of the survey interviewing myself and hiring UCLA graduate students to do the rest. I wrote to all the original respondents, explaining that I was now in California and enclosing a letter of endorsement from the UAW regional office. Of the 91 respondents in the first survey, 81 were reinterviewed about their circumstances in 1989, and 79 were interviewed once again regarding their status in 1991.[8] Thus, by 1991, the response rate had fallen to 61 percent of the original sample of 130, but 87 percent of the respondents to the initial survey were still participating in the study.[9] Of the 12 individuals lost between 1987 and 1991, 11 were white men and one was a Latina; indeed, these losses corrected for the underrepresentation in African Americans among the original respondents noted above.

Starting in 1989 and continuing through 1991, I made a series of trips back to New Jersey. On these occasions I was able to do a few more interviews with both management and union officials who had been particularly helpful earlier, and who remembered me from the earlier phase of the project. Some were puzzled by my continuing interest in them now that I no longer had official sponsorship of the company or the union. On the whole, however, my stated intention of "writing a book" seemed a much more comprehensible—and neutral—position to many individuals than the officially legitimate status Cydney and I had gone to such pains to achieve at the outset.

On these visits, my efforts were devoted mainly to conducting personal, open-ended interviews with both buyout takers and workers who were still in the plant. Most were with individuals who previously had responded to either the in-plant or buyout surveys, although I also interviewed several workers to whom I was referred by sample members. The subsamples I used at this point were far less random than the earlier survey samples. I tried to choose workers from a range of departments and to include both males and females, as well as a variety of racial and ethnic groups. At this stage I interviewed a total of 30 workers. Fourteen were buyout takers, all but 2 of whom had also been survey participants. The rest were still employed at Linden.

I explained to everyone I interviewed that I was now doing the research on my own, for the purpose of writing this book, but some workers' memories of the union and GM having sponsored the earlier project (and possibly the Labor Institute connection as well) put them on guard. Well trained in habits of distrust and dissimulation toward their employer, a few confessed after being interviewed that they initially had thought I still "worked for GM." For many, my involuntary shift from quasi-insider to outsider at this stage was a plus, and with some workers, I was able to establish enough rapport to allow them to reveal to me their involvement in various illegal or otherwise illegitimate activities.

Most of the interviews took place in workers' homes, or at local coffeeshops or restaurants. I used a very general interview guide but tried to be as casual as I could (my natural inclination in any case), and never discouraged anyone from going off on tangents. The interviews varied in length from 45 minutes to 4 hours, and all but two were tape-recorded and later transcribed.[10] Most interviews were with individuals, but in a few cases, workers offered to invite their friends from the plant as well, and I readily agreed. These turned out to be among the best interviews, since they developed a group dynamic in which my presence often became marginal. Although the tape recorder surely had occasional silencing effects, it had many advantages as well, most importantly allowing me to concentrate on and engage in the conversation rather than frantically note taking. In most cases it seemed quickly forgotten as workers became engaged in the conversation.

I came to feel that these interviews constituted the most valuable data I was able to obtain—indeed they are quoted extensively in the text. The surveys and my various earlier forays through the plant certainly provided the foundation for many of the ideas in this book and also helped me know what kinds of issues to focus on in the interviews. But in the end, the interview material—collected much more informally and after the period of official access to the field site had ended—proved richer and was a substantial source of insight. I leave it to the reader to assess the adequacy of my effort to mobilize and merge these disparate types of data. Hopefully, that task will be made easier by these comments on the social processes through which they were collected and constructed.

Notes

1. Introduction

1. The life histories recounted in the text are based on interviews with actual GM-Linden workers; only names and other identifying information have been altered to protect the privacy of individuals. All direct quotations are reproduced verbatim from tape-recorded interviews conducted by the author, unless otherwise indicated.

2. See, among many others, Barry Bluestone and Bennett Harrison, *The Deindustrialization of America: Plant Closings, Community Abandonment, and the Dismantling of Basic Industry* (New York: Basic Books, 1982); Katherine Newman, *Falling from Grace: The Experience of Downward Mobility in the American Middle Class* (New York: Free Press, 1988); Kathryn Marie Dudley, *The End of the Line: Lost Jobs, New Lives in Postindustrial America* (Chicago: University of Chicago Press, 1994); Carolyn C. Perrucci, Robert Perrucci, Dena B. Targ, and Harry R. Targ, *Plant Closings: International Context and Social Costs* (New York: Aldine de Gruyter, 1988); and Daniel S. Hamermesh, "What Do We Know about Worker Displacement in the U.S.?" *Industrial Relations* 28 (winter 1989): 51–59.

3. Ely Chinoy, *Automobile Workers and the American Dream*, 2d ed. (Urbana: University of Illinois Press, 1992 [first published 1955]).

4. *Work in America: Report of a Special Task Force to the Secretary of Health, Education and Welfare* (Cambridge: MIT Press, [1973?]).

5. For access to the debate about teams, see Harry C. Katz, *Shifting Gears: Changing Labor Relations in the U.S. Automobile Industry* (Cambridge: MIT Press, 1985); Mike Parker and Jane Slaughter, *Choosing Sides: Unions and the Team Concept* (Boston: South End Press, 1988); James P. Womack, Daniel T. Jones, and Daniel Roos, *The Machine That Changed the World* (New York: Rawson Associates, 1990).

6. Parker and Slaughter, *Choosing Sides,* 5.

7. This is part of the larger decline in research on workers lamented in Ida Harper Simpson, "The Sociology of Work: Where Have the Workers Gone?" *Social Forces* 67 (March 1989): 563–81.

8. Womack, Jones, and Roos, *Machine That Changed the World.*

9. The clearest example is Parker and Slaughter, *Choosing Sides.* A few recent critical case studies of unionized U.S. and Canadian auto transplants (partially Japanese- and partially locally owned) do include some discussion of rank-and-file workers' views. See Joseph J. Fucini and Suzy Fucini, *Working for the Japanese: Inside Mazda's American Auto Plant* (New York: Free Press, 1990); Laurie Graham, *On the Line at Subaru-Isuzu: The Japanese Model and the American Worker* (Ithaca: Cornell University Press, 1995); James Rinehart, Chris Huxley, and David Robertson, "Team Concept at CAMI," in *Lean Work: Empowerment and Exploitation in the Global Auto Industry,* ed. Steve Babson (Detroit: Wayne State University Press, 1995), 220–34; and Steve Babson, "Whose Team? Lean Production at Mazda U.S.A.," in Babson, *Lean Work,* 235–46.

10. See Saul Rubinstein, Michael Bennett, and Thomas Kochan, "The Saturn Partnership: Co-Management and the Reinvention of the Local Union," in *Employee Representation: Alternatives and Future Directions,* ed. Bruce E. Kaufman and Morris M. Kleiner (Madison, Wis.: Industrial Relations Research Association, 1993), 339–70; and Barry Bluestone and Irving Bluestone, *Negotiating the Future: A Labor Perspective on American Business* (New York: Basic Books, 1992), 191–201.

11. Positive evaluations come from Womack, Jones, and Roos, *Machine That Changed the World;* Clair Brown and Michael Reich, "When Does Cooperation Work? A Look at NUMMI and GM-Van Nuys," *California Management Review* 31 (summer 1989): 26–44; and Paul Adler, "The 'Learning Bureaucracy': New United Motor Manufacturing, Inc.," in *Research in Organizational Behavior,* ed. Barry M. Staw and Larry L. Cummings (Greenwich, Conn.: JAI Press, 1992, 111–94). Critiques include Parker and Slaughter, *Choosing Sides;* Christian Berggren, *Alternatives to Lean Production: Work Organization in the Swedish Auto Industry* (Ithaca: ILR Press, 1992); Stephen Wood, "The Japanization of Fordism?" *Economic and Industrial Democracy* 14 (November 1993): 538–55; and Ulrich Jürgens, Thomas Malsch, and Knuth Dohse, *Breaking from Taylorism: Changing Forms of Work in the Automobile Industry* (New York: Cambridge University Press, 1993).

12. Parker and Slaughter, *Choosing Sides,* 19.

13. Although their focus is a Japanese-owned plant in England, Philip Garrahan and Paul Stewart make a similar point in *The Nissan Enigma: Flexi-*

bility at Work in a Local Economy (New York: Mansell Publishing, 1992), especially chapter 4.

14. Parker and Slaughter, *Choosing Sides,* 111. Lowell Turner makes a similar point in regard to NUMMI in *Democracy at Work: Changing World Markets and the Future of Labor Unions* (Ithaca: Cornell University Press, 1991), 53–62.

2. Prisoners of Prosperity

1. Among the most valuable discussions of this history are Nelson Lichtenstein, *The Most Dangerous Man in Detroit: Walter Reuther and the Fate of American Labor* (New York: Basic Books, 1995), especially chapter 13; Nelson Lichtenstein, "UAW Bargaining Strategy and Shop-Floor Conflict, 1946–1970," *Industrial Relations* 24 (fall 1985): 360–81; and Howell John Harris, *The Right to Manage: Industrial Relations Policies of American Business in the 1940s* (Madison: University of Wisconsin Press, 1982).

2. The best account is Stephen Meyer III, *The Five Dollar Day: Labor Management and Social Control in the Ford Motor Company, 1908–1921* (Albany: State University of New York Press, 1981). See also Joyce Shaw Peterson, *American Automobile Workers, 1900–1933* (Albany: State University of New York Press, 1987); and David Gartman, *Auto Slavery: The Labor Process in the American Automobile Industry, 1897–1950* (New Brunswick, N.J.: Rutgers University Press, 1986).

3. See Carl Gersuny and Gladis Kaufman, "Seniority and the Moral Economy of U.S. Automobile Workers, 1934–1946," *Journal of Social History* 18 (spring 1985): 463–75; Nelson Lichtenstein, "The Union's Early Days: Shop Stewards and Seniority Rights," in Mike Parker and Jane Slaughter, *Choosing Sides: Unions and the Team Concept* (Boston: South End Press, 1988), 65–73; Lichtenstein, *Most Dangerous Man,* 150–51, 292; Michael J. Piore and Charles F. Sabel, *The Second Industrial Divide: Possibilities for Prosperity* (New York: Basic Books, 1984), 114–15.

4. *1987 Agreement between Chevrolet-Pontiac-GM of Canada, Linden Plant, General Motors Corporation and Local No. 595, United Auto Workers, Region 9* (privately published), 37–42. The narrowing of wage differentials at GM was among the UAW's cardinal achievements in the first decades of its existence. Between 1940 and 1960, relative wage differentials within GM's production workforce declined by 60 percent. See Lichtenstein, *Most Dangerous Man,* 140.

5. Harry C. Katz, *Shifting Gears: Changing Labor Relations in the U.S. Automobile Industry* (Cambridge: MIT Press, 1985), 22–23. As auto workers' wages rose relative to those of others in manufacturing, leaving the auto

industry for other industrial jobs became increasingly unattractive to workers, a development that indirectly undermined workers' power and that of the UAW. As the option to "exit" the industry became less practical, the "voice" of the workers was less likely to be heard. I am grateful to Nelson Lichtenstein for suggesting this point to me.

6. The literature on auto workers is vast, although relatively few works deal directly with the quality of shop-floor experience from the perspective of workers themselves. Among the best of those that do are Ely Chinoy, *Automobile Workers and the American Dream,* 2d ed. (Urbana: University of Illinois Press, 1992 [first published 1955]); Harvey Swados, *On the Line* (Boston: Little, Brown, 1957); Stanley Aronowitz, *False Promises: The Shaping of American Working Class Consciousness,* 2d ed. (Durham, N.C.: Duke University Press, 1992 [first published 1973]), chapter 1; Richard Feldman and Michael Betzold, *End of the Line* (New York: Weidenfeld and Nicolson, 1988); and Ben Hamper, *Rivethead* (New York: Warner Books, 1991). Other such accounts of auto workers in other countries include Huw Beynon, *Working for Ford* (London: Allen Lane, 1973); and Robert Linhart, *The Assembly Line,* trans. Margaret Crosland (Amherst: University of Massachusetts Press, 1981); originally published as *L'établi* (Paris: Editions de Minuit, 1978).

7. "General Motors Opens New Plant," *New York Times,* May 28, 1937, 31; "A Friendly Welcome: The Linden Plant" (pamphlet in author's possession, 1973); Charles Emerson, "Building Assembly Automation," *American Machinist & Automated Manufacturing* 131 (March 1987): 71.

8. Women are better represented in the auto-parts industry, where wages are considerably lower, than in assembly plants like Linden. For a historical account of the crystallization of postwar employment patterns in the auto industry by gender and race, see Ruth Milkman, *Gender at Work: The Dynamics of Job Segregation by Sex during World War II* (Urbana: University of Illinois Press, 1987). The best history of blacks in the auto industry is August Meier and Elliott Rudwick, *Black Detroit and the Rise of the UAW* (New York: Oxford University Press, 1979). The 1985 Linden data were supplied by local management. For the rise in women's employment at Linden in the 1970s, see Frank J. Prial, "G.M. Workers Say Layoffs in Linden Presage an End to Big American Car," *New York Times,* January 4, 1974, 33.

9. The 1984 local contract (in effect in 1985) listed a total of 137 production-worker classifications, but in 1985, only 89 of these actually had workers employed in them.

10. In a 1988 in-plant survey conducted by the author and Cydney Pullman at GM-Linden, 39 percent of respondents in the trim department and 30 percent in the chassis department said they could "bank" their work in

the pre-1985 period, compared with only 13 percent in the paint shop and 9 percent in the body shop. See appendix 3 for details on the survey and the sampling technique.

11. The correlation coefficient is $-.13$ ($P = .000$), for the 4,334 workers for whom 1985 wage and seniority data are available.

12. See appendix 1 for the detailed data on this point.

13. By contrast, Ely Chinoy's study of another GM plant in the late 1940s found that workers ranked custodial jobs at the very bottom of the "informal hierarchy of desirability." See Chinoy, *Automobile Workers,* 65. A few of the workers I interviewed at Linden had this negative view of janitor and sweeper positions, but most seemed to concur with Block's characterization in the text below. The fact that GM workers could get good pensions after thirty years in the plant by the 1980s, whereas this option did not exist at the time Chinoy did his research, may explain the contrast between my findings and his on this point. In other respects the informal hierarchy of desirability is largely similar between the two cases.

14. Outside the four main production departments, there was 1 worker in a waste water treatment classification in the maintenance department with only 1 year's seniority in 1985. With that exception, there were no production-worker job classifications in the entire plant where median seniority was less than 6 years. The metal grind classification, also in the body shop, shared the distinction (with the spot-welding classification mentioned in the text) of having a median seniority level of 6 years. See appendix 1 for a complete listing of job classifications and seniority levels for each.

15. Actually women and minorities were hired earlier in the 1970s as well, but when GM laid off the entire second shift at Linden in early 1974, these low-seniority workers were disproportionately affected. Union officials at the time claimed that 60 percent of those laid off in 1974 were blacks, Puerto Ricans, and women. Everyone hired after February 1968 was laid off at this time, and the top seniority among women in the plant was 1970. See Prial, "G.M. Workers."

16. The percentages cited are based on the total female and male workforce for whom job classification information is available (601 female and 3,744 male workers); for 56 women and 88 men, information on this variable is missing. The other four classifications involved are: all instrument panel operators (trim department); body assembly operator B (paint department); final assembly (chassis department); and fender and radiator (chassis department).

17. The transfer procedures are spelled out in Paragraph 63 of the GM-UAW National Agreement, which reads in part, "where ability, merit and capacity are equal, the applicant with the longest seniority will be given preference."

18. As appendix 1 shows, the median seniority for the 112 workers in the car driver classification (chassis department) in 1985 was 15 years.

19. This type of "premium" classification (labeled thus because, like relief and utility work, it came with a small amount of extra pay) existed in a form organizationally distinct from the job classifications listed in table 2 and appendix 1 that include the term *repair* in the title, even though the workers involved often performed substantively similar functions.

20. See the discussion of this issue in Robert Schrank, *Ten Thousand Working Days* (Cambridge: MIT Press, 1978).

21. The in-plant survey mentioned above, which was conducted on company time, benefited from this impulse, as is further discussed in appendix 3.

22. This practice is mentioned in Aronowitz, *False Promises;* and in Hamper, *Rivethead.*

3. Adversarialism and Beyond

1. See Thomas A. Kochan, Harry C. Katz, and Robert B. McKersie, *The Transformation of American Industrial Relations* (New York: Basic Books, 1986), 85.

2. Michael Massing, "Detroit's Strange Bedfellows," *New York Times Magazine,* February 7, 1988, 20–27, 52. See also Glenn Perusek, "Leadership and Opposition in the United Automobile Workers," in *Trade Union Politics: American Unions and Economic Change, 1960s–1990s,* ed. Glenn Perusek and Kent Worcester (Atlantic Highlands, N.J.: Humanities Press International, 1995), 169–87.

3. "To Open Assembly Plant," *New York Times,* May 27, 1937, 40; "General Motors Opens New Plant," *New York Times,* May 28, 1937, 31; and Norman Beasley, *Knudsen: A Biography* (New York: McGraw Hill, 1947), 177.

4. Of 2,485 valid votes cast in the GM-Linden representation election supervised by the NLRB on April 17, 1940, 2,135 (86 percent) were for the UAW-CIO, 65 for the UAW-AFL, and 285 for neither union. Similar elections were held on the same date at GM plants around the nation; in most cases the results overwhelmingly favored the UAW-CIO. See U.S. National Labor Relations Board, *Decisions and Orders of the National Labor Relations Board* 24 (May 29–June 30, 1940): 159–79.

5. "2100 Strike at Plant of General Motors," *New York Times,* November 7, 1941, 6; "Linden Strikers Seeking a Parley," *New York Times,* November 10, 1941, 9; "Automobile Strike Ends," *New York Times,* November 17, 1941, 11.

6. "Walkout of 44 Halts Big Jersey Car Plant," *New York Times,* July

18, 1953, 10; Ralph Rodney, "Rank and File Strike Flares at Linden over GM Plant Grievances," *Militant,* July 27, 1953, copy in folder titled "UAW—Locals/Local 595," VF Collection, Wayne State University Archives of Labor History and Urban Affairs (hereafter cited as WSU Archives).

7. See Minutes of Shop Committee–Management Meeting, February 17, 1954, 9–10, in folder titled "Local 595, Linden, New Jersey, January 1954–March 1954," box 28, UAW Local 216 Collection, WSU Archives.

8. Stanley Aronowitz, *False Promises: The Shaping of American Working Class Consciousness,* 2d ed. (Durham, N.C.: Duke University Press, 1992), 368; "Strikers at G.M. Sabotage Talks, Reuther Warns," *New York Times,* June 9, 1955, 1, 25.

9. "Grievance Move Rejected," *New York Times,* September 26, 1958, 15; see also "Auto Stoppages Keep 82,545 Idle," *New York Times,* September 27, 1958, 26.

10. "2,600 in Jersey Quit G.M. Plant a 2nd Time," *New York Times,* May 2, 1961, 40.

11. Nelson Lichtenstein, "UAW Bargaining Strategy and Shop-Floor Conflict, 1946–1970," *Industrial Relations* 24 (fall 1985): 376.

12. A more sophisticated yet congruent perspective holds that grievances and other such institutionalized forms of shop-floor struggle reinforce the overall consent of workers to the terms of capitalist production even as they challenge those terms at the margin. See Michael Burawoy, *Manufacturing Consent* (Chicago: University of Chicago Press, 1979), chapter 7.

13. Lichtenstein, "UAW Bargaining Strategy," 374–75.

14. This generalization is based on interviews with management and union officials, shop committee minutes for the period between January 1978 and September 1981 (in author's possession), and also on a collection of 666 actual grievances filed between December 1979 and November 1982 by one committeeman and his alternate, which is also the source of the grievances reproduced in the text below. This collection was kindly provided to the author by former Committeeman Carl Block (pseudonym). By all accounts Block was unusually aggressive about filing and pursuing grievances, so that these data may not be entirely representative of the plant as a whole, but they do suggest the sorts of issues that most often led workers to make use of the grievance mechanism in this period.

15. Paragraph 78 of the national GM-UAW contract reads in part, "Production standards shall be established on the basis of fairness and equity consistent with the quality of workmanship, efficiency of operations, and the reasonable working capacities of normal operators. The Local Management of each plant has full authority to settle such matters."

16. This is the text of an actual grievance from the collection provided

by Carl Block. The examples that follow are from the same source, unless otherwise indicated. All are reproduced verbatim except that the names of any persons mentioned in the text are omitted.

17. These cases are not from the grievances in the Block collection but appear in shop committee minutes from March and April 1978.

18. This is step 2 in the grievance procedure specified in Paragraphs 28 to 45 of the national *Agreement between General Motors Corporation and the UAW* (privately published, various years).

19. This is based on analysis of shop committee–management meetings for which minutes are in author's possession, held between January 25, 1978, and April 27, 1979; and between July 29, 1981, and September 30, 1981. In addition to the 31 meetings mentioned in the text, this collection of minutes includes 21 meetings where no grievances were discussed.

20. Ely Chinoy, *Automobile Workers and the American Dream*, 2d ed. (Urbana: University of Illinois Press, 1992 [first published 1955]), 97, 101, 105.

21. "Plant Guard Assaults President," *Local 595 Shop News Bulletin*, May 8, 1978, copy in author's possession.

22. Although the workers' names are not cited here to protect their privacy, the two names appearing in the shop committee minutes from which the extracts above are taken also appear on a plant roster for 1985 in author's possession.

23. The now classic report *Work in America*, by a Special Task Force to the Secretary of Health, Education and Welfare (Cambridge: MIT Press, [1973]), was important in shaping public awareness of blue-collar discontent at this time. The best account of events at Lordstown, emphasizing the generational aspect, is chapter 1 of Aronowitz, *False Promises*. See also Emma Rothschild's prophetic *Paradise Lost: The Decline of the Auto-Industrial Age* (New York: Random House, 1973), which includes the quotation from *Business Week* (17). Perusek, "Leadership and Opposition," argues for a somewhat different chronology, locating the emergence of rank-and-file revolt in the UAW in the late 1960s, and highlighting its links to the wider wave of social protest of that period. This may be accurate for groups like the League of Revolutionary Black Workers and perhaps more generally in Detroit auto plants, but at least at Linden (which had relatively few African-American workers before 1976), the upsurge came a bit later.

24. General Motors Corporation and Michael McCarthy, Craig H. Livingston, Roland Beish, Cases 22-CA-5831, 22-CA-5875, and 22-CA-5948, June 16, 1975, Decision and Order, U.S. National Labor Relations Board, *Decisions and Orders of the NLRB*, vol. 218 (Washington, D.C., 1976), 472–79. These events are discussed and additional background information presented in Michael Hoyt, "LAW Comes to Linden: The Union that G.M.

Couldn't Bust," *Nation,* March 19, 1983, 332–35. Because Stevens's and Towell's names appear in this published article, as well in other sources cited below, I use their actual names here rather than pseudonyms.

25. General Motors and McCarthy, Livingston, and Beish, *Decisions and Orders,* vol. 28, 477, 475.

26. Ibid., 478. The disposition of the appeal by the U.S. Court of Appeals, on April 21, 1976, is noted in 535 F. 2d 1246 (3d Cir. 1976). A copy of the court's unpublished judgment order, docket 75-1750, was obtained by the author by means of a Freedom of Information Act request to the NLRB. Documents procured in this manner are hereafter identified as NLRB Historical Records (FOIA).

27. On the 1974 layoffs, see Frank J. Prial, "G.M. Workers Say Layoffs in Linden Presage an End to Big American Car," *New York Times,* January 4, 1974, 33. The second shift was fully restored by June 1976, as is evident from later seniority lists in author's possession.

28. The quotation is from an affidavit sworn before an NLRB representative on April 22, 1976 [name redacted], in NLRB Historical Records (FOIA).

29. General Motors and McCarthy, Livingston, and Beish, *Decisions and Orders,* 478.

30. These are excerpts from three redacted affidavits [from which all names have been deleted] dated December 6, 1977; November 18, 1977; and March 8, 1977, respectively; all in NLRB Historical Records (FOIA). There are about a dozen other affidavits with similar content.

31. The following extracts are from redacted affidavits dated April 22, 1976; January 26, 1977; November 7, 1977; August 26, 1976; and January 19, 1977, respectively; all from NLRB Historical Records (FOIA). The records also contain several other affidavits with similar complaints.

32. Arthur Eisenberg (regional director, NLRB Region 22) to Joseph E. DeSio (associate general counsel, NLRB), April 17, 1978, NLRB Historical Records (FOIA).

33. Craig H. Livingston, quoted in Hoyt, "LAW Comes to Linden," 334.

34. *National Labor Relations Board v. General Motors Corporation,* Judgement of U.S. Court of Appeals for the Third Circuit, Dec. 12, 1978, docket 78-2427 (unpublished), with attached Settlement Stipulation (signed by the parties on March 27, 1978), NLRB Historical Records (FOIA). The various delays preceding this settlement are described in Craig H. Livingston to John S. Irving (general counsel, NLRB), February 23, 1978, NLRB Historical Records (FOIA).

35. Notice to Employees Posted by Order of the National Labor Relations Board, August 8, 1978, copy in NLRB Historical Records (FOIA).

36. Information on local union elections has been culled from a fragmen-

tary collection of electoral flyers, mimeographed election results distributed by Local 595, and the local union newspaper, all in author's possession.

37. Craig H. Livingston to Arthur Eisenberg, August 24, 1978; Craig H. Livingston to Arthur Eisenberg, October 23, 1978; James J. Crowley (attorney for GM) to Arthur Eisenberg, October 31, 1978; all in NLRB Historical Records (FOIA).

38. "U.S. Aide Targets GM Labor Practices: National Labor Board Urged to Sue over Linden Plant Violations," *Sunday Star-Ledger* (Newark), October 12, 1980, sec. 1, 60; Arthur Eisenberg (regional director, NLRB Region 22) to Craig H. Livingston (attorney for parties bringing charges against GM), August 25, 1980, copy in author's possession; Arthur Eisenberg to Craig H. Livingston, December 2, 1981, copy in author's possession; "Labor Board Says 'Contempt of Court': GM Management Accused of Unfair Labor Practices!" *Local 595 UAW Assembler* 25 (December 1981): 1, 4.

39. Petition for Adjudication in Civil Contempt and for Other Civil Relief, *National Labor Relations Board v. General Motors Corporation*, U.S. Court of Appeals for the Third Circuit, dockets 75-1750 and 78-2427, December 17, 1981, NLRB Historical Records (FOIA). Carl Block, a pseudonym, is the same individual mentioned elsewhere in the narrative; other workers' names appearing in this document have been changed to pseudonyms here to protect their privacy.

40. *Local 595 UAW Assembler* 22 (October 1978): 4. Interestingly, this article was reprinted from another UAW local paper, the *Advocator* (Newcastle, Ind.: UAW Local 371, n.d.).

41. Flyers in author's possession. The flyer pointing to the prospect of "Russian governance" is dated June 1981; another flyer in support of anti-LAW candidates for the 1979 elections alleges that on May 1 of that year "on the night shift a group of Commies somehow got into the plant and staged a parade with banners and flags[,] ready to plant their flag and declare our plant for their own." Although this latter flyer does not explicitly accuse LAW of this action, it is clearly meant to imply such a connection by prefacing its attack on LAW with anti-Communist rhetoric inspired by this alleged event.

42. Tony Fernandez is a real name; it appears in print in many publications of the local union and for that reason has not been replaced by a pseudonym here.

43. On the Linden layoffs of 1974, see Prial, "G.M. Workers," 33. The data on auto-industry employment are for Standard Industrial Classification (SIC) 371 (motor vehicle and equipment), in U.S. Department of Labor, Bureau of Labor Statistics, *Employment and Earnings* (various issues).

44. Harry C. Katz, *Shifting Gears: Changing Labor Relations in the U.S. Automobile Industry* (Cambridge: MIT Press, 1985), chapter 3.

45. See Daniel J. B. Mitchell, "Shifting Norms in Wage Determination," *Brookings Papers on Economic Activity* 2 (1985): 575–99.

46. See Katz, *Shifting Gears,* chapter 3; Jane Slaughter, *Concessions— and How to Beat Them* (Detroit: Labor Education and Research Project, 1983); and Ruth Milkman with Douglas Stevens, "The Anti-Concessions Movement in the UAW," *Socialist Review* 65 (September–October 1982): 19–42. The account below is based on these sources, unless otherwise indicated.

47. Employment of auto-production workers fell from 781,700 in 1978 to 511,900 in 1982, according to the Bureau of Labor Statistics data cited in note 43 of this chapter.

48. See Stanley Aronowitz, "Union Contracts: A 'New Contract'?" *Nation,* April 24, 1982, 495–96; and Michael Harrington, "The Left Gropes for Options," *New York Times,* March 30, 1982, op-ed page.

49. The best and most recent account is chapter 11 of Nelson Lichtenstein, *The Most Dangerous Man in Detroit: Walter Reuther and the Fate of American Labor* (New York: Basic Books, 1995), 220–47.

50. Michael Goldfield, *The Decline of Organized Labor in the United States* (Chicago: University of Chicago Press, 1987), 10; U.S. Bureau of Labor Statistics, *Extent of Collective Bargaining and Union Recognition, 1945,* Bulletin 865 (Washington, D.C., 1946), 1.

51. The 1983 figures include both members and workers represented by unions and employee associations. They are not strictly comparable to the 1945 figures cited above, but the general deunionization trend is unmistakable. The 1983 data are from U.S. Department of Labor, Bureau of Labor Statistics, *Employment and Earnings* 32 (January 1985): 208–9.

52. See Seymour Martin Lipset, "Unions in the Public Mind," in *Unions in Transition: Entering the Second Century,* ed. Seymour Martin Lipset (San Francisco: Institute for Contemporary Studies, 1986), 287–321.

53. Douglas A. Fraser and Owen Bieber to UAW General Motors Members in the U.S., February 8, 1992, copy in author's possession; and Dan Luria (UAW Research Department), personal communication with author, 1982. See also David Bensman, "Labor's Painful Dilemma," *Commonweal,* March 26, 1982, 173–78.

54. Cydney Pullman, my collaborator on the early stages of the research for this book, was part of this effort. See appendix 3 for discussion.

55. Milkman with Stevens, "Anti-Concessions Movement," 32.

56. "Local 595 Hosts Anti-Concessions Conference," *Local 595 UAW Assembler* 25 (March 1982): 1–2.

57. Milkman with Stevens, "Anti-Concessions Movement," 33, 35.

58. "GM's Road to Survival: Con-crete or Con-Game," special issue of *Local 595 UAW Assembler* (1982).

59. "Many at G.M. Reluctantly Voting to Trade Money for Job Security," *New York Times,* April 9, 1982, A16.

60. Milkman with Stevens, "Anti-Concessions Movement," 37–38.

61. GM's share of U.S. retail car sales fell from 44 percent in 1984 to 34 percent in 1989, and then stabilized. For detailed data, see American Automobile Manufacturers Association, *Motor Vehicle Facts and Figures* (Detroit: various issues).

62. Stephen Herzenberg, "Whither Social Unionism? Labor and Restructuring in the U.S. Auto Industry," in *The Challenge of Restructuring: North American Labor Movements Respond,* ed. Jane Jenson and Rianne Mahon (Philadelphia: Temple University Press, 1993), 314–36.

63. Milkman with Stevens, "Anti-Concessions Movement," 39.

64. On the politicization of the NLRB under Reagan, see Penn Kimble, "The New Anti-Union Crusade," *New Republic,* September 1983, 18–20; U.S. Congress, House, Subcommittee on Labor-Management Relations of the Committee on Education and Labor, *The Failure of Labor Law: A Betrayal of American Workers,* 98th Congress, 2d sess., Report 98 (Washington, D.C., 1984); and the same subcommittee's oversight hearings, *Has Labor Law Failed?* 98th Cong., 2d sess., June 21, 25, and 26, 1984. Hoyt, "LAW Comes to Linden," notes that the NLRB case against GM was dropped on February 22, 1983 (335), although he fails to mention the changes at the NLRB itself that occurred simultaneously with this move. In a personal communication with the author, an official in the historical records division of the NLRB noted that most NLRB case records are destroyed after six years, except for a small number of cases that are chosen for preservation in the National Archives (including the 1978 Linden cases discussed above).

65. John Holusha, "13 G. M. Factories Struck by Locals," *New York Times,* September 16, 1984, 1, 26.

66. "President Fernandez Appointed to International Staff," *Local 595 UAW Assembler* 27 (May 1985): 1.

67. Massing, "Detroit's Strange Bedfellows," 23.

68. Herzenberg, "Whither Social Unionism?" is the single best published account of the intra-union debate.

4. Farewell to the Factory

1. U.S. Congress, Office of Technology Assessment, *Technology and Structural Unemployment: Reemploying Displaced Adults,* OTA-ITE-250 (Washington, D.C., 1986), 3.

2. Figures are for all employees in motor vehicle and equipment manu-

facturing (SIC 371), from U.S. Department of Labor, Bureau of Labor Statistics, *Employment and Earnings* (various issues).

3. The classic study is Barry Bluestone and Bennett Harrison, *The Deindustrialization of America: Plant Closings, Community Abandonment, and the Dismantling of Basic Industry* (New York: Basic Books, 1982).

4. Avery F. Gordon, Paul G. Schervish, and Barry Bluestone, "The Unemployment and Reemployment Experiences of Michigan Auto Workers" (prepared for the Office of Automotive Industry Affairs, U.S. Department of Commerce and the Transportation Systems Center, U.S. Department of Transportation, by Social Welfare Research Institute, Boston College, December 4, 1984, mimeographed), 21, 27, 69.

5. This study, based on a mail questionnaire, had only a 26 percent response rate. Jacob J. Kaufman, Stephen Levine, and Alice Beamsderfer, "The Closing of a Ford Motor Company Plant in Mahwah, New Jersey" (prepared for the New York State Department of Labor by the New York State School of Industrial and Labor Relations, Division of Extension and Public Service, Cornell University, Ithaca, January 1983), 49, 50, 60.

6. See Bluestone and Harrison, *Deindustrialization;* Katherine Newman, *Falling from Grace: The Experience of Downward Mobility in the American Middle Class* (New York: Free Press, 1988); Carolyn C. Perrucci, Robert Perrucci, Dena B. Targ, and Harry R. Targ, *Plant Closings: International Context and Social Costs* (New York: Aldine de Gruyter, 1988); and Daniel S. Hamermesh, "What Do We Know about Worker Displacement in the U.S.?," *Industrial Relations* 28 (winter 1989): 51–59.

7. In 1990, 53 percent of the U.S. civilian labor force 25 to 64 years of age had 12 or less years of formal education; as recently as 1970, the figure was 74 percent (Bureau of the Census, *Statistical Abstract of the U.S., 1993* [Washington, D.C., 1993], 394).

8. Frank Levy and Richard J. Murnane, "U.S. Earnings Levels and Earnings Inequality: A Review of Recent Trends and Proposed Explanations," *Journal of Economic Literature* 30 (September 1992): 1355. See also Bennett Harrison and Barry Bluestone, *The Great U-Turn: Corporate Restructuring and the Polarizing of America* (New York: Basic Books, 1988), chapter 5; and Lawrence Mishel and Jared Bernstein, *The State of Working America, 1994–95* (Armonk, N.Y.: M. E. Sharpe, 1994), chapter 3.

9. See, for example, David Bensman and Roberta Lynch, *Rusted Dreams: Hard Times in a Steel Community* (New York: McGraw Hill, 1987); Gregory Pappas, *The Magic City: Unemployment in a Working-Class Community* (Ithaca: Cornell University Press, 1989); and William Serrin, *Homestead: The Glory and Tragedy of an American Steel Town* (New York: Random House, 1992).

10. The SUB program was the ersatz version of the Guaranteed Annual Wage program the UAW had proposed in the 1955 negotiations. See Nelson Lichtenstein, *The Most Dangerous Man in Detroit: Walter Reuther and the Fate of American Labor* (New York: Basic Books, 1995), 284–86.

11. See Harry C. Katz, *Shifting Gears: Changing Labor Relations in the U.S. Automobile Industry* (Cambridge: MIT Press, 1985), 22–23, 57.

12. The description of the program in this paragraph and those that follow draw on Howard Young, "The 1984 Auto Negotiations: A UAW Perspective"; and Sheldon Friedman, "Negotiated Approaches to Job Security"; both in *Proceedings of the 1985 Spring Meeting, Industrial Relations Research Association,* in *Labor Law Journal* 35 (August 1985): 454–57; and 553–57, respectively. The program provisions are detailed in the *Agreement between General Motors Corporation and the UAW* (privately published, September 21, 1984), appendix K, 185–215; and in the pamphlet *Job Opportunity Bank–Security Program* (UAW-GM Skill Development and Training National Office, March 1985), which reproduces the contract language, along with detailed commentary.

13. These were the payment amounts specified in the 1984 contract; they were increased in later contracts.

14. Lydia Fischer (UAW Research Department), personal communication with author, February 28, 1995. About 10 percent of these VTEPs occurred in the first three years of the program (1984–1987); over 60 percent of them occurred between 1987 and 1990. Since 1994, when GM reluctantly began hiring new workers (under pressure from the union, which protested the extensive overtime requirements imposed that year), VTEPs essentially stopped.

15. Donald F. Ephlin, "How the UAW-GM JOB Bank Operates—an Insider's View," *World of Work Report* (newsletter of the Work in America Institute), (February 1985): 5–6.

16. The cap was increased in 1987 and again in 1990.

17. For a more detailed description and evaluation of the Linden jobs bank, see Ruth Milkman, "Technological Change and Job Security: A Case Study of GM-Linden" (based on research done in collaboration with Cydney Pullman) (Labor Institute, New York, 1987, mimeographed). The next several paragraphs of the text draw on this report.

18. The contract language reads in part: "Job security will be provided for an eligible employe [*sic*] in the event technology is introduced which would otherwise result in the permanent layoff of an employe [*sic*]. Technology for the purposes of this document only is defined as any change in product, methods, processes or the means of manufacturing introduced by management at a location which reduces the job content of existing work at that location" (*Agreement between General Motors and the UAW,* 185).

19. Fischer, personal communication.

20. Workers with less than ten years' seniority were entitled to only one year of SUB and thus had no income for up to 3 months between the expiration of their SUB pay in August and their recall (unless they had found a job elsewhere during the layoff period). There were also gaps in fringe benefits. Depending on seniority, laid-off workers received from 2 to 24 months of paid health insurance benefits, although all could purchase additional months of coverage as needed. Dental coverage was suspended entirely for most of the changeover period. On the other hand, during the layoff Linden workers were eligible for up to $5,000 in tuition reimbursement, and hundreds took advantage of this opportunity.

21. While workers could choose to simply sit in the building and not attend classes, few did so. By contrast, at some other jobs-bank locations idleness was a common experience. See "GM Pays Workers with No Jobs but They Aren't Sitting Pretty," *Detroit Free Press*, February 1, 1988, sec. C, 1, 8.

22. The acceptance rate for buyouts was 22 percent at Linden, compared with 14 percent at GM's assembly plant in Wilmington, Delaware; 9 percent at the Rochester, New York, parts plant, and 2 percent in the Anderson, Indiana, parts plant, all of which offered the VTEP buyout and the special early retirement program linked to JOBS around the same time. In contrast, Linden had the lowest acceptance rate for early retirements among these four plants: 26 percent of those eligible accepted early retirement at Linden, compared with 33 percent at Rochester, 36 percent at Anderson, and 38 percent at Wilmington. These differences are statistically significant ($p < .000$).

23. This is based on data provided by local management for the first 841 buyouts at Linden in late 1986 or early 1987 (whereas the survey described later in this chapter is based on a somewhat larger population of 905, including a group who took the buyout a bit later in 1987). The payment schedule and seniority distribution of the 841 is as follows:

Years of Seniority	Payment Amount ($)	Number of Workers	Percentage
1 but less than 2	10,000	5	0.5
2 but less than 5	15,000	84	10.0
5 but less than 10	25,000	476	57.0
10 but less than 15	35,000	230	27.0
15 but less than 20	45,000	39	5.0
20 but less than 25	50,000	7	0.8
25 or more	55,000	0	0.0
Total		841	100.0

24. Doron P. Levin, "A G.M. Jobless Fund Is out of Money, 2nd Solvent," *New York Times*, February 26, 1993, C3; "GM Employees in Jobs Bank Face Furlough on March 1," *Daily Labor Report*, February 26, 1993, A8. Funding for the program was restored later in 1993, in the new GM-UAW contract that took effect that fall.

25. I have no systematic information on the degree to which buyout takers were former LAW activists, although I do know that most of the former LAW leaders explicitly mentioned in chapter 3 did not take the buyout and indeed are still employed at GM-Linden. One of them, Charlie Ferraro, runs a small business on the side, however. "I'd rather be out there saving the world, but I tried that already, and it didn't work too good," he told me. "I'm trying to be a capitalist here." I am grateful to Nelson Lichtenstein for pointing out to me that political radicalism and entrepreneurial skills are often linked.

26. Although these data are for a population (rather than a sample) and thus significance tests may not be appropriate in the strict technical sense, it has become common to generate significance tests for such data. I leave it to the reader to assess their value.

27. The average seniority of women who took the buyout was 7.7 years, compared to 8.4 for men; women who remained in the plant averaged 8.8 years of seniority, compared to 14.0 years for men.

28. In these data (obtained from GM-Linden management, white, African-American, and Latino (called black and Hispanic, respectively, in GM's rendition) are mutually exclusive categories—despite the fact that Hispanics or Latinos can be of any race.

29. Because the buyout decision is dichotomous, the appropriate statistical technique is logistic regression. This is particularly convenient because the results can be expressed in terms of odds ratios. (More precisely, the exponentiated coefficients from logistic regression can be interpreted as odds ratios.)

30. Not only were workers hired in or after 1976 much more likely to accept the buyout (see table 3), but also this cohort is demographically quite different from the pre-1976 one. Most important, there are only 5 women in the older group. If the problem were merely the nonlinearity of the relationship between seniority and buyout taking, a dummy variable would be an adequate solution for the regression model. But the colinearity of the cohorts with the crucially important gender variable in the analysis renders this solution inadequate. Thus the two cohorts are modeled separately here.

31. This effect is cumulative: the odds of acceptance for a worker who is $x + 10$ years old are about one-third those for one who is x years old. As the table below shows, for this pre-1976 cohort, all coefficients are negative, except that for Latinos. Here are the full results of this logistic regression

model for workers hired before January 1, 1976 (N = 1421). The dependent variable is buyout acceptance.

Variable	Coefficient	Standard Error	Odds Multiplier
Intercept	−0.61	0.47	0.54
African American	−0.29	0.37	0.75
Latino	1.25*	0.33	3.49
Age	−0.12*	0.02	0.89
Less than high school education	−0.27	0.29	0.76
More than high school education	−1.24	1.00	0.29

*Significant at p < .01.

32. The full results of the logistic regression models for workers hired on or after January 1, 1976 (N = 2683), are shown below. Two models are shown: one with no interaction effects—from which the odds statement about women in relation to men is derived—and a second (described in the remainder of the text) where the full range of possible interactions between gender and other variables is modeled. The dependent variable for both models is buyout acceptance. Age is calculated from a base of 0, with 0 equal to the age of the youngest member of the population. Omitted categories are males, high school graduates, and whites.

	Model 1		Model 2	
Variable	Coefficient (Standard Deviation)	Odds Multiplier	Coefficient (Standard Deviation)	Odds Multiplier
Intercept	−0.70 (0.11)*	0.50	−0.76 (0.12)*	0.47
Hired after 6/22/77	0.89 (0.09)*	2.44	0.91 (0.11)*	2.49
African American	−0.16 (0.11)	0.85	0.03 (0.14)	1.03
Latino	0.40 (0.14)	1.50	0.48 (0.16)*	1.61
Less than high school	0.14 (0.10)	1.15	0.17 (0.11)*	1.19
More than high school	0.22 (0.15)	1.25	0.20 (0.17)	1.22
Age	−0.06 (0.01)*	0.38	−0.06(0.01)*	0.94
Female	0.70 (0.11)*	2.01	1.06 (0.29)*	2.89
Female & hired after 6/22/77			−0.16 (0.21)	0.85
Female & African American			−0.61 (0.24)**	0.54
Female & Latina			−0.37 (0.35)	0.69
Female & less than high school			−0.17 (0.23)	0.85
Female & more than high school			0.17 (0.36)	1.18
Female & age			0.00 (0.01)	1.00

*Significant at p < .01.   **Significant at p < .02.

33. This is the exponent of the sum of the three coefficients (for model 2 in the table in note 32): .03 (for African-American); 1.06 (for female); and -.61 (for the interaction of African-American and female).

34. For more details on the survey design and response rates, see appendix 3.

35. In this regard, a study conducted twenty-five years ago of auto workers who accepted early retirement (after 30 years' service), then a new program, is of interest. The study found that neither "satisfaction with job and with place of work, ease or difficulty in getting along with superiors, extent to which the work was repetitive, [nor] ability to control the pace of the work were found to be systematically related to having retired early." In this case the projected size of retirement income was found to be the key determinant of whether a worker chose to retire early. See Richard Barfield and James Morgan, *Early Retirement: The Decision and the Experience* (Ann Arbor: University of Michigan Survey Research Center, 1969), 4.

36. Significant at $p < 0.000$, using Fisher's exact test on the underlying cross-tabulation. This question was only asked in the first survey. Data are reported here only for the 79 workers who answered both the question about information and the one about whether they regretted their decision, with indefinite answers (e.g., "not sure," "don't know") omitted.

37. *Mary R. Wells et al. v. General Motors Corporation,* 881 F. 2d 166–76 (5th Cir. 1989).

38. In October 1986, the state's unemployment rate was 4.8 percent, falling to 4.3 percent by March 1987. See U.S. Department of Labor, Bureau of Labor Statistics, *Employment and Earnings,* table D-1 (various issues). See also Roger Lowenstein and Robert Guenther, "New Jersey Rides the Tide of an Economic Upswing," *Wall Street Journal,* August 6, 1987, 6; Robert D. Hershey Jr., "Jobless Figure Is Stable at 5.9% despite Increase in Employment," *New York Times,* September 5, 1987, 29.

39. By the time of the second survey, 3 of the 24 respondents who had been self-employed in 1987 had turned to wage and salary employment, though 1 kept the small business as a second job. Meanwhile, 4 people who had been wage and salary workers in 1987 had established businesses of their own by 1989. Of the 24 respondents who were self-employed in 1987, 5 were among those we were unable to reinterview in 1989.

By 1991, at the time of the third survey, 14 of the 20 respondents who were self-employed in 1989 were still self-employed, and 1 respondent who had been in wage and salary employment in 1989 had entered the self-employed group. Among the 20, 4 others were now in wage and salary employment, 1 was unemployed, and 1 was among those we failed to reach in 1991. In the third survey, then, respondents who were self-employed in 1989 were underrepresented among those we were unable to recontact.

40. George Steinmetz and Erik Olin Wright calculate that the self-employed comprised 12 percent of the labor force for 1984 in their article "The Fall and Rise of the Petty Bourgeoisie: Changing Patterns of Self-Employment in the Postwar United States," *American Journal of Sociology* 94, no. 5 (March 1989): 1010. A lower estimate of 7.5 percent of persons in nonagricultural industries in 1985 can be found in Sheldon E. Haber, Enrique J. Lamas, and Jules H. Lichtenstein, "On Their Own: The Self-Employed and Others in Private Business," *Monthly Labor Review* 110, no. 5 (May 1987): 17.

41. See Steinmetz and Wright "Fall and Rise,"; Haber, Lamas, and J. H. Lichtenstein, "On Their Own."

42. The classic study is Seymour Martin Lipset and Reinhard Bendix, *Social Mobility in Industrial Society* (Berkeley: University of California Press, 1959). See also Kurt B. Mayer and Sidney Goldstein, "Manual Workers as Small Businessmen," and Ivar Berg and David Rogers, "Former Blue-Collarites in Small Business," both in *Blue Collar World: Studies of the American Worker,* ed. Arthur B. Shostak and William Gomberg (Englewood Cliffs, N.J.: Prentice-Hall, 1964), 537–66.

43. Ely Chinoy, *Automobile Workers and the American Dream,* 2d ed. (Urbana: University of Illinois Press, 1992), 82–83, 86. See, however, Marx's remarks in the first volume of *Capital* (New York: International Publishers, 1967), on what later would be called American exceptionalism. In this passage Marx's observations about the United States in the nineteenth century are more consistent with Chinoy's perspective on the twentieth: "The wageworker of today is to-morrow an independent peasant, or artisan, working for himself. He vanishes from the labour-market, but not into the workhouse. This constant transformation of the wage-labourers into independent producers, who work for themselves instead of for capital, and enrich themselves instead of the capitalist gentry, reacts in its turn very perversely on the conditions of the labour-market. Not only does the degree of exploitation of the wage-labourer remain indecently low. The wage-labourer loses into the bargain, along with the relation of dependence, also the sentiment of dependence on the abstemious capitalist" (769–70).

44. Chinoy, *Automobile Workers,* 94–95.

45. Muriel Ray, "Renault et ses filleules," *Le Monde Dimanche,* June 1, 1980, v. Thanks to Daniele Kergoat for bringing this to my attention.

46. Below are the specific figures and the p-values (using Fisher's exact test) for the underlying cross-tabulations. Results are shown for all employed respondents answering the question "Do you make more, less or about the same now than when you worked at GM?" (The proportion answering "less" or "about the same" is not shown here; results are also statistically significant for all three years when the data are divided between "less" and the other possible responses at $p < .1$ for all three years.)

Percentage Earning More than at GM	1987 (N = 74)	1989 (N = 68)	1991 (N = 64)
Self-employed respondents	50	55	53
Wage & salary respondents	20	19	14
p =	.0137	.0071	.0039

Another way to analyze the earnings differences between the wage and salaried respondents and the self-employed is to directly compare their self-reported earnings. However, the figures reported by self-employed informants cannot be used with great confidence. In many cases, as informants themselves noted, these figures were rough estimates, since it was often difficult to distinguish personal earnings from business revenues in these microenterprises, many of which functioned on an all-cash basis. This should be kept in mind in interpreting the figures below, which show average self-reported hourly earnings (converted from annual earnings self-reported by the self-employed, using hours worked per week in the computation) for each group. The differences are statistically significant (using two-tailed t-tests with pooled variance) for all three years.

Year	Mean Hourly Earnings Wage & Salary Workers ($)	Mean Hourly Earnings Self-Employed Workers ($)	p-value
1987	10.18	29.09	.0000
1989	12.20	18.31	.0013
1991	11.94	18.35	.0223

47. Below are the data and the p-values (using Fisher's exact test) for the underlying cross-tabulations. Results are shown for all employed respondents answering the question "Aside from the pay, do you like this [your present] job more, less or about the same as your old job at Linden-GM?" (The proportion answering "less" or "about the same" is now shown.)

Percentage Who Like Present Job More	1987 (N = 76)	1989 (N = 66)	1991 (N = 66)
Self-employed respondents	96	95	93
Wage & salary respondents	60	66	69
p =	.0001	.0151	.0905

48. Here are the data and the p-values (using Fisher's exact test) for the underlying cross-tabulations. Results are shown for all employed respondents answering the question "If you had the chance to make the decision over again, would you still take the buyout?"

Percentage Who Would Not Take the Buyout Again	1987 (N = 75)	1989 (N = 68)	1991 (N = 66)
Self-Employed Respondents	8	5	0
Wage & Salary Respondents	22	23	28
p =	.2035	.0936	.0298

49. The business survival rate may be overstated here, however, since in the 1989 survey, respondents who were self-employed in 1987 were over-represented among those we were unable to reinterview (5 of the 10 respondents we lost had been self-employed in 1987); and in the third survey (1991), 1 of the 2 respondents we lost had been self-employed in 1989. Also, note that some respondents who had previously been in wage and salary jobs moved into self-employment between the surveys. This was the case for 4 respondents between 1987 and 1989 and for 1 between 1989 and 1991. See figure 1.

50. See U.S. Small Business Administration, *The State of Small Business: A Report of the President* (Washington, 1990), 25; and Arnold C. Cooper, William C. Dunkelberg, Carolyn Y. Woo, and William J. Dennis, Jr., *New Business in America: The Firms and Their Owners* (Washington, D.C.: The NFIB Foundation, 1990).

51. See Michael A. Curme, Barry T. Hirsch, and David A. MacPherson, "Union Membership and Contract Coverage in the United States, 1983–1988," *Industrial and Labor Relations Review* 44 (October 1990): 5–26. The only contiguous states with higher union density than New Jersey in 1988 were Michigan, New York and Washington (as well as the noncontiguous states of Alaska and Hawaii).

52. This is a much higher regret rate than among the self-employed. See note 48.

53. For means and comparisons with the self-employed respondents, see note 46 above.

54. Here are the data and the p-values (using Fisher's exact test) for the underlying cross-tabulations. Results are shown for all employed wage and salaried respondents answering the question "If you had the chance to make the decision over again, would you still take the buyout?" Note that the 1987 results are not statistically significant.

Percentage Who Would Not Take the Buyout Again	1987 (N = 49)	1989 (N = 48)	1991 (N = 49)
Respondents earning less than at GM	25	36	38
Respondents earning same or more than at GM	12	5	13
p =	.459	.0156	.0573

55. This is the insurance firm Robin Leidner describes in chapter 4 of her *Fast Food, Fast Talk: Service Work and the Routinization of Everyday Life* (Berkeley: University of California Press, 1993).

56. Of the 15 Latinos among the 91 respondents to the first, 1987 survey, 10 were foreign born, including all 4 of the females. Three respondents (1 male and 2 females) were from Spain; 4 (3 males and 1 female) were from Portugal; and 3 (2 males and 1 female) were from Cuba. While the Portuguese are neither Latino nor Hispanic, management at GM-Linden classified them as "Hispanic."

57. *1987 Agreement between Chevrolet-Pontiac-GM of Canada, Linden Plant, General Motors Corporation and Local No. 595, United Auto Workers, Region 9* (privately published), 37–42.

58. Here are the data and the p-values (using Fisher's exact test) for the underlying cross-tabulations. Results are shown for all employed respondents answering the question "Do you make more, less, or about the same now than when you worked at GM?" (The proportion answering "about the same" is not shown here.) The only result that is not statistically significant is for "earning less" in 1987.

Percentage Earning More Than at GM	1987 (N = 76)	1989 (N = 68)	1991 (N = 64)
White respondents	36	33	32
African-American respondents	0	0	0
Latino respondents	20	36	9
p =	.1067	.1013	.0732

Percentage Earning Less Than at GM			
White respondents	50	40	34
African-American respondents	75	89	89
Latino respondents	60	45	64
p =	.3855	.0239	.0049

59. See William J. Wilson, *The Truly Disadvantaged: The Inner City, the Underclass, and Public Policy* (Chicago: University of Chicago Press, 1987), 12, 135. None of the 6 African-American male respondents was unemployed in 1987 or 1989; 1 was unemployed in 1991; 2 of the 6 African-American female respondents were unemployed in 1987; and 1 was in 1989. The fact that none of the 12 African-American respondents to the 1987 study was lost in the follow-up phases of the study also is reassuring on this point.

60. Here are the data and the p-values (using Fisher's exact test) for the underlying cross-tabulations. Results are shown for all employed respondents answering the question "If you had the chance to make the decision over again, would you still take the buyout?"

Percentage Who Would Not Take the Buyout Again	1987 ($N = 90$)	1989 ($N = 81$)	1991 ($N = 79$)
White respondents	17	15	11
African-American respondents	50	42	50
Latino respondents	20	14	21
$p =$	.0592	.0925	.0104

61. Using Fisher's exact test on the cross-tabulation of gender by self-employment, $p = .0502$ for 1987. Due to the small number of employed women in the sample, the fact that there was 1 self-employed woman in the two subsequent surveys, and the fact that the self-employment rate for men fell over time, there is no statistically significant gender difference in the rate of self-employment in the 1989 and 1991 data.

62. For 1987, $p = .0047$, using two-tailed t-test pooled variance. Women wage and salary workers averaged $9.61 in 1989, compared with $12.78 for men ($p = .1031$); in 1991, the figures are $9.99 for women and $12.43 for men ($p = .0886$).

63. This was the case for 2 Latinas and 3 white women in 1987; and for 2 Latinas, 4 white women, and 1 African-American woman in both 1989 and 1991. There were originally 4 Latinas in the sample, 1 of whom was lost to the study; there were 10 white women and 6 African-American women in the sample all three years. Significance was tested using Fisher's exact test on the cross-tabulation (for female respondents only) of the two variables of regretting the buyout and leaving the labor force voluntarily.

64. Kathryn Marie Dudley, *The End of the Line: Lost Jobs, New Lives in Postindustrial America* (Chicago: University of Chicago Press, 1994), 83.

5. The "New Linden"

1. The best account, despite its early publication date, remains Emma Rothschild, *Paradise Lost: The Decline of the Auto-Industrial Age* (New York: Random House, 1973).

2. Maryann Keller, *Rude Awakening: The Rise, Fall and Struggle for Recovery of General Motors* (New York: William Morrow, 1989), 204.

3. See Harry C. Katz, *Shifting Gears: Changing Labor Relations in the U.S. Automobile Industry* (Cambridge: MIT Press, 1985); and Thomas A. Kochan, Harry C. Katz, and Robert B. McKersie, *The Transformation of American Industrial Relations* (New York: Basic Books, 1986).

4. See Paul Osterman, "How Common Is Workplace Transformation and Who Adopts It?" *Industrial and Labor Relations Review* 47, no. 2 (January 1994): 173–88; and Eileen Appelbaum and Rosemary Batt, *The New American Workplace: Transforming Work Systems in the United States* (Ithaca: ILR Press, 1994).

5. The most comprehensive account is Paul Adler, "The New 'Learning Bureaucracy': New United Motors Manufacturing, Inc.," in *Research in Organizational Behavior,* ed. Barry M. Staw and Larry L. Cummings (Greenwich, Conn.: JAI Press, 1992), 111–94. See also the critical analysis of Mike Parker and Jane Slaughter, *Choosing Sides: Unions and the Team Concept* (Boston: South End Press, 1988).

6. See Saul Rubinstein, Michael Bennett, and Thomas Kochan, "The Saturn Partnership: Co-Management and the Reinvention of the Local Union," in *Employee Representation: Alternatives and Future Directions,* ed. Bruce E. Kaufman and Morris M. Kleiner (Madison, Wis.: Industrial Relations Research Association, 1993), 339–70; Barry Bluestone and Irving Bluestone, *Negotiating the Future: A Labor Perspective on American Business* (New York: Basic Books, 1992), 191–201; and for a more critical view, Mike Parker and Jane Slaughter, *Working Smart: A Union Guide to Participation Programs and Reengineering* (Detroit: Labor Notes, 1994), 94–106.

7. James P. Womak, Daniel T. Jones, and Daniel Roos, *The Machine That Changed the World* (New York: Rawson Associates, 1990), 13. For a more technical discussion of the system, see Yasuhiro Monden, *Toyota Production System: Practical Approach to Production Management* (Norcross, Ga.: Industrial Engineering and Management Press, 1983).

8. Womack, Jones, and Roos, *Machine That Changed the World,* 101–2, 225.

9. Shoshana Zuboff, *In the Age of the Smart Machine: The Future of Work and Power* (New York: Basic Books, 1988), 395.

10. Larry Hirschhorn, *Beyond Mechanization: Work and Technology in a Post-Industrial Age* (Cambridge: MIT Press, 1984), 97. See also Fred

Block, *Postindustrial Possibilities: A Critique of Economic Discourse* (Berkeley: University of California Press, 1990).

11. Michael J. Piore and Charles F. Sabel, *The Second Industrial Divide: Possibilities for Prosperity* (New York: Basic Books, 1984), 278.

12. Piore and Sabel, *Second Industrial Divide,* 307; on the UAW, see page 244. Piore and Sabel cite Katz, *Shifting Gears,* in support of this view.

13. Robert J. Thomas, *What Machines Can't Do: Politics and Technology in the Industrial Enterprise* (Berkeley: University of California Press, 1994), 243.

14. Appelbaum and Batt, *New American Workplace,* 148.

15. Guillermo Grenier, *Inhuman Relations: Quality Circles and Anti-Unionism in American Industry* (Philadelphia: Temple University Press, 1988), 194.

16. Parker and Slaughter, *Choosing Sides,* 19. See also Mike Parker, "Industrial Relations Myth and Shop-Floor Reality: The 'Team Concept' in the Auto Industry," in *Industrial Democracy in America: The Ambiguous Promise,* ed. Nelson Lichtenstein and Howell John Harris (New York: Cambridge University Press, 1993), 249–74.

17. Parker and Slaughter, *Choosing Sides,* 111. Lowell Turner points this out as well in his *Democracy at Work: Changing World Markets and the Future of Labor Unions* (Ithaca: Cornell University Press, 1991), 60.

18. Harry C. Katz, Thomas A. Kochan, and Jeffrey H. Keefe, "Effects of Industrial Relations on Productivity: Evidence from the Automobile Industry," *Brookings Papers on Economic Activity* 3 (1987): 709. Clair Brown and Michael Reich make a similar point in their "When Does Cooperation Work? A Look at NUMMI and GM-Van Nuys," *California Management Review* 31 (summer 1989): 26–44.

19. The rest of this chapter includes some material from my joint work with Cydney Pullman. For more detailed, jointly authored discussions of the data summarized here, see Ruth Milkman and Cydney Pullman, "Technological Change in an Auto Assembly Plant: The Impact on Workers' Tasks and Skills," *Work and Occupations* 18 (May 1991): 123–47; and Ruth Milkman and Cydney Pullman, "Technological Change and Job Security: A Case Study of GM-Linden" (Labor Institute, New York, August 1988, mimeographed).

20. See Michael G. Gabriele, "GM's Top Automated Plant Hits Full GM25 Output," *Metalworking News* 18 (May 18, 1987): 10–11; and Charles Emerson, "Building Assembly Automation," *American Machinist & Automated Manufacturing* 131 (March 1987): 67–72.

21. Maryann Keller quoted in Amal Nag, "Tricky Technology: Auto Makers Discover 'Factory of the Future' Is Headache Just Now," *Wall Street Journal,* May 13, 1986, 1. See also Keller, *Rude Awakening,* 202–15; "Gen-

eral Motors: What Went Wrong," *Business Week,* March 16, 1987, 102–10; and Robert S. Harvey, "Misfiring with High Technology," *Metalworking News* 18 (May 4, 1987): 30–31.

22. Managers in different plant departments provided somewhat different data on this point. A source in industrial engineering estimated that the large cars had about 9,000 parts, compared to 3,000 for the Chevrolet models. The material department estimated that about 10,000 parts were stocked for the large cars, but only about 2,500 for the Chevrolets. Some of the reduction in parts is probably a result of the increased use of subassemblies put together in parts plants (many of them nonunion operations), but unfortunately, no specific data on this could be obtained.

23. Quoted in the *1987 Agreement between Chevrolet-Pontiac-GM of Canada, Linden Plant, General Motors Corporation and Local No. 595, United Auto Workers, Region 9* (privately published), 54.

24. That so many more production than skilled-trades classifications were eliminated probably reflects the continuing differential in power between the two groups of workers, with skilled trades much better able to protect their interests than their production-worker counterparts.

25. For the 1985 data, see appendix 1. The 1987 data were supplied by GM-Linden management.

26. Derived from the data shown in table 6. Other studies of auto-assembly plant modernizations have found similar increases in the ratio of skilled-trades to production workers. See, for example, Steven M. Miller and Susan R. Bereiter, "Modernizing to Computer-Integrated Production Technologies in a Vehicle Assembly Plant: Lessons for Analysts and Managers of Technological Change" (paper presented at the Conference on Productivity Growth in the United States and Japan, National Bureau of Economic Research, Cambridge, Mass., August 1985); Ulrich Jürgens, Thomas Malsch, and Knuth Dohse, *Breaking from Taylorism: Changing Forms of Work in the Automobile Industry* (New York: Cambridge University Press, 1993); and Paul Windolf, "Industrial Robots in the West German Automobile Industry," *Politics and Society* 14 (1985): 459–95.

27. Harley Shaiken reports similar evidence in his *Work Transformed: Automation and Labor in the Computer Age* (New York: Holt, Rinehart and Winston, 1984), 185–86.

28. This figure is from the skilled-trades portion of the 1988 in-plant survey conducted by the author and Cydney Pullman. See appendix 3 for details on the survey methodology.

29. These data are from the 1988 in-plant survey described in appendix 3.

30. According to data obtained from GM-Linden management, the injury rate for body-shop production workers doubled from 7.2 percent in the

January to August 1985 period (just before the changeover) to 14.5 percent in the January to August 1987 period. In both years, body-shop injury rates were at least double those in any other department. There was little change in injury rates in the other production departments. According to these data, injury rates actually declined among skilled-trades workers over this period, despite the dangers discussed above.

31. These findings are from the in-plant surveys conducted by the author and Cydney Pullman described in appendix 3.

32. These findings on boredom and task repetition are statistically significant ($p < .01$) using a two-tailed paired t-test.

33. The term "flexible Taylorism" is from Christian Berggren, " 'New Production Concepts' in Final Assembly—the Swedish Experience," in *The Transformation of Work?* ed. Stephen Wood (London: Unwin Hyman, 1989), 171–203. The term "Toyotism" is from Knuth Dohse, Ulrich Jürgens, and Thomas Malsch, "From 'Fordism' to 'Toyotism'? The Social Organization of the Labor Process in the Japanese Automobile Industry," *Politics and Society* 14 (1985): 115–46.

34. Katz, Kochan, and Keefe, "Effects of Industrial Relations"; Steve Babson, "Lean Production and Labor: Empowerment and Exploitation," in *Lean Work: Empowerment and Exploitation in the Global Auto Industry*, ed. Steve Babson (Detroit: Wayne State University Press, 1995), especially 17–18.

35. *1984 Agreement between Chevrolet-Pontiac-GM of Canada, Linden Plant, General Motors Corporation and Local No. 595, United Auto Workers, Region 9* (privately published), 8–9. The identical language appears in the *1987 Agreement*.

36. Louis E. Tice, *Making Meaningful Changes*, audiotape 6 of *Investment in Excellence* (Seattle: Pacific Institute, 1983).

37. Louis E. Tice, *Motivating Yourselves and Others*, audiotape 5 of *Investment in Excellence*.

38. *1987 Agreement*, 79. This language also appears in the 1984 local contract.

39. Of the skilled-trades respondents, 35 percent reported pressure to work harder "often" or "all the time" before the changeover, compared with 23 percent afterward. This has borderline statistical significance ($p = .110$) using a two-tailed paired t-test. There was no statistically significant difference in the extent to which skilled-trades respondents characterized supervision in their department as "cooperative" before and after the changeover, nor in how often respondents said they were "treated with respect" by supervision.

40. *1987 Agreement*, 54–55.

41. By 1988, fewer grievances were being filed than in 1985. According

to summary data provided by local management, there were 4 grievances filed monthly per 100 workers in the first five months of 1988, compared to 6.6 for the equivalent period in 1985. Although there was a slight increase in grievance rates immediately following the changeover (in the first five months of 1987, the monthly rate averaged 8.4 grievances per 100 workers), most of these were attributable to the initial adjustment to the new technology, either Paragraph 78 (overwork) complaints about the newly designed jobs or skilled-workers' protests about new subcontracting arrangements associated with outsourcing. Once these matters were resolved, grievance rates subsided to a new low. Nonetheless, virtually all informants agreed that the decline in grievance rates associated with the changeover was modest; a far more dramatic decline had occurred in the early 1980s as a result of the sudden reversal of fortune experienced by the union described in chapter 3.

42. The study was done by Harbor and Associates, and is summarized in John McElroy, "Productivity Comparison," *Chilton's Automotive Industries* 171 (April 1991): 52–54.

43. By contrast, only 37 percent of skilled-trades respondents indicated that they expected a decrease in the number of workers in their department, while 33 percent predicted an increase. And even if GM didn't need them, the skilled-trades workers felt confident that they would be in demand somewhere. As electrician Peter Finney said, "There's always going to be a need for this type of work. You're not going to have a robot repair another robot in an area like this. In Japan maybe they can do it, but not here."

Appendix 3

1. Although the main purpose of this effort was to refine the survey questions, I have quoted occasionally from the comments of focus-group participants in the text, using pseudonyms to protect individuals' privacy.

2. For reasons of space, the in-plant survey questionnaires (there were separate versions for the skilled-trades and production workers) are not reproduced here. Interested readers can obtain copies from the author.

3. Unfortunately, the two-year delay in securing access to the plant meant that our research on the impact of technological change had to be retrospective, whereas originally, we had hoped to do "before" and "after" assessments. Although workers seemed to have vivid memories of their earlier job experiences, some retrospective bias may have shaped the results. In any case, production workers who had changed departments and skilled-trades workers hired in the course of the changeover were excluded from the populations sampled, because our goal was to compare, retrospectively, the situation before and after the plant modernization.

4. The buyout-survey questionnaires (the initial survey and the two follow-ups) are not reproduced here for reasons of space, but copies are available on request from the author.

5. For 12 percent of the sample, the addresses supplied by management were incorrect; another 15 percent had unlisted phone numbers. Only 4 sample members (3 percent) contacted refused to participate in this first buyout survey.

6. African Americans are 17 percent of the total sample but only 13 percent of the respondents. Whites are 65 percent of the total sample but 70 percent of respondents; for Latinos the figures are 18 percent and 17 percent, respectively. The difference between whites and African Americans is statistically significant ($p < .05$).

7. Actually the documents I did obtain contain numerous workers' names, and in most cases, I have altered these in the text. The only exception is that actual names are used for Douglas Stevens, Thomas Towell, and Tony Fernandez, simply because these particular names have already been published elsewhere in connection with the events recounted in chapter 3.

8. I made more extensive efforts to keep in touch with the 1987 respondents in the two follow-up surveys than we had with the original sample respondents back in 1987. With the help of professional locator services and by offering honoraria to respondents (not provided at the earlier stages of the research), I eventually found and interviewed some individuals who could not initially be located for the follow-up surveys. In a few cases this meant that the interviews about the circumstances of respondents in 1989 and 1991 were retrospective.

9. Of the 10 respondents lost between 1987 and 1989, 7 refused to be reinterviewed; the other 3 could not be located, or had unlisted phone numbers and did not respond to letters. Of the 2 additional individuals lost between 1989 and 1991, 1 had left the country and could not be located, and the other failed to respond to telephone messages and letters.

10. Where these interviews are quoted in the text, I have used pseudonyms to protect individual privacy. In creating these pseudonyms, however, I tried to preserve any ethnic identification linked to the person's actual name.

Index

African Americans: buyout takers, 13, 95, 104, 107–8, 115–16, 132–33; and postwar division of labor, 28, 36–37, 208n23. *See also* Race
Air controllers' strike (1981), 52, 80, 85
Alcohol, 49
Alienation, 43–44; and buyout acceptance motivations, 96; and postwar division of labor, 12–13, 18, 32; and self-employment, 121; worker resignation to, 26, 44; and work reorganization, 145, 154, 227n32. *See also* Worker degradation
Anti-Communism, 76, 210n41
Appelbaum, Eileen, 144
Apprenticeship programs, 40
Aronowitz, Stanley, 54
Automobile Workers and the American Dream (Chinoy), 12–13, 121
Automotive industry decline, 3, 45, 52, 79–80, 81, 93
Auto parts sector, 20, 204n8

Batt, Rosemary, 144
Benefits: and deindustrialization, 94; post-buyout wage/salary workers, 127–28, 131; postwar, 25, 26, 42; and self-employment, 122; and transformation of UAW in 1980s, 81
Boredom. *See* Alienation
Build-in-station concept, 6–8, 9, 14, 149–50, 170–72, 174
Business Week, 63
Buyout acceptance motivations, 3, 108–13, 218n35; vs. buyout decline motivations, 6, 114; self-employment, 109, 112–13; and seniority, 96, 102–4,

114, 216n27; worker degradation, 13, 96, 109–10, 111–12, 118, 120
Buyout takers, 98, 101–8, 134–36; acceptance rate, 6, 101, 105–6, 107–8, 215n22, 215n23, 216–17n31, 217n32; buyout program design, 98, 99, 101–2; demographics, 11–12, 13, 95–96, 104, 105–6, 107–8, 136, 216n30; and Linden Auto Workers, 103, 216n25; satisfaction/regret rates, 2–3, 13–14, 95–97, 108, 113–14, 115–16, 122, 221n52. *See also* Buyout acceptance motivations; Post-buyout employment trajectories

Chinoy, Ely, 12–13, 59, 121
Chrysler Corporation, 80, 81, 82, 83–84, 87
Custodial jobs, 32, 205n13

Degradation. *See* Worker degradation
Deindustrialization, 11, 93–95, 136
Democratic Party, 82
De-skilling, 23–24, 154, 155–57, 159
Doubling up, 48–49
Drugs, 49
Dudley, Kathryn, 134

Earnings. *See* Benefits; Wages
Education, 94–95, 100, 107, 213n7
Employee Development Bank, 98
Employee Involvement Groups (EIGs), 7, 161–62; failure of, 8, 9, 172–74, 175
Energy crisis, 52, 65, 79
Ephlin, Donald F., 53, 91, 98

Family connections, 35–36
Fernandez, Tony, 79, 91

231

Compositor:	J. Jarrett Engineering, Inc.
Text:	11/13.5 Caledonia
Display:	Caledonia
Printer and Binder:	Thomson-Shore, Inc.